First Nations in the Twenty-First Century

Contemporary Educational Frontiers

John W. Friesen

Virginia Lyons Friesen

DETSELIG
ENTERPRISES LTD

First Nations in the Twenty-First Century:
Contemporary Educational Frontiers

Library and Archives Canada Cataloguing in Publication

Friesen, John W.

First Nations in the twenty-first century : contemporary educational frontiers / John W. Friesen and Virginia L. Friesen.

Includes bibliographical references and index.
ISBN 1-55059-293-9
1. Native peoples – Education – Canada. I. Friesen, Virginia Agnes Lyons, 1952- II. Title.

E96.2.F743 2005   371.829′97071   C2005-901424-5

DETSELIG
ENTERPRISES LTD

Detselig Enterprises Ltd.
210, 1220 Kensington Road NW
Calgary, Alberta T2N 3P5

Phone: (403) 283-0900
Fax: (403) 283-6947
Email: temeron@telusplanet.net
www.temerondetselig.com

We acknowledge the support of the Government of Canada through the Book Publishing Industry Development Program (BPIDP) for our publishing program.

We also acknowledge the support of the Alberta Foundation for the Arts for our publishing program.

Cover art by David J Friesen

Cover design by Alvin Choong

ISBN 1-55059-293-9   SAN 113-0234   Printed in Canada

To our grandson,

Jonathan Leo

On the occasion of his arrival in this world,
March 4, 2005

Contents

Preface

We don't live in teepees or longhouses anymore, we are university
graduates, we are entrepreneurs, we are the future of our own people . . . once corporate Canada realizes the many benefits, together
we can build a stronger country for everyone. (Rodney Thomas,
Alberta Native News, August, 2004: 13)

There is no doubt that the First Nations of Canada made great
strides in several significant areas during the latter half of the twentieth century, but there is much more to be done. Some land claims
have been settled, health care and educational achievement have
improved somewhat, and even a semblance of self-government is
visible in some Aboriginal communities. Literature pertaining to
these modest successes, both academic and informal has burgeoned,
much of it emanating from the Native sector.

World's Largest Teepee, Medicine Hat, Alberta

That's the good news. On the more challenging side of the ledger is the difficult task of transferring authority for community alleviation of problematic concerns from government bureaucracy to local control. This is a very complicated undertaking because bureaucrats are not known for wanting to go out of business. Adequate financial resources to facilitate easy transfer and take over of governing authority are not readily available. When moneys are transferred, strings are often attached, special training may be required, and proposals have to be prepared, discussed, and mulled over. The end result of this long established democratically-anchored process is that settlements of any kind are always drawn out. Lengthy blocks of valuable time are consumed in discussion, not all of it particularly beneficial to either side. Still, if the record of the past half century is any indication, some progress will likely be made in this century on several important fronts.

It would take several volumes to describe the intricacies of government/Aboriginal bargaining in such vital areas as economics, resource allocation, governance, health, welfare, etc. Some of them are summarized in the next chapter as a means of providing background information. The purpose of this book is to highlight several key educational frontiers which Indigenous leaders and educators have identified and which they wish to define and resolve on their own terms. Many of them have been working hard to delineate what effect locally-elaborated approaches will have on their communities in the long term. While the primary goal has been to achieve educational equity with the rest of Canadian citizenry, Indigenous leaders do not want to sacrifice their traditional beliefs and values in the process.

Thus the stage is set for some very complicated and heavy-going research, discussion, and bargaining. Elders will be consulted, prayers will be said, and ceremonies will be observed, all of them essential to peaceful and consensual resolution of these important issues. It is our hope that we have done justice in providing an adequate background to the topics under scrutiny and clarified the related frontier. It is also our hope that this treatise might motivate interested parties (Native and nonNative) in patiently pursuing workable approaches to these important challenges. The first half of the twenty-first century should be interesting to watch in this regard. Perhaps we may also be invited to participate in the process.

As Cree elder Joseph E. Couture (1985: 6) once wrote;

Native cultures are dynamic, adaptive, and adapting, not limited to the past. These cultures are authentic and valid, inherently creative, capable of distinctive and sophisticated human development and expression, and, therefore, they can invent structural forms and institutions as needed to ensure and strengthen individual/group survival.

John W. Friesen
Virginia Lyons Friesen
The University of Calgary

One

The Way Things Are

The good news today is that the Aboriginal peoples of Canada-are *in* the news. For the most part press coverage is positive, although a rugged political frontier still lies before the nation's original peoples. Encouragingly, the First Nations of Canada are making significant progress on several fronts, but they still have a long ways to go in terms of achieving equity in major social sectors such as health, education, and socioeconomic status.

Recent gains made by the Indigenous people would not have happened a half century ago because the twentieth century was not kind to them. Negative statistics pertaining to their welfare abounded. The life expectancy for Indians in Canada in the repertoire of the 1960s was 36 years; infant mortality was more than twice that of the national average, and health conditions were poor. More than half of

"Ah, that Morning Juice!" Children at Morley United Church, Stoney (Nakoda Sioux) First Nations Reserve, Morley, Alberta

11

Canada's Aboriginals were living below the poverty level, and their children spent very little time in school. The suicide rate among Native peoples was 19.7 per 100 000 population while that of the nation generally (including Natives) was 9.7. Unemployment among Native people was 50 percent while the nation was enjoying an unemployment rate of only 6 percent.

Good News

Today some improvement in the overall socioeconomic status of Canada's First Nations is evident. Life expectancy of Aboriginals is up. The average Native male in Canada can expect to live 69 years, compared with 75 years for Canadian males as a whole. Native women can expect to live 76 years compared with 82 years for Canadian women as a whole (Frideres and Gadacz, 2001: 66-67).

The economic picture for Canada's First Nations is brighter as Native band councils begin to involve themselves in negotiations with resource companies for local industrial development. Many bands are currently partnered with resource companies and manufacturing firms with plans to build economically sustaining industries on site and provide employment for their increasing populations. Even the federal government is relinquishing its hold on decision-making regarding First Nations, and is actively consulting and bargaining with Indian leaders. No policy changes are being inaugurated without full consultation with all parties concerned from

Band Council Chambers, Tsuu T'ina First Nations Reserve near SW Calgary, Alberta

local band councils to national Indian organizations. Canada's First Nations are finally being heard.

There is also good news on the front of post-secondary education. Although the tendency for Native students to pursue post-sec-

College Class, Old Sun College, Siksika (Blackfoot) First Nation Reserve, Gleichen, Alberta

ondary education is of fairly recent origins, progress is being made. Aboriginal students only began to attend post-secondary institutions in any significant numbers during the 1970s. By 1981, the Canadian census revealed that two percent of the Aboriginal population held university degrees, compared with 8.1 percent of the nonAboriginal population. By 1990 the percentage of Native people holding university degrees rose to 2.6 percent compared with 12.6 for the nonNative population. When the Royal Commission on Aboriginal People (RCAP) was published in 1996, it indicated that 4.2 percent of Aboriginal people held university degrees compared with 15.5 percent of nonAboriginals. Data showed that 21 percent of Aboriginals had completed a college certificate compared with 25.5 percent of nonAboriginals. In the years following the RCAP Report statistics have kept rising; the number of Status Indians and Inuit enrolled in postsecondary institutions almost doubled between 1988/89 and 1997/98, rising from 15 572 to 27 100. Since then these numbers have held constant.

Casual observers of Native culture are not usually aware of the legal and cultural subcategories of the Aboriginal community, namely that several statutory distinctions are important. To begin with, there are now nearly 700 000 Status Indians in Canada, that is, persons so designated by terms outlined in the Indian Act. In addition, some experts estimate that there are at least a million other Native people in Canada who are considered nonStatus in legal terms. Sometimes these individuals are also called Métis or "mixed peoples," the former designation having its roots in the fur trade era of the 17th century.

Métis people are actually the descendants of marital unions between French fur traders and Woodland Cree and Ojibway Indian women. A shortage of women among incoming peoples, most of whom were fur traders, prompted immigrant males to turn their eyes toward Indigenous communities for mates. Aboriginal women of various eastern Canadian tribal affiliations sometimes married these newcomers and these unions produced offspring of mixed racial identity. Further inland, Woodland Crees and Ojibway women were ready targets of amorous attention because of the direct involvement of their people in the fur trade. Thus, when the French and Aboriginals mingled, a new people was born for the new nation, comprising a mixture of the old and the new. In the words of Bruce Sealey;

> These Métis are the true Natives of Canada. First Nations and Europeans were immigrants, and only the millennia separated their penetration into the New World. The meeting of the two races produced a mixture which was not from another land, but whose sole roots were in the New World. (Friesen and Lusty, 1980: vii)

Contemporary nomenclature fails to differentiate among the various designations of Native peoples, and some of the most popular choices are Aboriginals, AmerIndians, First Nations, First Peoples, Indians, Indigenous People, Native people, or North American Indians. Some have even suggested the term "PreCanadians" is most apt. The term "Native people" usually applies to people with some Indian bloodlines and thus includes Métis and nonStatus Indians. Interestingly, on November 19, 2003, the Supreme Court of Canada ruled that the Métis should be recognized as Aboriginal people which would imply that they could soon receive health, education, and welfare services through federal auspices.

The case was resolved on the basis of two separate instances involving Métis hunting rights, one in Ontario and the other in Manitoba, both occurring in 2003 (Friesen and Friesen, 2004: 7). Alberta immediately followed suit on October 6, 2004, when Métis Aboriginal hunting rights were affirmed in that province (*Alberta Native News*, October, 2004: 6). Earlier, in September 2004, at a Special Meeting between First Ministers and Aboriginal leaders, Prime Minister Paul Martin laid out an inclusive strategy on Aboriginal health which will for the first time even include Métis as equal partners in federal health programming (*Alberta Native News*, September, 2004: 2). There are currently nearly 300 000 people in Canada whose status could potentially be affected by subsequent federal legislation and action.

In 1972 the Government of Canada recognized the Métis as having separate legal status, but did not identify any special rights they might be entitled to. The Dominion Bureau of Statistics, on the other hand, to date has not recognized the separate existence of the Métis, and there are no population statistics of birth, morbidity, or death rates pertaining to the Métis in the territories. In effect, the northern Métis have probably been included in the categories of "Native Indians, Eskimo, White and Others," but those designations have depended on the location of their residence. The Métis were included in the 1941 census and again in 1981, but for the most part, the identity of the Métis exists by implication in the annals of Canadian history. Too often, they have been, as Sealey notes, "Canada's forgotten people" (Sealey and Lussier, 1975). Perhaps the recent supreme court decision will make amends in this regard.

Basic Statistics

While a significant percentage of Canadians can lay claim to Indigenous ancestry, the official roll count of Status Indians is around 700 000. This number is subject to significant change, however, due to the high birth rate among Native peoples (nearly 3 percent annually), and the fact that Aboriginal longevity has steadily increased over the past several decades. In addition, with the passing of Bill C-31 in 1985, those who previously lost their Status through various means could apply to regain it. More than 105 000 individuals have regained their Status since 1985 (Frideres and Gadacz, 2001: 33).

About one-fourth of Canada's Native people live in Ontario while Saskatchewan and British Columbia each play host to another 16 percent. Less than two-thirds (58%) live on Indian reserves, while the rest (42%) live in various cities and towns, and the move to urban centres is increasing. There are more than 2000 reserves in Canada, providing habitat to over 600 residential bands. Most bands consist of about 500 members and there are only eleven bands in Canada with a population of over 2000. Most of these are located in Ontario and Alberta. The largest reserve in Canada is that of the Blood (Kainai) Nation in southern Alberta, and the most populated reserve is Six Nations at Brantford, Ontario.

Living conditions on most Indian reserves are still less than desirable. The infant mortality rate is double that of the rest of the nation (17.5 per 1000 births versus 7.9 per 1000 births), poverty, unemployment, inadequate housing and poor health conditions are a harsh reality, and educational attainment is low. Although positive changes are slowing occurring, the major challenge is accessibility to adequate services which is both difficult and costly (Frideres and Gadacz: 2001: 78). Coupled with these realities is the fact that Native people are continuing to migrate to urban areas where they are having to contend with a myriad of other challenges, such as cultural alienation, racism, and economic deprivation (Buckley, 1993; Fox and Long, 2000).

Canadian First Nations were not able to participate fully in the Canadian economy during the twentieth century. Some 50 years ago when the country's financial base moved from an agricultural base to one of science and technology, First Nations productive powers lagged behind, many times restricted by law from engaging in economic development. In some cases Aboriginals were refused licences to act as commercial big game hunting outfitters in areas where nonNatives had established ventures. They were also forbidden to take homestead lands which were reserved for incoming nonNative settlers. Finally, when the Canadian northlands opened up inland commercial fisheries, the Indigenous people were restricted from competing with nonNatives (Frideres, 1993: 464). Against this background it has been very difficult for the First Nations people to make satisfactory adjustments to changing economic conditions.

Treaties and Reserves

It is sometimes confusing to readers unfamiliar with Native history to decipher the legal complexities of such phenomena as Indian Treaties, the Indian Act, and the ownership of Indian reserves. Treaty-signing, by the way, was not a new phenomenon for Native people at the point when the Canadian government decided to engage in such negotiations. It is estimated that after the 1700s, close to 500 formal "deals" were signed between the French and the First Nations alone (Purich, 1986: 96). Between 1871 and 1899 a total of ten formal treaties were signed by the Crown (acting for the Canadian Government) with Indigenous people.

Welcome to Peguis (Ojibway) First Nation Reserve, Location of Signing of Treaty No. 1, Fisher River, Manitoba

Treaty No. 1, was dated August 3, 1871, and signed by the British Government with the Ojibway and Swampy Cree of Manitoba. The act of treaty-signing implied that the government would make available to First Nations small allotments of ground known as reserves, as well as provisions of cattle, seed, agricultural equipment, guns, and ammunition. In return the Indians would give up their rights to most of their hunting grounds so that incoming settlers could occupy them. Essentially the treaties were agreements about surrendering lands and government payments for such. The terms of Treaty No. 1, for example, included the following components:

18 *First Nations in the Twenty-First Century*

1. The relinquishment of the Indian right and title to specified lands;
2. Certain hunting privileges;
3. Annual payments of five dollars as compensation to every Indian person involved in these dealings (head chiefs and councillors of each received $25.00 and $15.00 respectively), as well as a suit of clothes, a British flag and silver medals;
4. Certain lands allocated as "Indian reserves" amounting to 160 acres per family;
5. Agricultural implements, oxen and cattle to form the nuclei of herds were offered on a one-time basis to the tribes; and
6. Provision for the establishment of schools for the instruction of Indian children.

It is of some interest to note that Treaty No. 6 made provision for "a Medicine Chest to be kept at the house of the Indian agent" for the care of Indian people (*Citizens Plus*, 1970: 57). Aboriginal leaders today insist that the gist of that clause implies free medicare for Native people. Government officials, on the other hand, have tried to interpret the phrase in a literal sense.

First Nations leaders emphasize that while their forebears engaged in treaty deliberations on a nation-to-nation bases, the full understanding of what it meant to "surrender land" was alien to them. They also point out that church leaders whose best interests were not for the Natives' benefit, were often involved in these deliberations, so in the end the government came out the winner. The element of bias was certainly evident in subsequent actions particularly with regard to educational provisions. The government was quick to turn that responsibility over to religious orders and church denominations. This arrangement gave church leaders the right to promote religious indoctrination along with cultural assimilation backed by government funds. Some religious leaders regarded this as a windfall of sorts, but their joy turned to consternation later on when it became evident that Indigenous cultures would not easily be assimilated.

The traditional Indigenous concept of land ownership was simply that land could not be owned. The land belonged to the Creator and people were merely stewards of it. There were ways to acknowledge this. For example, among Plains Indians the spoils of a hunt, were to be graciously received from the Creator with appropriate thanks rendered. This was done by placing a serving of meat into the ground, accompanied with a prayer of thanksgiving.

According to some sources Native leaders endorsed treaty-signing because they thought they were signing peace treaties. After all, "stewards of the land" could not bargain its ownership away (Snow, 1977: 28-29). Additional confusion about land negotiations arose because the First Nations stance of negotiation was rooted in the tradition which fur trading nations had established with Native people. These dealings were done in good faith between two mutually-respecting and independent nations. The fact that European fur companies, both French and English, regarded the various bands of First Nations as separate political entities is recognized in the literature (Driver, 1968; Jenness, 1986; Frideres, 1988; Josephy, 1968; and Patterson, 1972). This attitude was certainly not the position of treaty negotiators of the new Canadian government of 1867 who saw Aboriginals in a different light.

By the 1870s when treaties were being signed, government attitudes toward First Nations took a decidedly negative tone. At the time of first contact Indians had been viewed as providers of fur, but that perception soon changed to one of mutual negotiation as the fur trade developed its own institutional structure. By the time the fledgling Canadian government took over, the fur trade was history and government officials viewed the First Peoples as victims of the times. It was perceived that Aboriginals should be grateful for anything that the government could do for them. In fact, government officials saw themselves as engaged in acts of reluctant benevolence. Suddenly, the Indian became the "White man's burden" who was in need of civilization and in need of His Majesty's Christian influence (Surtees, 1969). This attitude ushered in the missionary era.

The impact of treaty-making severely jarred the Indigenous community when it was discovered that traditional hunting domains were now off limits. Even after the tribes were ushered onto their respective reserves, many hunting parties in search of food drifted off their reserves but were rounded up and brought back by members of the Northwest Mounted Police. In some instances First Nations were rudely herded onto reserves and the police were charged with seeing to it that they stayed there. Little sensitivity was shown to tribespeople in this undertaking. It was simply announced that Aboriginals would live on reserves and eventually assume a government approved form of self-government (Wuttunee, 1971: 111).

The formation of Indian reserves was motivated by a series of factors, not necessarily free from paradoxical reasoning. One of the prime motivations for creating these geographic ghettos was to place the First Peoples on lands which would not be designated for incoming settlers. The poorer lands, not readily suitable for farming were left to the First Nations; after all, they were not expected to make "proper" use of the lands. A more humane reason for the creation of reserves was that they would afford management ease in administering custodial care to the Indians. It was sometimes frustrating to try to "do something for the Indians" when they travelled nomadically across the plains in search of buffalo. One could hardly build portable schools or churches. One priest, charged with working among the Indian people remarked in frustration, "When the last buffalo is dead, it may be possible to do something for the Indian" (Friesen, 1983: 45-46; McDonald, 1974: 152).

Conceptualizations of Aboriginal peoples which motivated the formation of reserves also varied. Some officials saw reserves as a temporary essential political necessity since Indigenous populations were dying out anyway. Others sincerely believed that European-like communities of civilization could be developed among the First Nations once an agricultural means of livelihood could be stabilized. There were even those who regarded Indian culture as a remnant of the bygone days of pre-civilization when people were happy and carefree so Aboriginal culture should therefore be salvaged as a token of the past.

Cultural changes forced upon Native communities by the clash with European civilization were almost insurmountable. Many of them remain and the resultant agenda for adjustment includes a variety of challenges ranging from Aboriginal self-government to spirituality (Krotz, 1990; Ponting, 1986; Richardson, 1989; York, 1989). As the past has shown, however, Aboriginal people will undoubtedly prevail, and will handle the various threats and challenges to their existence with a measure of dignity and perpetuity.

Key Issues

As the twenty-first century gets underway, a number of crucial challenges continue to haunt any notions of progress for Canada's Indigenous peoples. At the top of the list of concerns are land claims, industrial development in Native communities, Indian residential school litigations, and the possible attainment of some form of Aboriginal self-government. Complex as these issues are, some progress is being made on all fronts but not without hard bargaining and involved confrontations and discussions. Although these challenges are not the major concern of this book, a good example of the complexity of resolution is illustrated with regard to residential school litigations. For example, on July 12, 2001, the Supreme Court of British Columbia authorized an award of half a million dollars to a group of six Aboriginal litigants for damages suffered because of their experiences in a residential school run by the United Church of Canada. Originally the group had asked for five million dollars, but even with an award of half a million dollars, when the dust had settled, it appeared doubtful that the litigants would actually receive any of the money. Their lawyers would deduct 40 percent for their expenses, and when court costs were calculated, the prosecutors would "hardly see a dime of the awards" (*Calgary Herald,* April 14, 2001). The court ruled that in this case the United Church of Canada was 25 percent responsible for these crimes and the federal government was 75 percent responsible.

In addition to laying claim to settlement funds for physical and sexual abuse in residential schools, some First Peoples are asking for damages pertaining to loss of language and culture. The federal government seems reluctant to bargain in that area, choosing to define the issues in narrower terms. If interpreted on a wider scale, such losses go well beyond the parameters of residential school cases. In July 2003, the federal government announced a fast-track program of cash settlements to residential school litigants, but lawyers for the claimants objected saying that the settlement would not address culture and language losses. A draft of the federal plan recommended that abuse victims in Ontario, British Columbia, and the Yukon be awarded an individual maximum of $245 000, compared with $195 000 elsewhere (*Calgary Herald,* November 7, 2003: A13).

The settlement of land claims is proceeding slowly. The following are examples of limited success. On June 21, 1996, the Minister of Indian Affairs and Northern Development, Ron Irwin, announced that an agreement-in-principle regarding land claims with 19 First Nations in Manitoba had been reached. In March, 2001, the government announced a treaty process had been established for the Atlantic provinces. On May 1, 2001, the federal government announced that settlements had been reached with 21 First Nations in British Columbia. That province has the highest number of outstanding land claims because the two treaties that were signed in that province, Treaty 8 and the Douglas Treaty accounted for only a small territorial area. A provincial task force to assist in the delicate matter of protecting provincial rights pertaining to land and renewal resources, was appointed in December, 1990. A British Columbia Treaty Commission was set up in 1992. The saga continues.

Self-Government

When the Penner Report was released in 1983 it called for the induction of some form of Aboriginal self-government and introduced the concept of a third order government to follow federal and provincial jurisdictions. Since then the struggle to define self-government has been ongoing. Essentially, Native people have been asking for independence and self-determination within Canada, but a workable application of that concept has not been realized.

A case of interest occurred recently when the Dene Nation put forth their demands for self-determination based on very clear underlying principles. The Dene sought recognition of their right to practice and preserve their language, traditions, customs, and values. They claimed the right to develop their own institutions and enjoy their rights as a people in the framework of their own institutions. They also insisted that a Dene government could function within confederation with jurisdiction over geographical area and over subject matters that in the past were within the jurisdiction of either the federal government or that of the Northwest territorial government. Here progress has been made.

The Union of British Columbia Indian Chiefs under the leadership of George Manuel defined their position on self-government this way;

We must be masters in our own house, in order to survive as Indian people. There is no basis in the laws of Canada to restrict the recovery of Aboriginal rights because we have never given up our rights to control our own lives and means to live. (Wall, 2000: 144)

Although the Canadian Constitution makes reference to Aboriginal rights, no definition of it was included in the document when it was repatriated in 1982. Attempts to do so were made in 1992 in the Charlottetown Accord which did not reach fruition. One of the central themes of the Report of the Royal Commission on Aboriginal Peoples was that the Liberal Government of Canada recognized the inherent right of Aboriginal people to self-government. Again, the validity of the concept was recognized but it was not defined or elaborated.

The third order of government referred to in the Penner Report has some Native leaders worried that even if some form of it were initiated, it would reduce First Nations governments to that of glorified municipal governments with very limited powers. In the meantime, the quest for definition has left plenty of fodder for political discussion, Aboriginal worry, and academic rumination.

An outspoken critic of Aboriginal self-government, Thomas Flanagan (2000) of the University of Calgary, suggests that Native militants tend to define the concept in racial terms. He warns that because the Aboriginal population is so small in comparison to the total Canadian population, if a third order of government were instituted, it would represent a special privilege for a very small number of people. Its very existence would be a standing invitation for other ethnic minority groups to request similar status (Flanagan, 2000: 194).

Flanagan cautions that the Aboriginal concept of self-determination contributes to cultural exclusiveness. It encourages First Nations to withdrawn unto themselves, under their own "self-governments," on their own "traditional lands," and with their own "Aboriginal economies." Flanagan believes that this is the wrong direction for a healthy economic order to take since it will enable political and professional elites to do well for themselves at the expense of the good of the majority (Flanagan, 2000: 195). Flanagan is in consensus with the late Howard Adams that the contemporary status of neocolonialism in Indigenous communities encourages upper echelon Natives to adopt conservative middle class ideologies and superimpose them on their unsuspecting peers. Adams claimed that universities which house Aboriginal studies departments often foster neocolonialism by educating the Native elite to fill the role previously abandoned by government bureaucrats. As Adams stated;

> In short, it involves giving some benefits of the dominant society to a small, privileged minority of Aboriginals in return for their help in pacifying the majority. This use of an educated Native elite to help governments deal with the 'Native problem' has its parallels around the world (Adams, 1999: 54).

Boldt echoes a similar sentiment when he observes that blind faith is often placed in Native leaders for economic development or for the resolution of problematic situations with unfortunate results (Boldt, 1993: 141). These individuals may attempt to justify their actions by suggesting that "they learned the art of corruption from their nonNative counterparts," but, hopefully this unwarranted form of self-justification will satisfy only a few for a very brief time (Friesen, 1995a: 128).

A related concern to defining Aboriginal self-government is that a format of operation could be elaborated prescribing separate legal status for First Nations. Such an arrangement might satisfy some, but it might also backfire in the sense that it would a encourage Canadians to absolve themselves of any responsibility for Aboriginal welfare. Frideres and Gadacz (2001: 251) suggest that such status will never be attained by First Nations because the federal government will see to it that any arrangement for self government will have to harmonize with existing Canadian laws.

Urban Reserves

Many First Nations have in recent years migrated to large cities where urban reserves have been established. Baron and Garcea (1999) postulate three reasons for the creation of urban reserves, the first being that they are directly related to treaties and treaty land entitlement. In Saskatchewan, for example, nearly thirty bands were short-changed when land entitlements for reserves were negotiated. As a result, the provincial government settled with the bands by offering them compensatory funds with which to buy private real estate holdings.

The second reason why urban reserves have been created is closely associated with the desire of First Nations to develop and diversify economic opportunities. An acreage of federal land for development was found in Saskatoon, for example, and negotiations for transfer to Indian ownership were undertaken. The result was the creation of an urban reserve with all the rights and privileges pertaining thereto.

Third, the creation of urban reserves is an expression of the inherent right of self-government for First Nations. Many Aboriginals want to be full players in dominant society, not necessarily as assimilated Indians, but as people with a separate cultural integrity. Theoretically, the principle of inherency is based on the notion that self-government is practiced by a national community living on a land base and exercising all the primary social functions true of any national community. Translating this definition to reality postulates the formation of an urban reserve that functions as an extension of a band's national land patrimony and authority.

Many off-reserve Aboriginals have essentially integrated with dominant society. The question as to how the introduction of Aboriginal self-government would affect them is probably only remotely relevant, as is the fact that most of them will likely choose to remain off-reserve. What then is the point of pumping additional monies into reserve economies when the trend is to move away? As is currently the case, most reserve economies do not support the people who live in there. Most reserve income for Canada's more than 600 Indian bands is generated off-reserve by nonNatives. Is there any validity to the definition of self-government if it simply means that people living on a reserve have the privilege of spending money generated by someone else? (Miller, 2000: 347). As Boldt (1993: 261) suggests;

> Any proposal that Indian political autonomy and culture should be financed by another government makes a mockery of Indian nationhood. It is a manifestation of the "culture of dependence" in the political sphere. Such an arrangement is a design for continued subordination and paternalism.

Boldt goes on to state that if Indigenous cultures are to have any validity in their own right, they must first develop a clear vision and consensus about who they want to be, culturally, in the future. They must assess the damage that colonialists have inflicted on them in the past (which continues to this day), and invent ways to stop the processes of assimilation and acculturation. They must critically evaluate what must be done to mobilize their people in an effort to make that identity a reality. "Such a process of cultural revitalization will necessitate a purge of corrupting colonial institutions, and of traits derived from the culture of dependence and from Euro-Western acculturation" (Boldt, 1993: 219).

Few observers of the Aboriginal self-government phenomenon are optimistic about fast results. McDonnell and Depew (1999: 353) suggest that the processes associated with self-government are so powerfully unilateral in their focus that they have all but displaced considerations relating to self-determination. Henderson (2000: 167) accuses legal bureaucrats of unreflectively asserting colonial privileges and power when dealing with the issue, but some observers are a bit more optimistic. Hylton (1999) notes that some progress towards Aboriginal self-government has been made both in terms of federal attitude and experiences reported by some Indian bands. He notes that

> Aboriginal people in Canada are increasingly engaged in the practice of self-government. . . .a number of Aboriginal nations have already negotiated far-reaching self-government agreements. . . . the federal government appears more ready than previous administrations to enter into new arrangements with Aboriginal people .(Hylton, 1999: 432)

The Indian Act

The distinctions inherent in the Indian Act are of great legal importance and are responsible for the creation of several subcategories of Native Peoples. Combining the implications of treaty-signing with the Indian Act has created such distinctions as Treaty-Status Indians, nonTreaty Status Indians, and nonStatus, nonTreaty Indians. Some members of the latter group claim Métis heritage and reject the nomenclature of being nonStatus. Sometimes Status Indians are also called "Registered Indians," although historically that term refers specifically to the individuals who were enrolled at the first "Indian census." Additional legislation also designates some peoples of the north as Dene and Inuit, the latter formerly being called Eskimos.

As federal, Native and provincial leaders continue to wrestle with the meaning of Aboriginal self-government, complex political action is being proposed on other fronts. On May 14, 2001, Robert Nault, Minister of Indian Affairs and Northern Development, proposed changes to the Indian Act which was originated in 1876. In a letter to his Aboriginal constituents Nault wrote:

> You and your leaders have told me that you want legislation that offers your council more freedom and responsibility with respect to the day to day operations of your communities. You have to decide what the right mechanisms are to ensure you have access to your government, and that your government is effective and accountable to you. Our collective challenge is to come up with an approach that works for everybody.

Nault's letter was accompanied by a questionnaire and packet of materials entitled, *Communities First: First Nations Governance under the Indian Act* (2001). A discussion paper included in the packet raised three key issues: (i) legal and standing and capacity; (ii) leadership selection and voting rights; and, (iii) accountability to First Nation members. First, the discussion paper notes that under the Indian Act, the powers of chief and council are not clear. The Indian Act does not set out the legal standing and capacity for Indian bands and band councils in such areas as the capacity to sue, to contract, to borrow, etc., all of which make it difficult for band councils to conduct the day-to-day business of their bands.

A second concern has to do with leadership selection and voting rights. Currently there are two systems in place—those bands that follow the procedure outlined in the Indian Act via the election of chiefs and councils, and those that follow an hereditary system of appointment. The government has no power to interfere in the latter procedures under the Indian Act. Although the Indian Act now allows off-reserve indians to vote in band elections, they cannot run for the office of councillor. This does not apply to the office of chief. In fact, one does not have to live on a reserve nor even be a band member to run for that office. It is the government's impression that many First Nations people want these requirements to change.

The third item of concern has to do with accountability. The Indian Act says almost nothing about rules needed to see that First Nations communities are run in a fair and equitable manner. Many First Nations bands already operate their own system of accountability, but they vary in structure and function. As it is, Aboriginal band members have virtually no say in such matters as band management of funds or incurred debt load and the government wants to change this. Band council recommendations, for example, can be made without giving notice to band members, and the same goes for by-laws, annual reports, accounting and band budgeting. Often local members have no idea what goes on in band council meetings.

Opposition to the government's intention to changing the Indian Act has been strong, particularly from nationally-recognized Indian leaders. Matthew Coon Come, former Grand Chief of the Assembly of First Nations (AFN), stated that his organization does not oppose replacing the Indian Act, but they want the government to abandon their attempts to reach the grass roots, and instead work with the AFN which represents about half of Canada's Aboriginal people. AFN leaders want talks to concentrate on Aboriginal self-government, treaty rights, and social and economic concerns. Coon Come threatened to launch campaigns to barricade highways and engage in other disruptions if the government would not desist. Legislation to replace the Indian Act has been tabled and the government has set aside a budget of 13 million dollars for the project.

Walter Robinson, federal director of the Canadian Taxpayers's Federation objects to complaints by Native leaders that conditions on reserves are solely the fault of the federal government (Calgary Herald, July 21, 2001). He points out that the combined bill for Aboriginal health, education and welfare spent by federal and provincial initiatives amounts to 10 billion dollars annually. Yet the number of Indian bands who are in financial receivership or under third party management is mounting. Mismanagement is not the result of ignorance, capacity, or lack of training; it is blatant colonization by Native leaders. Many Aboriginal leaders are educated and articulate and well acquainted with fiscal procedures. Thus there is an urgency to change the law towards ensuring greater accountability and transparency.

Future Outlook

As our industrial society continues to compel changes in First Nations communities, Aboriginal complaints that they have been hard done by are beginning to be heard. When Native leaders make claims about their youth having been poorly trained in inadequately-equipped schools, managed by unsympathetic administrators, and taught by insensitive teachers, the public appears to be listening. A few critics proffer objections such as these now and then;

Everyone has had it tough. If you cannot cope with the challenges of the modern technological age, you will simply have to join the group – get with the flow. Out-dated tribal practices have no relevance in a competitive society. Another objection is; "Call it assimilation, call it integration, call it adaptation, call it whatever you want; it has to happen" (Flanagan, 2000: 196).

There may be a temporary impasse while the divergency of opinion works itself out, but in the long run the strength of the Indigenous spirit will prevail. The First Nations have already lived through a long history of disrespect for and misunderstanding of their ways. The good news is that Canadian citizens may be starting to show interest in changing this stance and governments are engaging in meaningful negotiation with the First Peoples (Miller, 2000: 410). The resurgence of traditional Indian spiritual values has provided a positive base for deliberation and progress with possible benefits to anyone who will take time to examine their beliefs.

Verna Kirkness (1998b: 12-13), a Cree Professor Emeritus at the University of British Columbia, adds another dimension to this exchange when she urges her own people to meet the challenges of changing times by starting to "cut the mustard." Not all Native ills can be blamed on government inaction. Kirkness states;

> To illustrate a point, I would like to suggest that we consider a 4th "R," namely, rhetoric. It is common to hear our political leaders and educators speak eloquently about the importance of education and what we must do to improve it not only for today, but for future generations. We all know the right words; we sound like experts, but we fall short when it comes to putting our rhetoric into action . . . We say that culture is language and language is culture . . . yet we continue to teach our language for only a few minutes a day in our schools, knowing that this approach is ineffective.

The hope to develop a healthy social milieu for Canadian First Nations rests in the hands of both Natives and nonNatives. If Kirkness is correct, there is work to be done on both sides of the table. The Indigenous people must examine their own hearts and be willing to put their own house in order even if it means more pain. NonNatives must not only listen to Aboriginals but be willing to implement some of the solutions that the latter consider desirable.

The educational frontiers outlined in the chapters ahead will become better crystallized if they are grounded in historical awareness. The intent of the next chapter is to provide that background.

References

Adams, Howard. (1999). Tortured People: *The Politics of Colonization*. Revised edition. Penticton, BC: Theytus Books.

Boldt, Menno. (1993). *Surviving as Indians: The Challenge of Self-Government*. Toronto, ON: University of Toronto Press.

Buckley, Helen. (1993). *From Wooden Ploughs to Welfare: Why Indian Policy Failed in the Prairie Provinces*. Montreal, PQ: McGill-Queen's University Press.

Citizens Plus, The Indian Chiefs of Alberta. A Presentation by the Indian Chiefs of Alberta to the Right Honourable Pierre Elliott Trudeau, Prime Minister and the Government of Canada, June, 1970; also known as "The Red Paper."

Couture, Joseph E. (1985). Traditional Thinking, Feeling, and Learning. *Multicultural Education Journal*, 3:2, 4-16.

Driver, Harold E. (1968). *Indians of North America*. Chicago, IL: University of Chicago Press.

Flanagan, Thomas. (2000). *First Nations? Second Thoughts*. Montreal, QC: McGill-Queen's University Press.

Fox, Terry and David Long. (2000). Struggles within the Circle: Violence, Healing and Health on a First Nations Reserve. *Visions of the Heart: Canadian Aboriginal Issues*. Second edition. David Long and Olive Patricia Dickason, eds. Toronto, ON: Harcourt Canada, 271-301.

Frideres, James S. (1983). *Native Peoples in Canada: Contemporary Conflicts*. Third edition. Scarborough, ON: Prentice-Hall.

Frideres, James S. (1993). *Native Peoples in Canada: Contemporary Conflicts*. Fourth edition. Scarborough, ON: Prentice-Hall.

Frideres, James S., and Réne R. Gadacz (2001). *Native Peoples in Canada: Contemporary Conflicts*. Sixth edition. Scarborough, ON: Prentice-Hall.

Friesen, John W. (1983). *Schools With a Purpose*. Calgary, AB: Detselig Enterprises.

Friesen, John W. (1995). *You Can't Get There From Here: The Mystique of North American Plains Indians' Culture & Philosophy*. Dubuque, IA: Kendall/Hunt.

Friesen, John W. (1998). *Sayings of the Elders: An Anthology of First Nations' Wisdom*. Calgary, AB: Detselig Enterprises.

Friesen, John W., and Virginia Lyons Friesen. (2004). *We Are Included: The Métis People of Canada Realize Riel's Vision*. Calgary, AB: Detselig Enterprises.

Henderson, James (Sa'ke'j) Youngblood. (2000). Postcolonial Ledger Drawing: Legal Reform. *Protecting Indigenous Knowledge and Heritage*. Marie Battiste and James (Sa'ke'j) Youngblood, eds. Saskatoon, SK: Purich Publishing, 172-178.

Hylton, John H. (1999). Future Prospects for Aboriginal Self-Government in Canada. *Aboriginal Self-Government in Canada*. John H. Hylton, ed. Saskatoon, SK: Purich Publishing. 432-455.

Jenness, Diamond. (1986). *The Indians of Canada*. Toronto, ON: University of Toronto Press.

Josephy, Alvin M. Jr. (1968). *The Indian Heritage of America*. New York: Alfred A. Knopf.

Kirkness, Verna J. (1998). Our Peoples' Education: Cut the Shackles; Cut the Crap; Cut the Mustard. *Canadian Journal of Native Education*, 22:1, 10-15.

Krotz, Larry. (1990). *Indian Country: Inside Another Canada*. Toronto, ON: McClelland and Stewart.

McDonald, N.G. (1974). Alexandre Tache: Defender of the Old Regime. *Profiles of Canadian Educators*. Robert S. Patterson, John W. Chalmers, and John W. Friesen, eds. Toronto, ON: D. C. Heath, 141-166.

McDonnell, R.F. and R.C. Depew. (1999). Self-Government and Self-Determination in Canada: A Critical Commentary. *Aboriginal Self-Government in Canada*. John H. Hylton, ed. Saskatoon, SK: Purich Publishing, 352-376.

Miller, J.R. (2000). *Skyscrapers Hide the Heavens: A History of Indian-White Relations in Canada*. Third edition. Toronto, ON: University of Toronto Press.

Patterson, E. Palmer. (1972). *The Canadian Indian*. Toronto, ON: Macmillan.

Ponting, J. Rick, ed. (1986). *Arduous Journey: Canadian Indians and Decolonization*. Toronto, ON: McClelland and Stewart.

Purich, Donald. (1986). *Our Land: Native Rights in Canada*. Toronto, ON: James Lorimer.

Sealey, D. Bruce and Antoine S. Lussier. (1975). *The Métis: Canada's Forgotten People*. Winnipeg, MB: Manitoba Métis Federation Press.

Snow, Chief John. (1977). *These Mountains Are Our Sacred Places: The Story of the Stoney Indians*. Toronto, ON: Samuel Stevens.

Surtees, R.J. (1969). The Development of an Indian Reserve Policy in Canada. *Ontario Historical Society*, LXI, 87-99.

Wall, Denis. (2000). Aboriginal Self-Government in Canada: The Cases of Nunavut and the Alberta Métis Settlements. *Visions of the Heart: Canadian Aboriginal Issues*. Second edition. David Long and Olive Patricia Dickason, eds. Toronto, ON: Harcourt Canada, 143-166.

Wuttunee, William I.C. (1971). *Ruffled Feathers*. Calgary, AB: Bell Books.

York, Geoffrey. (1989). *The Dispossessed: Life and Death in Native Canada*. Toronto, ON: Lester & Orpen Dennys.

Two

The Way Things Used to Be

In the olden days no one would have dreamed of laying claim to the land. It belonged, not just to the Dene, but to the moose, caribou, bears and birds as well. The river was shared by the fish in it and the people on it." – Andrew Chapeskie, Elder, Alaskan Dene Nation, (Friesen, 1998: 34).

As the twentieth century unfolded anthropological literature pertaining to First Nations continued to burgeon, following the lead of 17th century French philosopher, Jean Jacques Rousseau who chose the term, "noble savage" to describe North American Indians. Rousseau argued that "this creature" ought to be saved as a remnant of the bygone days of pre-civilization when people were happy and carefree. He argued that the excessive use of reason had corrupted mankind and a return to the days of pre-civilization, such as that practiced by the First Nations, was the only remedy for societal ills (Surtees, 1969: 90; Friesen and Boberg, 1990: 8-9). Although later perceptions of the Indigenous peoples deviated from Rousseau's romantic version in diverse ways, until recently the ways of the First Peoples were never viewed with the respect they deserved.

Negative Images

The First Nations of North America have struggled with the effects of European invasion in many ways, including the tendency of observers to print mainly critical stories about Aboriginal people. Newspaper reporters have especially been motivated by the fact that many happenings in Native communities can so easily be sensationalized. Today the orientation to print negative stories has diminished somewhat, the penchant to do so having been squelched out of fear of being accused of character assassination or running the risk of a lawsuit. It has also been influenced by more authentic descriptions of Native ongoings by Aboriginal writers. The image of

Indigenous people as part of a quaint but less than ideal subculture is slowly disappearing.

The Media

An Aboriginal writer Gilbert Oskaboose, once composed a brief essay in answer to the question, "What's is like to be an Indian?" He wrote;

> Well, . . . on one of my bad days I would say that . . . to be Indian is to be expected to be an expert on all things pertaining to the Great Outdoors. An Indian must be totally familiar with the Indian, English and Latin names of all Canadian flora and fauna, by fully cognizant of their medicinal properties . . . and aside from knowing most moose by their first names, be able to converse fluently with at least 15 separate species." (Oskaboose, 1980: 8)

Oskaboose went on to denigrate typical stereotypes about Indians, namely that Aboriginal spirituality consisted of worshipping totem poles and rocks, their war losses were always heavy in re-run western movies, and their situation (or "plight"), was subject to endless commiseration by Canadians (Oskaboose, 1980). Obviously weary of constantly encountering an endless array of erroneous portrayals of First Nations, Oskaboose chose to fight back in an essay of objection through exaggeration.

Thirty years ago, a Calgary newspaper addressed an editorial to a lecture about First Nations given by Dr. Harry Hawthorn of the University of British Columbia. Hawthorn lamented the passing of Indian culture while the local paper reciprocated by suggesting it would not be a bad thing if Aboriginal culture became a part of the Canadian mainstream because;

> . . . too much of Indian culture is really nothing but a poverty culture in this day and age. It spells out human suffering and reserve degradation, and the sooner it disappears the better." (*Calgary Herald*, February 17, 1971)

The editorial did allow that certain elements of Indigenous culture should be preserved, "the arts, the crafts and some of the traditions," and this should be undertaken in the same manner that other Canadians have remained conscious of their heritage. Fortuitously, we have come a long way since the days of the *Calgary Herald* editorial, and most media reports about Aboriginal communities are now more understanding. Note for example, a sympathetic comment by Julian Beltrame (June 16, 2003: 38) in *Maclean's;*

> They're angry because they've been left out of a process to trans-
> form the way Natives live. . . . An underlying fault with legislation
> is that it begins with a false premise—that the Native leadership's
> incompetence, or worse corruption, is a major contributor.

Academics

Native peoples have not always fared well at the hands of well-meaning social scientists, many of whom were no doubt influenced by their own cultural perspectives. Writing about the Indigenous people at the turn of the twentieth century, George Bird Grinnell, noted that;

> The Indian has the mind of a child in the body of an adult. . . . his
> mind does not work like the mind of the adult white man . . . by
> this I mean that it is a mind in many respects unused, and absolute-
> ly without training as regards all matters which have to do with
> civilized life. (Grinnell, 1900: 7-8)

Grinnell may have been correct in his observation that tradition-al Indigenous cultures thrived on different kinds of knowledge than their European counterparts, but he did not seem to recognize that cultural differences do not necessarily merit classification. Grinnell did admit that in terms of matters familiar to Aboriginals the First Nations manifested insights that apparently astonished even the white man, "who is here on unfamiliar ground." On the whole, however, Grinnell could not refrain from making remarks that implied the superior cultural repertoire of his own nationality.

Another late nineteenth century writer, John MacLean, was less subtle than Grinnell, and entitled one of his publications, *Canadian Savage Folk,* thereby castigating Aboriginal culture as uncivilized. MacLean delineated six types of religion among North American Indians, namely: (1) Shamanism; (2) Totemism; (3) Sun Worship; (4) Sabianism or Sky Worship; (5) Hero Worship; and, (6) Ancestor Worship. MacLean contended that Shamanism was the lowest form of religion, and it was practiced by the Inuit (Eskimos), the Tinne tribes of Athabasca, and certain tribes in British Columbia. (MacLean, 1986). Today anthropologists are a bit chagrined that MacLean would designate any religious form as "lowest." It is obvi-ous that MacLean's own bias got the better of him when he developed the paradigm by which to rank the various religions. In MacLean's defence, however, he did admit that a faithful study of Indian languages and customs would compel anyone to acknowledge that ". . . underneath the blanket and coat of skin there beats a human heart. . . . there is beauty, sweetness and wisdom in their traditions and courage, liberty and devotion in their lives" (MacLean, 1986: iv).

One of the pioneers of American anthropology, Ruth Benedict, sparked a minor furore when she decided that Indigenous cultures could be classified in terms of modal personality types. She suggested that Northwest coastal Indians were "Dionysian" in personality which meant that they were aggressive, prestige-seeking, and competitive. The southwest pueblo Indians, on the other hand, were "Apollonian" or peace-loving, laid back, and more reconciled to nature (Benedict, 1934). Benedict went on to denounce the potlatch feast of the west coast kwakwaka'wakw (Kwakiutl) First Nation as "wasteful" and observed that it ranked low on the human scale of values. She was brought up short by a colleague who demanded to know where she got the scale by which to evaluate that cultural practice and she was forced to admit that it was of her own making.

As it turned out, for many years anthropologists followed similar lines of thinking when it came to First Nations cultures. Robert Lowie entitled a book on Indian beliefs, *Primitive Religion* (Lowie, 1924), and Diamond Jenness could not resist describing Indian religion as "crude" and "curious" (Jenness, 1924: 181-183). These statements are not intended to denigrate the work of anthropologists as much as to point out that observers of Indigenous culture, regardless of their professional affiliations, have for a long time made judgments about Indigenous cultures from purely ethnocentric perspectives. While it may be true that some headway has been made in this respect, there is still much to do in rectifying past misjudgments.

There is evidence to indicate that the tone of writing about Indigenous history is gradually changing, and the Aboriginal people of North America may be getting a bit of a break. Representative of the trend to provide a more balanced view is the work of Olive Dickason whose two major works shifted the attention of Canadian historians to a new perspective. In Dickason's (1984) first book, *The Myth of the Savage and the Beginnings of French Colonialism in the Americas,* she investigated historical developments during European contact from the perspective of the peoples who were already resident here. The mandate perceived to be Divinely-granted to them caused the French to create an ideology that AmerIndians were savages. This description justified one of the greatest land grabs in human history as well as the squelching of the foundations of a well-established civilization. Historical accounts of the First Peoples encountered were penned by fur traders, explorers and missionaries, all of whom perceived Indigenous people as inferior and just targets for exploitation. All subsequent writings were attempts to justify the imperialism of France (and later England), religious or otherwise, and permit the ruthless transcendence of all national boundaries.

Dickason's (1993) second book, *Canada's First Nations: A History of Founding Peoples from Earliest Times* was targeted at filling the gap of the silent years before the Europeans came. Dickason pled for a wider scope and greater diversity of research for historians to study, other than just being document-bound. Because the First Peoples relied on an oral tradition, their recounts of past events were often ignored and a great deal has been lost. Today, thanks to mounting archaeological evidence, much of what was claimed about Native history via the oral tradition, has been substantiated. It is regrettable that a more appreciative stance for the oral tradition could not have been developed sooner so that the richness of Indigenous history could have been supplemented by the recorded sayings of Native elders. Dickason's work combined the historical documentary approach with the oral tradition, thereby enabling her to develop a fairly complete composite of Aboriginal life in Canada before the arrival of the French.

Dickason's tack has not gone unnoticed, and has definitely influenced two separate prongs of historical inquiry; first, the inclusion of First Nations' data before first contact; and, second, the provision of firsthand elder narratives to round out the program. Two books that illustrate the first influence are *Origins: Canadian History to Confederation* by Douglas Francis, Richard Jones and Donald Smith (1988), and *History of the Canadian Peoples: Beginnings to 1867*, by Margaret Conrad, Alvin Finkel, and Cornelius Jaenen (1993). Although both volumes offer only single chapter outlines of Native life before the Europeans arrived, the fact of their having made the attempt to include such information shows definite improvement over earlier historical surveys. Basically, Francis and colleagues offer one paragraph descriptions of such major themes in AmerIndian history as the moundbuilders, the buffalo, and the horse under the guise of surveying the major culture areas of Canada. Still, theirs is a noble effort in an enterprise too long neglected by North American historians.

Margaret Conrad and colleagues fare a bit better by recognizing that historians have only recently attempted to offer a fuller picture of Canadian history researching First Nations happenings before the European invasion. These authors caution that a reverse look into our historical past could give birth to the danger of romanticizing the past life of the First Peoples who actually behaved much like other nations in their approach to life. True, some First Nations were warlike, others had slaves, and still others engaged in wasteful hunting practices which may have caused the death of certain species of animals, but these shortcomings could easily be paralleled in other societies. Many historians generously admit that until recently members of their profession relied only on the written tradition as a valid form of accumulating information about the past, and those sources were usually penned by an elite group of nonNative males who had very specific agendas.

Recent historical releases have increasingly devoted space to the precontact lifestyles of First Nations. Miller (2000) entitles the first three chapters of his book: "Indians and Europeans at the time of first contact, Early Contacts in the Eastern Woodlands," and "Commercial Partnership and Mutual Benefit." Steckley and Cummins (2001) offer these first four chapter titles: "The Oral Tradition, Connections to the Land, Native Languages," and "The Peopling of the Americas" as introductory to their work. Higham (2000), on the other hand, chooses to honor the precontact cultures of First Nations by belittling the work of Christian missionaries. All of these authors reference Dickason's works.

Publications devoted solely to portraying aspects of Indian life-today offer an advanced degree of sophistication and authenticity. Miller (1995: ix), for example, attempts to provide information that will build a foundation on which to answer fundamental questions raised by the public; "Just what do the Natives want?" or "Why should they have special rights in Canada?" McMillan labels the colonialist policies of past governments a dismal failure and pleads for the recognition of Indian cultures and rights. The tone of his work is paralleled by Bruce Morrison and Roderick Wilson of the University of Alberta and James Frideres of the University of Calgary. Morrison and Wilson (1995: 14) build their case for a more objective look at Indigenous cultures on three assertions: (i) an understanding of Native peoples must start from an appreciation of Aboriginal society as it existed and as it continues; (ii) perceptions which Native peoples have of themselves must take into account the political dimensions of the history of relationships between Native cultures and Canadian society; and, (iii) scholars who describe the nuances of Native societies always bring an element of the subjective to the printed page. Frideres echoes these sentiments by providing a critical interpretation of the "person on the street's" thinking about Native people (Frideres, 1993: viii).

Alternate Images

Ironically, a quite positive source describing the First Nations of North America came from the pen of the imperialist explorer, Christopher Columbus in his first letters to Spain's royal court;

> So tractable, so peaceful are these people that I swear to your Majesties that there is not in the world a better nation. They love their neighbours as themselves, and their discourse is ever sweet and gentle, and accompanied with a smile . . . their manners are decorous and praiseworthy. (Brown, 1981: 1)

Columbus' positive impression was paralleled by other nonNatives, for example, missionary Father A.M. Beede, who described the Sioux (parent tribe of the Assiniboines), as a "true church of God" with a religion of truth and kindness. He suggested that the Sioux had no need for missionaries so he abandoned the role and devoted his life to the study of law so he could help the Sioux in the capacity of legal adviser. He was subsequently defrocked by the church and spent the rest of his life in service to "the downtrodden race of America" (Seton and Seton, 1966: 38). Father Wilhelm Schmidt (1965) supplemented Beede's observations by careful analysis of the theological system of various Indigenous Peoples, and argued that there were no grounds on which to label the foundations of their beliefs as less valid than those emanating from Europe. Schmidt vigorously propounded the theory that at the time of the first arrival of the Europeans, the First Nations had in place a monotheistic theological system that paralleled in sophistication and complexity any system imported from across the ocean (Schmidt, 1965: 21-33).

Of Assiniboine extraction, Chief John Snow of the Wesley Band of the Stoney Nation (Nakoda Sioux), observed that when Christian missionaries arrived in Stoney country their message was readily heeded. He claimed that this was because of the similarity of beliefs between the two parties. The Stoneys perceived the Creator as a caring, healing Being whose attention could be secured by faith through prayer and fasting. The medical skills of the Stoneys reinforced their belief that the Creator's teachings and lessons would be learned by observing the universe around them. They studied the laws of nature and lived by them. In addition, the creations of the Great Spirit revealed many mysteries to the Stoneys and enhanced their respect for the earth (Snow, 1977: 7).

McDougall Methodist Church (1873) near Morley, Alberta

Anthropological surveys of North American Indians that followed the flagship lead of Grinnell and MacLean slowly began to reflect a degree of respect for Native ways. One such classic by Paul Radin, first published in 1927, was entitled, *The Story of the American Indian*. Although relatively objective in describing the various facets of AmerIndian culture, Radin could not refrain from ridiculing some elements of Aboriginal etiquette. As Radin noted;

> Etiquette, however, seemed to reach its most ridiculous culmination in the case of a man's mother-in-law. Whenever possible he sat

with his back to her. Not one word did he address to her nor, for that matter, did she address any to him. (Radin, 1937: 18)

In analyzing the spiritual context of North American Indian cultures, Radin discounted the assumption that Indian peoples were theologically monotheistic. He argued that monotheism was not a commonly-practiced perspective among AmerIndians, but rather the result of philosophical speculations by a small segment within the community, notably shamans or priests. Radin contended that the Supreme Beings identified by these individuals were not meant to be worshipped, and in cases where they did become the object of spiritual adulation their position was quickly transformed into the highest position within a pantheistic realm (Radin, 1937).

A contemporary of Radin, anthropologist Clark Wissler, exhibited a bit more sensitivity, noting that the North American First Nations were often accused of engaging in extreme measures when involved in war. Wissler pointed out that while the Aboriginal way of making war might have been unique, it was certainly not as pagan as modern "civilized" wars where people are bombed ". . . from the air, mostly by raids to burn, mutilate, kill and spread terror, with no regard for age, sex or condition" (Wissler, 1966: 17). Although he may have hoped for it, Wissler did not anticipate the assimilation of AmerIndians in the near future, emphasizing that they should be respected for the specialized knowledge they had accumulated, such as the domestication of wild plants. He conceded that Indigenous knowledge had enabled the First Peoples to live on this continent for thousands of years. By contrast, Wissler's contemporary, Diamond Jenness, traversed Canadian soil from east to west, and to the far north, writing about Native people. Jenness speculated that among other things, some day the Eskimo race, for example, would amalgamate ". . . with white trappers and traders and produce the hardy and resourceful stick necessary for the development of Canada's far North" (Jenness, 1986: 422).

Bering Strait

No one really knows the exact origins of Canada's First Nations; they may well have always been here, as some of AmerIndian tribes have claimed. Many archaeologists believe the First Peoples of Canada (at least in the west), came to this continent from Asia via Alaska across the Bering Strait as many as 30 000 years ago. Those who adhere to this interpretation estimate that at that time the 80 kilometre wide strait may have stretched to 1 500 kilometres in width. Deloria (1995: 88-89) debunks this theory on the basis that an ocean water level drop of 60 metres would have been necessary to form the isthmus on which the people could cross. At that time Siberia was locked in huge glaciers and its population would have had to be minute. Furthermore, Siberian temperatures would have been such that "it would have been impossible for people to move without freezing to death or falling into glaciers" (Deloria, 1995: 89).

The case for arguing that the Indigenous Peoples have a very old history on this continent usually relies on archaeological evidence. The case has been weakened somewhat by the recent redating of two identified early Canadian sites. One, the Old Crow site, in northern Yukon, was originally dated as being at least 17 000 years old. More recent dating in 1985 showed located artifacts to be only 1 300 years old. A reexamination of a second site at Taber, Alberta, did not verify claims of it being 30 000 to 60 000 years old. Instead, scientists concluded that the site may be only 4 000 years old. Despite this, there are several other sites, particularly in the Yukon which provide evidence that Native cultures in that area were existent between 10 000 and 16 000 years ago (McMillan, 1988).

The oldest dated materials with clearly established associations of people and animals in the Great Plains are still those assigned to the Clovis or Llano peoples. These are mainly in the western and southern sections of the plains and consist of remains of mammoth kills which were accomplished by thrusting or throwing spears near waterholes or springs. They often include bones of camels, horses, and giant bison as well as species which are now extinct. These remains date around AD 11 000 and are still without cultural antecedents (Wedel, 1978). More than anything these finds prove that the First Nations of Canada have been around for a long time. Perhaps the last word on the subject should go to the oral tradition of First Nations themselves whose many stories of how the world began deserve equal consideration with interpretations about origins from other world philosophical systems (Conrad, Finkel and Jaenen, 1993). In this context Spence (1994) notes that the origin stories of Aboriginal peoples are infinitely more rich in creative and deluge myths than those of any other race in the two hemispheres. Spence (1994: 106) states;

Tales which deal with the origin of man are exceedingly frequent, and exhibit every phase of the type of creative story. Although many of these are similar to European and Asiatic myths of the same class, others show great originality, and strikingly present to our minds the characteristics of American Aboriginal thought.

A half century ago, anthropologists began to eliminate inadvertent or implied ethnocentric observations about First Nations cultures, and produced works more readily oriented towards the acknowledgment of Indian contributions to the North American way of life. Many, however, like Ruth Underhill (1953), still clung tenaciously to the theory that the Indigenous Peoples migrated to North America via the Bering Strait. Driver was more hesitant; "Although we are certain that there was some contact between South Pacific Islands and South America before 1492, this came much too late to account for any principal peopling of the New World" (Driver, 1968: 4).

The lack of information about the fabled Bering Strait theory has not kept anthropologists from guessing about Indigenous origins on this continent, and they have plenty of company. The general presupposition on which the Bering Strait theory has been promulgated is that since archaeological evidence exists to identify the presence of Indigenous peoples 11 000 years ago in the Valley of Mexico, this means that their ancestors must have come to America via the Bering Strait thousands of years earlier. Anyone analyzing Vine Deloria, Jr.'s sarcastic repudiation of that theory is sure to agree with him that "the Bering Strait theory is simply shorthand scientific language for, 'I don't know, but it sounds good and no one will check'" (Deloria, 1995: 81). Sadly, if Deloria is correct, the most compelling reason for advancing the theory is to justify European colonization. If it can convincingly be argued that First Nations were also fairly recent immigrants to North America, they could lose their claim to being original inhabitants and with that the right of first occupancy.

By the 1960s generic works about the Indigenous peoples began to take on a degree of academic sophistication, but musings about the Bering Strait lingered. As Owen, Deetz, and Fisher (1968: 3) stated;

The dates of the earliest migration to the New World are still in question. . . . Regarded as even less likely are those fanciful contentions which suggest that the origin of American Indians can be attributed to sunken continents or wandering lost tribes.

Josephy (1968: 38)was more specific, and estimated that the bridge across the Bering Strait was probably part of a path that led to the New World some 12 000 to 35 000 years ago. Peter Farb (1968: 191) concurred; he estimated that the Aboriginal people of North America had lived on this continent at least 13 000 years ago. Jennings (1978: 1) was even more persistent, insisting that "There is no reasonable doubt as to the ultimate origin of the human population that finally covered the hemisphere." These scholars were joined by Carlson as late as 1998 (20) when he stated;

> Ancestors of the first humans to occupy the Great Plains came to America from Asia. They were hunters whose lifestyles reflected a dependence on big game. . . . Probably unaware that they had crossed to another continent, the migrants entered North America at different periods over a long span of time.

Carlson joins a long list of academics who still assert with some degree of confidence that thou believe the first North Americans were of Asian stock. Deloria was right; for "professionals" of this category, any form of "educated speculation" would appear to be much superior to what they might term pure fantasy, although the differences might not be evident to anyone else.

Indigenous Perspectives

Some hope for setting the record straight about Native origins and the nature of their traditional way of life emanates from the Aboriginal sector. There are increasing numbers of published works penned by Indigenous writers which describe the preinvasion lifestyle and Native hopes for the future. It would be premature to suggest that these works will necessarily produce an accurate picture of First Nations cultures since some of the writers will be tempted to paint a little brighter picture of their heritage if only as a means of retaliation (Friesen, 1985). However, these literary offerings comprise a step in the right direction, namely that the *Indigenous* side of things is at last being told.

Written descriptions of traditional Aboriginal cultures by Native writers are of considerably more recent origin than anthropological sources and they promulgate a bold and refreshingly new perspective. Relying heavily on information from contemporary elders, much of this information is speculative and in alignment with the oral tradition, not necessarily demonstrative of reliance on written historical documentation. Much of the past is clouded with mystery, and informants can only guess at the meaning of some traditional Indian values. The extent of preserved knowledge also varies from one community to another. Most of that which was recorded, and is currently utilized by Native writers, was undertaken by individuals who neither spoke Indigenous languages nor understood their cultures (LaRoque, 1975: 29). Writings by First Nations, recent as they are, tend to portray a somewhat idyllic picture of the old way of life rather than presenting a purely descriptive view or analyzing seeming inconsistencies or deficiencies therein. Perhaps this stance is adopted as a means of bolstering evidence against the negative stereotypes so much postulated about Native peoples. A few examples may illustrate this observation.

Writing at the time of the formulation of the infamous federal White Paper of 1969 which advocated the breakup of Indian reserves, Harold Cardinal called the policy pertaining thereto as a ". . . thinly disguised programme of extermination through assimilation," based on the philosophy that "the only good Indian is a non-Indian" (Cardinal, 1969: 1). Cardinal argued that the "good old days" of Indigenous life featured effective institutions of every kind and fostered a series of corresponding values. Cardinal postulated that the educational system in traditional Aboriginal communities functioned well because it was designed to prepare children for the life they were to lead. The end result was that Indian children knew who they were and how they related to the world and the people about them. Like other Native social institutions, the underlying currents of motivation were spiritual and based on "the philosophy of brotherly love, the principle of sharing in the purification of giving, in the good sense of forgiving . . . " (Cardinal, 1969: 81). Cardinal put forth the argument that many First Nations leaders believe if society returns to the old values, ethics and morals of Native beliefs, their social institutions would be strengthened.

Writing two years later from the standpoint of comprising a rebuttal to Cardinal's work, a fellow Cree, lawyer William Wuttunee (1971: 1) strongly denounced the concept of the Indian reserve as an outdated mode of living promoted by glorifying "a buckskin and feather culture." Wuttunee contended that modern Indian culture must move past traditional notions of "buckskin and feathers" and become flexible and relevant. However, like Cardinal and other of his counterparts, Wuttunee believed in the glory days of the buffalo hunt and in the virtues of traditional Indian life—peace and content-ment, a sense of relaxation in their concept of time, an appreciation of living close to nature without polluting one's surroundings, and a deep concern for fellow members in the community (Wuttunee, 1971: 117; Snow, 1977: 16). Apparently no race of people ever had a stronger love for their families. They never punished their children by corporal punishment, fully recognizing the harmful effects that come from manhandling children (Red Fox, 1971: 21; Pelletier and Poole, 1973). Even the condition of their physical health was enshrined as excellent. First Nations were described as healthy and strong, and seldom sick. The great outdoors provided them with dependable remedies for their few ailments, and they enjoyed life fully even though the rigors of the northern winters brought many hardships (Dion, 1979: 5).

Observers of the bygone Native cultural lifestyle sometimes fall into the trap of believing that because the nature of the structure of traditional Native cultures was so different and often invisible to the outsider, there was no inner structure. In fact, nothing could be fur-ther from the truth. In addition to having very specific rules govern-ing every aspect of their way of life, there were very strong founda-tional spiritual bases on which these rules were designed. Undergirded by the oral tradition, many of the interpretations of the various rituals and practices changed with the times and with the practitioner, but their persistence even in modified form gave struc-ture and meaning to the culture. In the final analysis, the strength to fulfil oneself lay within the individual. Religious purity was a state of being within self. "If you cannot be honest with yourself, you will never be honest with anyone else" (Manuel and Posluns, 1974: 36). Cochise of the Ciricahua Apache nation would have added, "You must speak straight so your words may go as sunlight into our hearts" (Friesen, 1998: 50).

There are a number of Aboriginal writers who convey a note of negativity and disenchantment through their portrayals of tradition-al Indian lifestyle, particularly with regard to its chances to endure. Frustrated with what they consider to be an relentless campaign of assimilation against them, they describe as purely paternalistic past and present institutional efforts to intervene in the Indian communi-ty, particularly efforts by government, educators, and religious personnel (Sealey and Kirkness, 1973: 198). Indigenous writers assert that efforts by Native peoples to improve their lot on these fronts are thwarted or hindered by interfering government officials and outside do-gooders (Campbell, 1973: 156). If these writers are correct, the future for Aboriginal people looks bleak, and their options are limited and negative. Some writers cast an air of despair about them (Cardinal, 1977: 219); others, disillusioned with the leadership emanating from within their own communities, predict the possibility of violence as an option (Adams, 1975; Sealey and Lussier, 1975: 194). Events that transpired at the 1990 armed standoff in the Mohawk community at Oka, Quebec, are one example of this reality. This happening resoundly underscored the fact that circumstances which birth conflict and discord find their origins as much in the nonNative world as they do in the Native community. Cultural misunderstandings emanate from within two opposing sectors just as meaningful dialogue and conflict resolution comprise a two-way street. The roots of misunderstanding are buried deep in First Nations history, usually thoughtlessly perpetuated by outside powerbrokers who see no need to understand the Native point of view. The resultant disregard for and manipulation of Native values are often propelled by an impatience for traditional (slower) ways which are seen to impede progress.

Some Native writers, though very aware of the atrocities worked against their people in the past, still manage to project an air of optimism and hope (Campbell, 1973: 156-57; Manuel and Posluns, 1974; Snow, 1977). Brascoupé (2000: 429) states that the Aboriginal peoples of Canada are major players in resource restoration and sustainable resource harvesting. He further posits that they "are also playing a greater role in nation building." Castellano, Davis, and Lahache (2000: 255) suggest that;

> Political gains in the area of Aboriginal self-government can provide breathing space while the spirit of Aboriginal people provides the impetus for cultural survival. . . . Traditional ecological knowledge is just one area in which the wisdom of Aboriginal people is gaining recognition around the globe.

Yazzie (2000) joins his Aboriginal colleagues by insisting that while Indigenous people may not necessarily experience success with "macro issues," they can succeed with "micro issues" such as effectively assuming control of and taking responsibility for their own personal lives. As he states (2000: 47);

We must exercise internal sovereignty, which is nothing more than taking control of our personal lives, our families, our clans, and our communities. To do that, we must return to our traditions, because they speak to right relationships, respect, solidarity, and survival.

These are not the writings of poets, but of reasonable observers, eager to participate in the process of maintaining and rebuilding. They are willing to cooperate with others in seeking to enhance the renaissance of Native ways (Lincoln, 1985). They are well aware that any changes to be effected in their communities will need to be a cooperative effort between Natives and nonNatives working side by side (Erasmus, 1989: 42). This will mean that if justice is to prevail, "ruling class Canadians" will have to give up something for cooperation to be birthed, psychologically as well as in material means (Riley, 1984: 163). The future of Native hopes for a better world is fraught with a painful challenge for all Canadians and all North Americans in fact. The question remains, "Do the power brokers of society possess enough of the human spirit of goodwill that they can 'move over' sufficiently, even though heavy costs may be involved, and assist Indigenous people in attaining their just due?"

First Contact

Unlike other cultural groups in Canada, the First Peoples have a long heritage of political conquest. Often targets of resource-hungry and insensitive governments and religious politics of cultural domination with which it is highlighted, First Nations history is certainly not dry reading. In fact, most of the initial intercultural happenings between locals and incoming Europeans were fraught with a view to eradicating Native cultures if necessary to prepare the new world for "civilization."

When the fur traders arrived they established the parameters by which Native cultures would be viewed during the centuries that followed. Aboriginals were viewed as a common culture with little regard for the inherent diversity among them. The newcomers did not realize that the cultural variations among resident Native peoples were as extensive as they were among incoming cultures. This fact is still somewhat difficult for observers to comprehend in light of the habit of describing Aboriginal cultures as an entity separate from the national cultural mainstream. It is another misconception to think of specific First Nations tribes as always having occupied the areas in which they currently reside. Many tribes historically engaged in substantial migrations. For example, linguistic patterns indicate that the two main Cree peoples today (Plains and Woodland), had a common origin. Originally they were part of an eastern Woodland configuration. Today, however, the designation between the Woodland or Bush Cree and Plains Cree is well established. The Crees first came west with the fur trade and gradually formed two subdivisions of Woodland and Plains cultures. The former group comprised the mainstay of the fur trade, while the latter group became primarily a buffalo people. In making this adaptation, they developed a culture not unlike that of the Blackfoot who presumably came west from the Great Lakes region (Patterson, 1972; Dempsey, 1979).

Initially the Crees welcomed the fur trade because it gave them access to goods not locally obtainable. They liked to hunt, and the added impetuous of trading off their goods enhanced their motivations for that undertaking. The Blackfoot were less directly involved in trading, preferring instead to act as suppliers of food (chiefly buffalo meat), and sellers of horses to trading posts. The animosity ascribed to Cree-Blackfoot relations today originated in the fur trade, each nation being very jealous of their traditional hunting territories.

If there were differences in the way the original occupants accepted the fur traders there were even greater differences in the way fur trading personnel regarded them. To the south, the Spanish attempted to dominate the First Nations for economic purposes which resulted in a campaign of colonization. Religious missions were an important element in "civilizing" the Indians and intermarriage between Spanish and Aboriginals was commonplace. Further north, French traders acted in a similar fashion, even being encouraged to intermarry with the locals as a means of cementing relations for a continuing successful fur trade. This attitude quickly led to the origins of the Métis people.

English traders were not as accepting, preferring to hold their new acquaintances at arm's length, rarely allowing Indigenous hunters into their trading posts as visitors (Patterson, 1972: 92). Both the English and French, however, were interested in establishing permanent settlements in the new world, primarily as a means of obtaining lucrative economic rewards. Both nations needed the

Aboriginals as allies in their quest, and despite the more hospitable attitude on the part of the French, English military might eventually dominated. Their economic success was subsequently attributable to the efforts of the Hudson's Bay Company established in 1670. After a series of clashes between the Hudson's Bay Company and the French-established Northwest Company, things came to head when the English officially gained control of the Hudson's and James Bays through the Treaty of Utrecht in 1713 (Francis, Jones, and Smith, Vol. 1, 1988: 340-341).

The Fur Trade

The fur trade precipitated a series of major cultural upheavals among Native peoples characterized, perhaps by intermarriage. Social, political, and economic changes also occurred, many of them subtle enough to escape first glance. Other changes like the introduction of the horse and the gun were immediately obvious. The effect of these diffusive elements was significant, for example, in the redefinition of the role of the Indian chief or headman. Accustomed as they were to functioning according to European social structures, fur traders usually sought out persons in authority when beginning the bargaining process, and thus the office of chief soon took on an added element of economic importance among Natives. Traditionally, the role of chiefs as tradespeople was limited, and maintained primarily on the basis of his/her successes as a warrior or hunter. When fur traders concentrated their efforts on chiefs as a negotiators, and lavished gifts on them in order to enhance their chances of good trade, the office of chief began to take on new responsibilities. Trade negotiators preferred to deal with the same individual each subsequent year, and thus the chief's office grew to be a political force not previously recognized as such by First Nations themselves (Ray, 1974: 137). That prestige has been maintained to this day, accompanied by the traditional expectation that chiefs will also supply and care for their people.

Ascribing economic responsibilities to the office of chief worked to the advantage of fur traders in another way. If a tribe brought in a lower number of furs than expected, company negotiators withheld gifts from Native leaders as a means of motivating them to encourage their hunters to work up to quota. Unfortunately, some of the gifts used to motivate fur production worked devastation among the locals, particularly the gifts of alcohol (firewater) and tobacco. As gift-giving became more important in motivating the fur trade, larger quantities of both were given out. As Ray notes, competition also encouraged larger gift-giving which in turn lessened the motivation for hunting and influences Aboriginals hunters to spend more of their time indulging in an "indolent lifestyle" (Ray, 1974: 122). The result was that the attempt to obtain more furs through gift-giving contributed toward the weakening of traditional Indigenous culture. Traders tried to stock up and trade more liquor and tobacco to enhance the trade market while the Indians continued to rely increasingly on products which ultimately damaged the success of the fur trade.

"Family Comes first,"Trudy and Ivan Wesley and family, Stoney (Nakoda Sioux) First Nation, Morley, Alberta

As an indication of economic value differences between the first North American residents and the invaders, European explorers aimed for territorial aggrandizement, unlike their Native hosts who fought for prestige, honor and booty. Radin (1937: 5) describes the extent to which chiefs were traditionally exhorted to serve their people;

> Try to do something for your people. . . . have pity on your people and love them. If a man is poor, help him. Give him and his family food, give them whatever they ask for. If there is discord among your people, intercede. Take your sacred pipe and walk into their midst. Die if necessary in your attempt to bring about reconcilia-

tion. Then when order had been restored and they see you lying on the ground dead, still holding in your hand the sacred pipe, the symbol of peace and reconciliation, then assuredly will they know that you have been a real chief.

Traditionally, the First Nations sought to produce only enough food supply for their immediate or seasonal needs, and they did not hoard. In fact, they shared whatever they had with anyone who had need. By contrast, their invading captors collected everything and anything in surplus amounts and placed great store on who possessed what property. A large amount of material goods was equated with spiritual prowess and assignments of stratified importance were correlated with material success. Value orientation differences such as these still persist between the worldviews of Natives and nonNatives in North America, and indicate just how wide a cultural gulf is yet to be crossed if meaningful communication is to be attained.

Horse and Gun

The introduction of the horse and the gun caused significant changes to the First Nations lifestyle. The horse culture actually began in the early 18th century in the southern United States with Spanish colonists who took up residence in northern Mexico and what is now the state of New Mexico. Later the horse migrated further north to the Great Plains. The animal fit in well with the nomadic moves of the Aboriginals since it was able to carry heavier loads, and travel faster than was the case with a dog travois. The horse was also a valuable means of transportation for hunting.

By the nineteenth century the demand for horses skyrocketed to unbelievable proportions. It became popular to steal horses as a means of proving one's qualities as a warrior; partially the deed was magnified in importance by the amount of danger involved. To steal the picketed horse of an enemy was a very brave act, to say nothing of the value which a good horse could bring in trade or as a sign of individual wealth (Driver, 1968: 233). Social distinctions were also made according to the number of horses a man possessed. Often horseless families would attach themselves to a family with horses and a band or subdivision of a tribe was thus formed. Social mobility of a new sort became a reality when a young man of a poor family rose to wealth and status by acquiring horses. This was done through raiding parties and even sons of wealthy families often participated because they were teased into joining a raiding party to show how brave they were (Patterson, 1972: 93). Undoubtedly, the interest shown in rodeos by First Nations today is a carryover from the status scale and significance which the horse wove into the fabric of Indian culture.

The introduction of the gun was a boon to the eager Native hunter and afforded an immediate superiority over a gunless enemy. This was not necessarily the case when the gun was first introduced because of the complications which developed because of the first gun's inadequate technology. However, as the instrument improved its users got to the point that they could hardly live without it. American historian, Walter Webb of the University of Texas surmised that technological elements as simplistic as the six-gun, the windmill and barbed-wire made the west inhabitable for emigrating settlers (Webb, 1931). Imagine the surprise on the enemy's face when he discovered that his foe had fired what he thought was his one-shot musket, only to discover that the enemy continued to keep firing. This was the superiority of the new gun. Not only could the hunter continue to stalk his prey if he missed the first time, he could also count on hitting his target from a much greater distance. To complete the account of the various elements of frontier development promulgated by Webb, he also postulated that the windmill made it possible to access water on the plains from deep wells, and barbed-wire secured private ranchland from invasion.

Early guns introduced problems of obtaining ammunition and weapon repair. If a gun failed it was useless to the owner until he could make a long trip back to the trading post, usually in spring when travel was possible. Repairing guns also made possible a new vocation for men at trading posts even though it was not easy to consult with repairmen during severe winters when travel was restricted. That was a problem confounded with technological ramifications which would require years of catch-up experimentation (Ray, 1974: 75).

The Crees were the first western First Nation to possess guns and soon after the Blackfoot acquired rifles. Each tribe was anxious to obtain firearms once they learned of their existence because of the subsequent superiority it would render them in hunting and war (Jenness, 1986: 254). It could also be said that the gun's very existence contributed to strife and warfare, particularly so if the enemy was not known to have guns.

Disease

Another biproduct of the fur trade was the transplantation of diseases from Europe, including illnesses now viewed as "common household" or "children's diseases," for example, measles, whooping cough, smallpox, and tuberculosis. A smallpox epidemic in eastern Canada in 1781-1782 almost wiped entire tribes out of existence. At the height of the epidemic, some family members lay unburied in their tents while survivors fled, unfortunately to spread the disease further. It became a fulltime occupation of inland trading post staff to care for sick Indians without even having time to ply their trade (Rich, 1976: 158-159). In the west another smallpox epidemic in 1837 wiped out two-thirds of the Blackfoot Nation, and again in 1857-1858 the dreaded disease hit epidemic proportions. Up till the 1900s it was largely believed by government officials that the Indigenous peoples would eventually die out from these causes. Thus the reserves on which the First People were placed were seen as convenient custodial areas to which services could be provided to residents on a temporary basis while their most certain destiny could unravel. Reserves were created for the government's administrative convenience, not to safeguard Indian lands. Their establishment was to render certain areas available for settlement by nonNatives. No reserves were created in areas where whites wanted to settle (Melling, 1967: 37-39).

Partially, the fur trade faltered because of the demise of desired furbearing animals. By the late 1800s, the buffalo had also vanished from the plains, and where huge herds of buffalo could once be seen all across the prairies, in just a few years there were only a dozen or so animals in a herd (Symington, 1969: 217). The reasons why the buffalo disappeared are more complex than merely laying the blame at overhunting. That there was overhunting is a fact. The Métis, for example, are credited with killing up to 100 000 animals in one season alone, exclusively for trade purposes. They also killed additional animals for their own use. Sportshooting by nonaffected hunters also took its toll on the lumbering beasts. A Sunday pastime would be to ride a slow-moving train through a herd of buffalo and see how many could be eliminated from a sportsman's gun. Some buffalo also died from a natural enemy, namely prairie fires, which were sometimes ignited by smoke-spewing, charcoal-spreading trains which rumbled across the prairies. What had been the "supermarket of the plains" met death by starvation as landspace became increasingly scarce due to its occupation by incoming settlers. With a severe restriction of grazing lands, it became harder for buffalo to follow their annual migration treks.

Trains

An important factor in effecting change in Aboriginal culture was the coming of the railway. The national tie of the Canadian railroad was completed in British Columbia in 1885, but its devastating effect on Native communities occurred earlier. During the earlier part of l880s, Winnipeg was viewed as the "Gateway to the West" and became the settlement where the rail ended and newcomers to the nation migrated to points west on horseback and by wagontrain. By 1882, a total of 133 000 settlers had arrived in Canada, two-thirds of whom chose the west as a place to live. The settlers came in response to government advertisements offering free land in dryland areas reputed to be excellent for farming. Each homesteader could obtain 160 free acres if buildings were erected and half of the land was tilled within three years (Friesen, 1989: 29; Palmer, 1982). During the peak of immigration as many as 2 500 settlers left the Winnipeg depot each week and this reality promoted the expansion of the railway to points west. By 1883 there were just 1 000 kilometres of track to be laid before the nation would be joined by a steel line.

There was, of course, an important corollary reason for expanding the railroad masterminded by one William Cornelius Van Horne of the Canadian Pacific Railroad. Van Horne saw railway expansion as a way to make Canada rich by attracting opulent travellers from Europe to experience the majesty of Canada's beauty by touring the prairies and mountain areas via train. Van Horne also supervised the building of luxury hotels in the west so that visitors could be accommodated in style (Hart, 1983: 28). Many of the specially constructed hotels still dot the downtown landscape of major western cities and smaller centres such as Waterton and Emerald Lake in Alberta.

One can only marvel at the discrepancy in lifestyles that existed between incoming immigrants and touring millionaires. Many of the settlers came from peasant cultures and undoubtedly their quickly constructed shacks or sodhouses may have fascinated the affluent tourists as an additional attraction of the Canadian wilds. The immigrants, however, were probably too involved in eking out

Former Lebret Residential School, largest in western Canada (350 children). Lebret, Saskatchewan

a living to notice the extent of wealth of the passing entourage of opulence.

For the First Nations the railway had greater significance. It meant more people in the west, more restrictions on hunting areas, a diminishing number of buffalo for food, and a growing realization that the traditional way of life was fast coming to an end. It would mean an end to a golden age which had only recently been liberated by imported horses and guns whose benefits were being suffocated by even more inventions. Soon a proud and fearless nomadic culture would be transformed into a "pathetic, half-starved creature, confined to the semi-prisons of the new reserves and totally dependent on government for his existence" (Berton, 1974: 374).

Churches and Schools

It would be misleading to foster the notion that missionary activity among First Nations was singularly religious. This thesis may be illustrated with reference to the career of one of the nation's first missionaries, Marguerite Bourgeoys, founder of the Order of Ursulines in 17th century New France. Bourgeoys visualized the education of Aboriginals as an admixture of humanitarian acts with Christian teaching (Chalmers, 1974). Jesuit day schools founded in the 17th century introduced agricultural education and manual training as a means of helping First Nations adjust to the impending cultural shift from hunting to farming and as a means of "preventing laziness among Indian children" (Brookes, 1990: 12). When the success of these schools maintained dismal results, the Jesuits built residential or boarding schools. The idea was that with forced attendance, students would disconnect with their heritage culture and experience greater academic success. Initially, parents were bribed to send their children to day schools, but they were reluctant to do so because of the long absences they experienced from their children. Manual learning opportunities were introduced including mathematics, marine navigation, and arts and crafts. The element of integration was also at play in these schools; while most of the students attending came from nonNative backgrounds, a few Aboriginal children did attend (Chalmers, 1972).

By 1830 the administration of the Federal Department of Indian Affairs was transferred from military to civil authority and a revised

Christian Education at Morley United Church, Stoney
(Nakoda Sioux) First Nation, Morley, Alberta

policy became evident with regard to First Nations schooling. Industrial schools specializing in trades were added to the agenda in Eastern Canada offering training for such occupations as black-smithing, carpentry, cabinet-making, and tailoring were offered to boys. Girls were taught sewing, knitting, cooking, and laundry work. An evaluation of the success of these schools was undertaken in 1858 and showed they had accomplished very little. As a result, they were soon abolished (Brookes, 1990: 21).

In the west, Roman Catholic missionaries under the leadership of Bishop Alexandre Tache (1823-1896), dedicated themselves to a rejuvenation of Indian civilization on the premise that while First Nations had once reached an advanced stage of civilization they had lost it because they had abandoned the "traditions which bound them to God" (McDonald, 1974: 151). Industrial schools were made part of the pedagogical package, founded with the secondary objective of recruiting young Amerindians for the priesthood. It was a matter of disappointment to the Bishop Tache that during his administration not a single Native person was ordained to the priesthood.

A Methodist missionary named James Evans began work among the northern Saskatchewan Indians in 1840, accompanied by the Rev. Henry Steinhauer, a Native convert. Evans is noted for his invention of Cree syllabics which provided Indigenous People with the Scriptures and hymns in their own language. Another missionary Rev. Robert Rundle, worked further south among the Blackfoot and Stoney Indians, largely learning their ways by accompanying them on their hunting expeditions. It was part of the work of missionaries George McDougall and his son, John, who worked among the northern Swampy Cree and the Stoney tribe near Calgary to build the first Methodist schools for Aboriginal children. Their first mission school opened at Whitefish Lake, Alberta, where they tried to effect a broader-than-religion-only kind of policy with this slogan, "Christianize, educate, and civilize." To Christianize meant infusing the Methodist version of the Gospel into Stoney culture; education, consisted of teaching the three "r's;" and, civilizing implied developing an allegiance to the British Crown. The latter also required the instilling of various "civilized practices" among the Stoney converts, including democratic procedures of operation, and the abolition of certain unacceptable (barbaric) practices such as the Stoney wolf-feast (Friesen, 1974).

Future Outlook

The repercussions of the historical cultural clash between Aboriginals and nonAboriginals are quite evident today. The conditions in most Indigenous communities, economically and socially, are in many instances well below the national standard. The fact that the original cultural "clash" resembled the takeover of one culture over another hindered a genuine exchange of ideas and practices. Now, backed by a newly emerging sophistication and experience in the realities of the EuroCanadian political world, the First People are fighting back. Mingling hope with political reality, their future conquests will undoubtedly find success in bridging the socioeconomic gap between theirs and the dominant culture.

Quoting from the Old Testament prophet Isaiah, Chief John Snow prognosticates that eventually the Canadian First Nations will "mount up with wings as eagles" in claiming their rightful destiny (Snow, 1977: 160). A Lakota Elder, Beatrice Medicine, hints at an Indigenous cultural revival based on the inherent qualities of traditional Indian philosophy combined with the "best of the white world, namely their educational system" (Medicine, 1987). Other Aboriginal writers are more persistent and suggest that First Peoples demand support for a rebirth of their way of life, spiritually, socially, and economically. They argue that if Canada's First Nations are to regain a rightful toe-hold in the forthcoming annals of this nation's history, that hope will be much more than an illusion. Its achievement will necessarily force a restructuring of the Canadian mainstream to hopefully result in a new form of cultural enrichment.

As the intercultural developments between Aboriginal and nonAboriginal communities unfold, there are a number of lingering educational frontiers that continue to challenge the Aboriginal community. These will be identified in subsequent chapters. The next chapter will outline the background to those frontiers and show how Native education in Canada has arrived at its present state of affairs.

References

Benedict, Ruth. (1934). *Patterns of Culture.* Boston, MA: Houghton-Mifflin.

Berton, Pierre. (1974). *The National Dream: The Last Spike.* Toronto, ON: McClelland and Stewart.

Brascoupé, Simon. (2000). Aboriginal Peoples' Vision of the Future: Interweaving Traditional Knowledge and New Technologies. *Visions of the Heart: Canadian Aboriginal Issues.* David Long and Olive Patricia Dickason, eds. Toronto, ON: Harcourt Canada, 411-432.

Brookes, Sonia. (1990). An Analysis of Indian Education Policy, 1960-1989. Unpublished M.A. Thesis, Calgary, AB: The University of Calgary.

Brown, Dee. (1981). *Bury My Heart at Wounded Knee.* New York, NY: Pocket Books.

Campbell, Maria. (1973). *Halfbreed: A Proud and Bitter Canadian Legacy.* Toronto, ON: McClelland and Stewart.

Cardinal, Harold. (1969). *The Unjust Society: The Tragedy of Canada's Indians.* Edmonton, AB: M.G. Hurtig.

Carlson, Paul H. (1998). *The Plains Indians.* College Station, TX: Texas A & M University.

Castellano, Brant, Lynne Davis, and Louise Lahache. (2000). Conclusion: Fulfilling the Promise. *Aboriginal Education: Fulfilling the Promise.* Marlene Brant Castellano, Lynne Davis, and Louise Lahache, eds. Vancouver, BC: University of British Columbia, 224-255.

Chalmers, John W. (1972). *Education Behind the Buckskin Curtain.* Edmonton, AB: University of Alberta.

Chalmers, J.W. (1974). Marguerite Bourgeoys: Preceptress of New France. *Profiles of Canadian Educators.* Robert S. Patterson, John W. Chalmers, and John W. Friesen, eds. Toronto, ON: D. C. Heath, 4-20.

Conrad, Margaret, Alvin Finkel, and Cornelius Jaenen. (1993). *History of Canadian Peoples: Beginnings to 1867.* Toronto, ON: Copp Clark Pitman.

Deloria, Jr., Vine. (1995). *Red Earth, White Lies: Native Americans and the Myth of Scientific Fact.* New York, NY: Scribner.

Dempsey, Hugh A. (1979). *Indian Tribes of Alberta.* Calgary, AB: The Glenbow Museum.

Dickason, Olive Patricia. (1984). *The Myth of the Savage and the Beginnings of French Colonialism in the Americas.* Edmonton, AB: The University of Alberta.

Dickason, Olive Patricia. (1993). *Canada's First Nations: A History of Founding Peoples From Earliest Times.* Toronto, ON: McClelland and Stewart.

Dion, Joseph F. (1979). *My Tribe, The Crees.* Calgary, AB: Glenbow Museum.

Driver, Harold E. (1968). *Indians of North America.* Chicago, IL: University of Chicago.

Erasmus, George. (1989). *The Solution We Favour for Change. Drumbeat: Anger and Renewal in Indian Country. Boyce* Richardson, ed. Toronto, ON: Summerhill, 295-302

Farb, Peter. (1969). *Man's rise to Civilization as Shown by the Indians of North America From Primeval Times to the Coming of the Industrial State.* New York, NY: E.P. Dutton & Co.

Francis, R. Douglas, Richard Jones, and Donald B. Smith. (1988). *Origins: Canadian History to Confederation.* Vol. 1, Toronto, ON: Holt, Rinehart and Winston.

Frideres, James. (1993). *Native People in Canada.* Second edition. Scarborough, ON: Prentice-Hall.

Friesen, John W. (Spring, 1974). John McDougall: The Spirit of a Pioneer. *Alberta Historical Review,* 2:2, 9-17.

Friesen, John W. (1977). *People, Culture and Learning.* Calgary, AB: Detselig Enterprises.

Friesen, John W. (1985). *When Cultures Clash: Case Studies in Multiculturalism.* Calgary, AB: Detselig Enterprises.

Friesen, John W. (1989). The Human Side of Prairie Settlement. *Multicultural Education Journal,* 7:2, November, 28-36.

Friesen, John W. (1998). *Sayings of the Elders: An Anthology of First Nations' Wisdom.* Calgary, AB: Detselig Enterprises.

Friesen, John W., and Alice L. Boberg. (1990). *Introduction to Teaching: A Socio-cultural Approach.* Dubuque, IA: Kendall-Hunt.

Friesen, John W., and Terry Lusty. (1980). *The Métis of Canada: An Annotated Bibliography.* Toronto, ON: Ontario Institute for Studies in Education.

Grinnell, George Bird. (1900). *The North American Indians of To-day.* London: C. Arthur Pearson.

Hart, E.J. (1983). *The Selling of Canada: The CPR and the Beginning of Canadian Tourism.* Banff, AB: Altitude.

Higham, C. L. (2000). *Noble, Wretched & Redeemable: Protestant Missionaries to the Indians in Canada and the United States, 1820-1900.* Albuquerque, NM: University of New Mexico.

Jenness, Diamond. (1986). *The Indians of Canada.* Toronto, ON: University of Toronto Press.

Jennings, Jesse D. (1978). *Ancient Native Americans.* San Francisco, CA: Freeman and Company.

Josephy, Alvin M. Jr. (1968). *The Indian Heritage of America.* New York, NY: Alfred A. Knopf.

Krotz, Larry. (1990). *Indian Country: Inside Another Canada.* Toronto, ON: McClelland and Stewart.

LaRoque, Emma. (1975). *Defeathering the Indian.* Agincourt, ON: The Books Society of Canada.

Lincoln, Kenneth. (1985). *Native American Renaissance.* Berkeley, CA: University of Berkeley Press.

Lowie, Robert. (1924). *Primitive Religion.* New York, NY: Grosset and Dunlop.

MacLean, John. (1896). *Canada's Savage Folk.* London, UK: William Briggs.

Manuel, George, and Michael Posluns. (1974). *The Fourth World: An Indian Reality.* Don Mills, ON: Collier Macmillan Canada.

McDonald, N. G. (1974). Alexandre Tache: Defender of the Old Regime. *Profiles of Canadian Educators.* Robert S. Patterson, John W. Chalmers, and John W. Friesen, eds. Toronto, ON: D.C. Heath, 141-166.

McMillan, Alan D. (1995). *Native Peoples and Cultures in Canada: An Anthropological Overview.* Revised edition. Vancouver, BC: Douglas & McIntyre.

Medicine, Beatrice. (1987). My Elders Tell Me *Indian Education in Canada, The Challenge,* Volume One: The Legacy. Jean Barman, Yvonne Hébert, and Don McCaskill, eds. Vancouver, BC: University of British Columbia, 142-152.

Melling, John. (1967). *Right to a Future: the Native Peoples of Canada.* Toronto, ON: T.H. Best.

Miller, Alan D. (1995). *Native Peoples and Cultures of Canada.* Revised edition. Vancouver, BC: Douglas and McIntyre.

Miller, J.R. (2000). *Skyscrapers Hide the Heavens: A History of Indian-White Relations in Canada.* Toronto, ON: University of Toronto.

Morrison, R. Bruce, and C. Roderick Wilson. (1995). *Native Peoples: The Canadian Experience.* Toronto, ON: McClelland and Stewart.

Oskaboose, Gilbert. (1980). To be Indian. *Indian News.* 21:8, (November), 3.

Owen, Roger C., James Deetz, and Anthony D. Fisher, eds. (1968). *The North American Indians: A Sourcebook.* New York, NY: The Macmillan Company.

Palmer, Howard. (1982). *Patterns of Prejudice: A History of Nativism in Alberta.* Toronto, ON: McClelland and Stewart.

Patterson, E. Palmer. (1972). *The Canadian Indian.* Toronto, ON: Macmillan.

Pelletier, Wilfred, and Ted Poole. (1973). *No Foreign Land: The Biography of a North American Indian.* Toronto, ON: McClelland and Stewart.

Radin, Paul. (1937). *Primitive Religion: Its Nature and Origin.* New York: The Viking Press.

Ray, Arthur J. (1974). *Indians in the Fur Trade: Their Role as Trappers, Hunters and Middlemen in the Lands Southwest of Hudson Bay, 1660-1870.* Toronto, ON: University of Toronto.

Red Fox, Chief William. (1971). *The Memoirs of Chief Red Fox.* New York, NY: McGraw-Hill.

Rich, E.E. (1976). *The Fur Trade and the Northwest to 1857.* Toronto, ON: McClelland and Stewart.

Richardson, Boyce, ed. (1989). *Drumbeat: Anger and Renewal in Indian Country.* Toronto, ON: Summerhill.

Riley, Del. (1984). What Canada's Indians Want and the Difficulties of Getting It. *Pathways to Self-Determinaiton: Canadian Indans and the Canadian State.* Leroy Littlebear, Menno Boldt, and Anthony Long, eds. Toronto, ON: University of Toronto, 159-163.

Schmidt, Wilhelm. (1965). The Nature, Attributes, and Worship of the Primitive High God. *Reader in Comparative Religion: An Anthropological Approach.* William A. Lessa and Evon Z. Vogt, eds. New York, NY: Harper and Row, 21-33.

Sealey, D. Bruce, and Verna J. Kirkness. (1973). *Indians Without Tipis: A Resource Book by Indians and Métis.* Vancouver, BC: William Clare.

Sealey, D. Bruce and Antoine S. Lussier. (1975). *The Métis: Canada's Forgotten People.* Winnipeg, MB: Manitoba Métis Federation.

Seton, Ernest Thompson, and Juliam M. Seton. (1966). *The Gospel of the Redman: A Way of Life.* Santa Fe, NM: Seton Village.

Snow, Chief John. (1977). *These Mountains Are Our Sacred Places: The Story of the Stoney People.* Toronto, ON: Samuel-Stevens.

Spence, Lewis. (1994). *North American Indians: Myths and Legends.* London, UK: Senate.

Steckley, John L., and Bryan D. Cummins. (2001). *Full Circle: Canada's First Nations.* Toronto, ON: Prentice-Hall.

Surtees, R. J. (1968). The Development of an Indian Reserve Policy in Canada. *Ontario Historical Society,* LX!, 87-99.

Symington, F. (1969). *The Canadian Indian.* Toronto, ON: McClelland and Stewart.

Underhill, Ruth M. (1953). *Red Man's Religion.* Chicago: IL: University of Chicago.

Webb, Walter Prescott. (1931). *The Great Plains.* New York, NY: Gosset and Dunlop.

Wedel, Waldo R. (1978). *The Prehistoric Plains: Ancient Native Americans.* Jesse D. Jennings, ed. San Francisco, CA: Freeman and Company, 183-220.

Wissler, Clark. (1966). *Indians of the United Sates.* Revised edition. New York: Doubleday and Winston.

Wuttunee, William I.C. (1971). *Ruffled Feathers.* Calgary, AB: Bell Books.

Yazzie, Robert. (2000). Indigenous Peoples and Postcolonial Colonialism. *Reclaiming Indigenous Voice and Vision.* Marie Battiste, ed. Vancouver, BC: University of British Columbia, 39-49.

York, Geoffrey. (1989). *The Dispossessed: Life and Death in Native Canada.* Toronto, ON: Lester & Orpen Dennys.

Three

How We Came to This Pass – Educationally

The ethnocentric bent of the early European explorers quickly led them to conclude that the Indigenous People of North America were in dire need of a European version of civilization. It never occurred to them that the First Nations had in place a series of functional institutions that governed every aspect of their lives. The means by which the newcomers hoped to accomplish their goal of cultural makeover was via instruction in schools designed by European architects of learning combined with heavy doses of religion.

Initial Explorations

French exploration of the St. Lawrence Valley began in 1534 with the three voyages of Jacques Cartier, followed by Samuel de Champlain in 1608. Although the first newcomers to the area that later became Canada were primarily explorers and imperialists, they were quickly followed by individuals who had specific religious purposes in mind.

The first missionaries who followed Cartier were a reform branch of Franciscans called Récollects who worked among the Hurons in New France as early as 1615. The Capauchins devoted themselves to educating the Mik'maq (also spelled Micmac) in Acadia as early as 1632, and their methods were quite unorthodox when viewed in light of later developments. Although their approach was more humane than that of Spanish priests in the American southwest, they basically saw their role fulfilling a God-given mandate. The Spanish priests who arrived in America via Mexico operated slave labor systems between the years 1680 and 1840, dominating local Natives while converting them to the Christian Gospel. The construction of mission stations in the southwest was accomplished by local Aboriginals who were allowed to

65

occupy a living space measuring seven feet by two feet sometimes described as "specially-constructed cattle pens" (Churchill, 1998: 141). The Aboriginals were forced to live in deplorable conditions, working hard to construct elaborate religious edifices while living on diets of less than 1 400 calories per day. An open pit served as a toilet facility for literally hundreds of people. The imperialist philosophy gradually translated itself into the concept of boarding schools.

Entrance to Huron-Ouendat Village, Midland, Ontario

The first legislation passed by the British Parliament concerning Aboriginal people in Canada occurred in 1670 and was quite unspecific in intent. The implicit message of the policy was that the government would look after or protect the Indians, principally because they were useful to the fur trade. A dramatic shift in policy occurred in 1830 when the fur trade waned and the government viewed First Nations from a different perspective. Almost overnight the mood shifted and the Indigenous people were suddenly depicted as living in a state of "barbarism and savagery," who must be brought to a state of civilization through education. The immediate plan by which to accomplish this was to establish Aboriginals in permanent settlements and commence instruction so that an agricultural form of lifestyle would be possible. Missionaries and schoolmasters were conscripted to instruct the children, to teach them to pray, to read the Scriptures, and to "pursue moral lives" (Friesen, 1991: 14). In 1857, legislation to design education for Indians was passed entitled, *An Act for the Gradual Civilization of the Indian,* followed by another act in 1858, called the *Civilization and Enfranchisement Act.* On attaining nationhood, Canada passed the first Indian-related legislation, the *Indian Act,* in 1876. The government also attempted to address the issues of Native education and local government by passing the *Indian Advancement Act* in 1884, but neither its provisions nor program were clear (Frideres, 1988: 29; Frideres and Gadacz, 2001: 25).

Wigwam, Old Fort William, Thunder Bay, Ontario

Maritime Campaign

The campaign to transform Aboriginal culture through the medium of schooling has a long history in Canada. It may be highlighted by a series of divergent thrusts even though religious instruction and the promotion of literacy topped the list of objectives. It was difficult to attain any degree of literary success since First Nations were nomadic peoples who did not often remain long enough in one area so their children could be "properly educated." Eventually, a wide range of program alternatives to day schooling was undertaken, perhaps best described in colloquial terms as consisting of fits and starts regarding initiation, operation, and failure. With each successive failure, a new program was devised and lasted only until it became clear to its organizers that their efforts and finances were literally being wasted. A brief description of developments in the various geographic regions of Canada will illustrate the shotgun approach to Native education that was undertaken with regard to the education of Indigenous children.

From the beginning, early French mission day schools were unsuccessful for lack of attendance; thus another approach was needed. One alternative plan was to send young Indian boys and girls directly to France for their education. It was conjectured that this way they would be "properly educated" and would return to their tribes and teach their families the superior French way of life. The results were not favorable; more often than not these young Aboriginals would return as misfits, unable to function in either milieu. By 1639 the practice was ended because scarcely a dozen Native young people had returned to the colony to assist the missionaries (Cornish, 1881; Hawthorn, 1967; Jaenen, 1986).

By the middle of the 17th century the Jesuits developed day schools known as "reductions" in permanent settlements in New France, and tried to lure Indigenous students with a view to teaching them the Catholic faith and French culture. The schools were built close to mission stations and French settlements, and First Nations were expected to remain near these settlements so their children could receive schooling. The primary objective of these efforts was to satisfy the mandate of the French government officials who expected the Jesuits to assist in the building of durable colonies in eastern Canada.

The curriculum of the Jesuit schools consisted of religious studies, agriculture, and manual trades. Aboriginal children *did* adapt to the French diet, manner of dress and other aspects of the French lifestyle, but they were never successful in agriculture or manual trades (Brookes, 1991). Simultaneous to Jesuit efforts, the Ursulines begun by Sister Marguerite Bourgeoys, instructed Indian girls in French manners and customs, household duties, reading and writing, and religion. Later they also added knitting and spinning. Indicative of the serious intent of the program and to the credit of the developers is the fact that they tried to provide instruction in these courses in Aboriginal languages. Bourgeoys arrived in New France in 1653 in response to a call from Governor Maisionneuve of Ville-Marie Montreal to start a school. Five years later she opened a school for girls in a converted stable and eventually enrolled Aboriginal students as well. Although her primary targets were children of fur traders and explorers whose families lived in nearby settlements. She later expanded her mission to include the education of the "King's girls," namely young women who came from France to New France to seek mates and reestablish themselves. Bourgeoys attempted to provide them with the knowledge needed to live on the frontier by emphasizing Christian values, social graces, the three "r's" and "housewifely skills" (Chalmers, 1974).

The schools designed and promoted by the religious orders were met with opposition from Aboriginal parents who objected to the omission of First Nations history and culture from the curriculum. The First Nations were proud of their heritage and did not want to give it up easily. Native parents also objected to sending very young children to school who they thought should remain at home for a few more years. Despite these objections, the program of francization continued. The methodology employed consisted of memory work, repetition, recitation, and the writing of examinations.

By 1763, New France was absorbed by the British Empire and the administration of Indian people was assigned to the British Imperial government. This policy continued until 1830. The British military initially assumed this responsibility and functioned with the sole purpose of maintaining Indian allegiance and cooperation. The education of Indigenous people was left to the religious sector, and one organization, the New England Company, for example, assumed control of schooling in New Brunswick. The leaders of the company stressed three themes in their programs of instruction— English language teaching, religion, and vocational training. Administration of the program was located in England and governed by a board made up of learned men representing the judiciary, the clergy, merchants, and government leaders.

The New England Company encouraged Native parents to reside near British settlements so that better management of their children could be facilitated. Since this arrangement forbad great indulgence in their preferred nomadic way of life, Aboriginal parents were sometimes supplied with food, clothing, and other provisions. The New England Company also experimented with a variety of educational approaches including an extensive use of Native languages such as Chippewa, Cree, and Mik'maq. One special feature was an apprenticeship program whereby Aboriginal children would be sent to live with selected nonNative families in hopes that the youngsters would learn a trade. After 15 years this program was shut down because on returning home not a single Indian youth had been successfully employed.

Muskowekwan Residential School in southern Saskatchewan

By the middle of the nineteenth century a number of church denominations were involved in Native education in eastern Canada with the double-edged objective of spreading the Gospel and "culturally rehabilitating the Indian." During the period from 1833 when missionary Peter Jones petitioned the Methodist Church to build a residential school among the Ojibway people of Ontario, to 1988 when last residential school in Canada closed (McKay Residential School in Dauphin, Manitoba), eighty such schools were in operation.

West Coast Campaign

With the fall of New France and the establishment of British sovereignty, a path was clear for the expansion of Protestant missions to other areas of the new country. By the mid-1800s most regions of Canada had been claimed by Anglican, Methodist, Presbyterian, and Roman Catholic missionaries. In British Columbia, Roman Catholic missions were established throughout the interior, while Anglican and Methodist missionaries competed for territory on the northern British Columbia coast. All three denominations joined Presbyterian efforts in western Canada.

The first recorded encounter of Europeans with the Aboriginal peoples of British Columbia is reported to have occurred in July 1774, when the Spanish navigator, Juan Pérez met a group of Haidas near Langara Island. Four years later, explorer Captain James Cook spent nearly a month refitting his ship at Nootka Sound, and engaged in trade with local residents. By 1792, the west coast fur trade was in full swing with efforts concentrated on the more heavily settled south coast and on Vancouver Island.

As had become the trend, missionary educators arrived in the new territory shortly after the first explorers. Although educational efforts among First Nations of British Columbia began in the latter part of the 18th century, mission schools for Aboriginals did not become populous in British Columbia until the middle of the nineteenth century. In 1838 a Roman Catholic missionary, Modeste Demers, undertook a reconnaissance survey of the interior of British Columbia and reported that the locals were quite receptive to educational endeavors (Furniss, 1995: 43). In 1849, The Reverend Robert Staines, a Church of England minister, began a school at Fort Victoria for children of Hudson's Bay Company employees, while a Roman Catholic priest, Father Lempfrit, began a school for Métis children (Johnson, 1968: 62).

Metlakatla

In 1856, a self-styled non-ordained Anglican missionary, William Duncan, built a mission school among the Tsimshian First Nation at Fort Simpson (Duff, 1997: 136). In 1872 the Oblates made Fort Thompson the headquarters for their missionary efforts among local First Nations. Born in England in 1832 to a very poor family, William Duncan became the manager of the first, if not the only,

Aboriginal commune in North America. While still a young man, Duncan emigrated to Canada with the Church of England Missionary Society. His objective was to establish a mission among the First Nations of British Columbia. He arrived in Vancouver in June 1857, and travelled to Fort Simpson, some 500 miles north, where the Anglican Church had already selected a site. A community of 2 300 souls awaited Duncan at Fort Simpson, one of the largest First Nations settlements in the province. Conveniently for Duncan, entire bands of Tsimshian people had left their traditional villages and moved their longhouses to Fort Simpson to be closer to where the fur trade flourished (Scott, 1997).

At first Duncan was a bit overwhelmed with his assignment. Although not ordained by the church, he began holding worship services and offering religious instruction wherever he could. He struggled with learning the Tsimshian language, eventually mastering a basic vocabulary of 1 500 words. Typical of missionaries of the time, Duncan bemoaned the deplorable state of Aboriginal culture, which he described as consisting of drunkenness, slavery, prostitution, and barbarous ceremonial dancing. He departed from collegial thinking when he observed that the Aboriginal people were an intelligent and industrious folk, and he resolved to build on those attributes in establishing his own mission.

Duncan began a school during his first year as a missionary and within two years had attracted a group of 50 adherents. He shared his vision of a utopian Aboriginal colony with the governor of the province, and with the latter's support, made plans to develop such a site a few miles south of Fort Simpson at a location known as Metlakatla, a Tsimshian word meaning "the place where two waters meet." An advance party began the work of building the village in May 1862, followed by a company of 300 who agreed to abide by Duncan's list of 15 regulations. Then a plague struck the colony and one-third of the members died. Still, the work proceeded, eventually to include 30 houses, and a 600-seat building that doubled as a church and school. The membership of the settlement was divided into companies, each governed by several councillors, elders, and constables. The primary governing body consisted of hereditary chiefs and Duncan himself.

The economy of Metlakatla included a sawmill, a fish-processing plant, and a store. Later soap and textile factories were added, as well as a tannery, a guesthouse, a fire hall and a dog pound. Native handicrafts and other products were taken south to the city of Victoria by a boat, which Duncan purchased, and then marketed the goods in Victoria without benefit of any middleman. This meant that Duncan essentially controlled the fur trade in the region. At its peak of development, Metlakatla was home to several other missionaries who arrived at Duncan's invitation. In 1874 the village became home to St. Paul's Church, the largest cathedral west of Chicago and north of San Francisco. It was equipped with a vestibule, gallery, belfry, and spire, groined arches, and solid timber frame. It had a seating capacity of 1 200.

The demise of Duncan's Metlakatla began when he developed a dislike for his superior, Bishop Hills of Victoria. The bishop wanted Duncan to be ordained, but the latter said he did not feel called to the ministry. Duncan also resisted providing the Eucharist (Holy Communion, or The Lord's Supper) to his converts on grounds that even the little bit of alcohol consumed in the Sacrament could be damaging to a people he was trying to cure of alcoholism. Another of Bishop Hill's complaints against Duncan was that he had not tried to groom local Aboriginals to become clergymen. Then unexpectedly, a revival of sorts flared up. A newly arrived Anglican clergyman, James Hall, began to preach with an emotional enthusiasm not previously heard in the colony. Duncan became concerned, but Bishop Hills supported Hall and would not back down to Duncan's protests. In an effort to break down Duncan's influence, the mission district of Metlakatla was divided into several regions governed by a local bishop, Bishop William Ridley, who also opposed Duncan. Duncan then took his quarrel to the federal government in Ottawa. Although not likely above board, Prime Minister John A. Macdonald influenced his party to award the settlement of Metlakatla to the Anglican mission society and put Duncan out of business (Scott, 1997: 36).

The loss of control over the affairs of Metlakatla did not deter the illustrious William Duncan. In 1887, after negotiating with President Grover Cleveland of the United States, Duncan managed to procure a prospective settlement in Alaska, some 75 miles north of Fort Simpson in American territory. The American government was impressed with Duncan's progress in "civilizing the Indians" and responded positively to his pleas. Eight hundred people followed Duncan to the new location. Within a few months, the new colony began to take shape. Most of the buildings at Metlakatla were dismantled and relocated to the new settlement by boat. Again, a variety of industries was established and a huge cathedral was erected. In 1908, however, there was mutiny in the ranks, with dissident individuals demanding their fair share of the assets so they could relocate elsewhere. Duncan, however, had formed a company with all Metlakatla assets held in his own name; it took seven years to dismantle Duncan's empire because the United States government was reluctant to "take harsh measures with a kindly old man" (Scott, 1997:39). Ultimately, things got progressively worse and Duncan became more possessive. In 1915 control of the colony was assigned to the local Indian tribal council, an arrangement that still prevails. Duncan died in 1918 at the age of 86 and was buried in front of his church.

West Coast Totem Pole in front of British Columbia Legislature
Building, Victoria, British Columbia

Today Metlakatla continues to be a typical thriving northern American Aboriginal neighborhood. Several denominations have established churches in the settlement and traditional Native spirituality has made a comeback. Spiritual leaders of nearby Aboriginal settlements have provided the locals with a wide range of traditional songs, prayers, and rituals to replace those they lost when Duncan first took over. Only a few village buildings of the old Metlakatla remain as testimony to Duncan's efforts.

Toward the Plains

Shortly after establishing settlements in selected areas of British Columbia, the missionaries moved inland towards the prairies. The Roman Catholic Church, represented by the Oblates, virtually dominated the early stages of the missionary education movement following their founding in the 1840s. They worked hand in hand with the Grey Nuns (Sisters of Charity) who were responsible for the education of Native girls. The first schools established by the Grey Nuns were at St. Boniface and Pembina, Manitoba, around 1817. The Pembina School lasted only six years while the one at St. Boniface lasted ten years. Within the decade more itinerant missionaries, both Roman Catholic and Protestant, were involved in teaching Native and nonNative children in fur trading posts stretching from the United States to the Arctic (Lupul, 1970).

In the west a host of well-known missionaries labored for the same cause including James Evans, Robert Rundle, Father Albert Lacombe, Father Joseph Hugonnard and Henry Steinhauer (a Native missionary). Typical of the educational philosophy of the time, Methodist missionaries George McDougall and his son, John, strove to "Christianize, educate and civilize" the Indians, in their case the Woodland Crees and the Stoneys (McDougall, 1903: 71). Father Hugonnard outlined his objective bluntly, namely to remove Indian boys and girls from their "savage milieu" and convert them to "civilized" habits through English language instruction (Gresko, 1986: 91).

The Hudson's Bay Company encouraged missionary efforts, hoping that the civilizing effect of religious efforts would auger well for their business interests. By 1857 the company was making annual grants to various religious denominations in an effort to encourage their educational endeavors. The Roman Catholics were the most aggressive, and after establishing the St. Boniface School, moved on to other locations. They began a school at Lac St. Anne in 1942, at Fort Edmonton in 1852, and at Lac La Biche in 1854. Father Albert Lacombe founded a permanent school in Fort Edmonton in 1860 with an enrollment of more than 20 children. Day schools generally turned out to be ineffective in terms of missionary objectives because these schools allowed only temporary contact with Aboriginal students. The missionaries argued that by removing students from their parents and incarcerating them in residential schools, "they could spend several years in acquiring regular habits of discipline and a taste and a liking for work" (Fisher, 1978: 138).

The first Protestant school in the North West Territories was initiated by Methodist James Evans on Playgreen Island at the Rossville Mission near Norway House. Two decades later George McDougall and his son, John, undertook missionary work among the Woodland Crees at Fort Victoria in northeast Alberta, and the Stoney (Nakoda Sioux) Indians at Morley, Alberta (Friesen, 1974: 59).

After the Riel War of 1885, the temporary tenor of relations established between the Canadian government and First Nations withered somewhat as additional settlers poured into Native territory. As a result, Aboriginal people began to be a minority in the west, so federal officials felt free to impose a rigorous pattern of cultural assimilation. This policy of "coercive tutelage" was based on the assumption that Native people did not know and perhaps could not know what was in their best interests. It fell to government to strip them of their civil, economic, and cultural rights under a regime of government paternalism. Subcontracting the operation of Indian schools to religious denominations not only shed government of the responsibility of working in an area in which they had no expertise, but transferred some of the cost to the churches. Whenever the churches opted for the building of more residential schools the government somewhat disinterestedly demurred (Dyck, 1997: 14).

During David Goggin's reign as the first Superintendent of Education in the North West Territories from 1893 to 1912, he sought to develop a universal school system. As a strong British national imperialist he had little patience with the values of ethnic minorities or First Nations. His concern was that the children of these communities should grow up to be Canadians and learn to speak the language. As he put it, "A common school and a common tongue are essential if we are to have a homogeneous citizenship" (McDonald, 1974: 178).

Policy Formation

Since confederation the creation of Indian education policy has consistently been a federal responsibility. As a prelude to his arrangement, in 1847 the Province of Canada published a report based on the ideas of Egerton Ryerson, Canada's first superintendent of English-speaking schools. Ryerson urged the government to adopt a policy whereby Aboriginals could be raised to the educational level of EuroCanadians. This perspective motivated the new Canadian government of 1867 to maintain control of Indian affairs rather than relegate them to provincial administration. Sadly, the government did not maintain its responsibility, but soon assigned it to other spheres.

Although the establishment of the Indian Act in 1876 authorized the federal government to provide schooling for First Nations, the responsibility was soon shifted to the church denominations, partly on grounds that they were already involved in the enterprise (Brookes, 1991: 168). The Canadian federal government had only been in operation for a decade so it was a simple matter to delegate some areas of governance rather than assume responsibility for them. The long-range forecast for Indigenous survival was perceived as inevitable genocide, so no one felt obligated to provide Aboriginal children with a first-class education. Canadian Indian education policy, therefore, evolved without too much government planning.

In 1879 the Davin Report urged the establishment of residential schools following the pattern set in the United States. Thus, during the 1880s, the Canadian government shifted its Indian education policy from the creation of additional day schools to residential schools, and a number of such schools were established in British Columbia. By 1894, eleven residential schools were operating in British Columbia including one at Alert Bay (Wolcott, 1967), Kamloops (Haig-Brown, 1993), and Williams Lake (Furniss, 1995). A residential school was established at Mopass in Yukon Territory in 1901 (King, 1967).

A short-lived experiment in Native education was the development of industrial schools (Titley, 1992). These schools were begun shortly after 1830 when the civil branch of government took over Indian matters from the military. Industrial schools differed from residential schools primarily by attempting preparation in various trades as a means of preparing Indian youth for a new way of life. The fur trade was over and in order to assist Aboriginal people to ward off destruction and ruin, their children would need to learn skills required in the new world. Boys were taught such trades as shoemaking, carpentry, blacksmithing, and tailoring, and girls learned sewing, knitting, washing, and cooking.

Essentially, the industrial schools failed. After a few years of operation it became evident that few of the students were applying the skills they learned in their daily lives. Various factors led to this dismal conclusion including late enrolment for many students, parental prejudice against the schools, short periods of attendance, and lack of funds to establish "graduates" when they completed their term of studies. Native parents basically resented residential industrial schools. They did not like their children being taken away from them, often very far away. They disliked deliberate attempts to "convert and civilize" their children whom they wanted to retain in the lineage of their cultural heritage. They also resented the restrictions on use of Indigenous languages and the teaching of "women's chores" to young men (Gresko, 1986: 98). Fortunately for them, only a small portion of First Nations young people attended residential schools although those who attended day schools were philosophically and culturally not much better off. Aboriginal children were provided with negative descriptions of their heritage in both settings. Parents who did relent to enrolling their children in either residential or day schools often did so because they thought their children were mainly being taught how to read and write (Miller, 1987: 3f). They objected to the work component of the industrial schools believing that their offspring were being shortchanged. After all, they were being sent to school to learn literary skills, not to become unpaid apprentices with fulltime jobs.

Twentieth Century Developments

By 1920 amendments to the 1876 Indian Act mandated compulsory schooling for Native children at either residential or day schools, but it was not until 1946 that concern about cultural genocide was raised. At that time, J. Allison Glen, Minister of Mines and Resources suggested that as much as possible, First Nations children should be given the opportunity to retain as many Aboriginal characteristics as possible while developing their ability to function as full-fledged Canadian citizens.

In 1947, New Zealand anthropologist, Diamond Jenness urged the Canadian government to "solve the Indian problem" by abolishing Indigenous reserves and establishing an integrated approach to schooling. The underlying intent of Jenness' plan was to assimilate the First Nations and thereby "eliminate the Indian problem within twenty-five years" (Haig-Brown, 1993: 32). Subsequent modifications to the Indian Act in 1951 changed little, except to make it possible for Aboriginal children to attend public schools. Before another line of attack was devised, plans were made to turn over the administration of residential schools directly into the hands of government bureaucrats instead of religious leaders. By the 1960s this arrangement had pretty well been concluded.

The process of transforming administration of residential schools to secular control actually began in 1949. That year a Special Joint Committee of the Senate and the House of Commons recommended that wherever possible Indian children should be educated in association with nonNative children (Friesen, 1983: 48). The committee solicited the advice of Native leaders and obtained 411 briefs in all. The proposals were distributed among Native communities for added input. Finally, government leaders thought they had achieved two-way communication. Now the path was cleared for integrated education. The bottom line was that education following the traditional European format was still perceived as the vehicle by which the assimilation of First Nations could come about (Hawthorn, 1967). Most Aboriginal parents would be invited to sit on advisory boards, but they would not have an official voice in either educational policy-making or school procedure. Integration in this mode was to be the order of the day.

On March 15, 1967, the Honorable Arthur Laing, Minister of Indian Affairs and Northern Development announced a seven-point integration program for Indian education. The plan was to work collaboratively with provincial departments of education to integrate Native children into provincial schools. Laing promised more consultation with First Nations parents than had been the case before, by inviting them to sit on school boards in districts where a significant number of Aboriginal children were enrolled (Burns, 1998). Standardized forms of provincial curricula were to be used and amended only when special needs of students became apparent. Federal schools were to follow suit. Residential schools were to continue in use only when absolutely necessary, and then with full consultation with the religious organizations that ran them (Ashworth, 1979: 39-40).

Laing's proposals were studied for four years and reported on in 1971 with the conclusion that the sooner Indigenous pupils left federal schools and entered provincial schools, the better their chances of enjoying academic advances. The key factor would be for Native students to become fluent in the official language of the school. It was also noted that unless the school offered instruction in Indigenous languages through the high school level, those students would lose knowledge of their Native language altogether.

Barman (1986) contends that nonNative Canadians have never wanted First Nations to enter their socioeconomic order, and this motivated the government to offer an inferior kind of education in Native communities. According to Barman, most Canadians are content to see that First Nations remain at the bottom rung of the economic ladder and not complete on even ground with their fellow nonNatives. This suggests that if Indian youth did triumph by surviving the impact of the residential school, they would only encounter additional roadblocks and discrimination further ahead. The bottom line is that Native children were originally enrolled in religious schools on the pretext of educating them, while in reality the intent was to squelch their potential to develop fully as members of either Native or nonNative society.

White Paper, Red Paper

When the Liberal government took office in 1968 under the leadership of Pierre Elliott Trudeau, Ottawa bureaucrats decided to adopt a brand new, modern oriented Aboriginal policy. The intent was to resolve once and for all the issue of Indian land claims so that the legal base for such claims would vanish forever. No longer would Aboriginals be treated differently from other Canadians, but regarded as full-fledged Canadian citizens. The economic status of Indian people would be ungraded so they could compete with other Canadians on an equal basis. Essentially, this implied the elimination of Indian Status in order to recategorize First Nations to the same legal plane as other Canadians (Boldt, 1993: 18).

The historical background to the White Paper, Red Paper controversy dates to 1963 when the federal government asked University of British Columbia anthropologist, Harry Hawthorn, to survey the living conditions of Canada's Native peoples. The observations made by Hawthorn's (1966-1967) team of researchers

stunned everyone, including government leaders. The report pointed out the devastating conditions under which most Canadian First
Nations were living. The report showed that Indigenous people suffered from unemployment, poverty, health problems, and even mal-
nutrition. Their housing was substandard, education was inadequate, and their life expectancy was dismally below that of other
Canadians. Hawthorn made a plea that Aboriginal people be
extended the same rights as other citizens and be assured that their
legal status be honored as well. This observation later gave rise to
the phrase, "Citizen's Plus," implying that First Nations were
Canadian citizens who had special additional rights.

During the 1960s in Canada there was a great deal of discussion
about human rights and fundamental freedoms of citizens in general. The American civil rights movement spilled over into Canada
and forced attention on neglected minorities. The Red Power movement and Vietnam War demonstrations in the United States threatened many Canadians who feared that similar protests might develop in this Canada. The armed occupation of Anicinabe Park in
Kenora, Ontario, and the near riot on Parliament Hill were seen as
proof that the same thing could happen here (Purich, 1986: 188). The
theme of the 1960s movement targeted needy minorities and
stressed the provision of opportunities for neglected communities in
an effort to bring them up to par with the rest of society.
Unfortunately, this implied that all responsibility to make recommendations to motivation or lifestyle to fit the mainstream lay within the minority camp. Central to this position was the assumption
that education would be the vehicle by which to accomplish this
goal. Good teaching and good education would serve to equalize
opportunity and minimize differences (Friesen, 1993: 7).

Against this background, in 1969 the Canadian federal government decided it was time for a radical shift in Indian policy. It was a
move that represented blatant assimilation. To implement this view,
the Honorable Jean Chrétien, Minister of Indian Affairs and
Northern Development, issued a White Paper outlining the government's new view on Indian affairs. The underlying assumption was
that the Aboriginal Peoples of Canada were to join the rest of
Canadians by having their special status eliminated via proposed
legislation. The major recommendations of the report included abolition of the Department of Indian Affairs and Northern
Development (DIAND), repeal of the Indian Act, and the transfer of

Indian programs to provincial administration. Management of Indian reserve lands was to be turned over directly to First Nations bands. The government also proposed to formulate a policy to eliminate Indian treaties. The insulting tone of the report became evident when Ottawa patronizingly agreed to recognize the contributions that the Indigenous People had made to Canadian society (White Paper, 1969).

The government White Paper was vigorously opposed by First Nations who were joined in their repudiation by a number of nonNative social and political organizations (Cardinal, 1969). The first official reaction to the White Paper came in the form of the Red Paper in 1970, authorized by the Indian chiefs of Alberta. The Red Paper debunked the validity of every one of the points made in the White Paper claiming that it was a document of despair, instead of hope. The framers of the Red Paper contended that if the proposals of the White Paper were initiated, within a generation or two First Nations would be left with no land and the threat of complete assimilation. Severe criticism of the Red Paper was launched in a book, *Ruffled Feathers,* by Cree lawyer, William Wuttunee (1971) of Calgary, who accused the writers of fostering a treaty mentality and supporting a buckskin and feather culture. It eventually became public that the Red Paper was actually prepared by M & M Systems Research of Alberta, an organization established by former Social Credit Premier, Ernest Manning, and his son (Wuttunee, 1971: 58).

A second major paper critical of the White Paper emanated from the Union of British Columbia Indian Chiefs, and became known as the Brown Paper. The Indian chiefs of British Columbia were concerned that the special relationship which had developed between First Nations and the federal government through the years should not be negated. The framers of the Brown Paper insisted that this relationship carried immense moral and legal force and should constitute the foundation for cooperative policy-making. Interestingly, the Brown Paper also made reference to the principle of self-determination and suggested that Indian bands take over aspects of reserve administration at local levels until self-government was attained. In this the British Columbia chiefs joined with other Native organizations who requested that the Indian Affairs Branch provide necessary financial resources to develop their plans, programs, and budgets towards that end.

First Nations Response

Yet another form of protest to the White Paper came from the National Indian Brotherhood (NIB), now known as the Assembly of First Nations (AFN). The NIB originated during the 1960s when the federal government decided to fund political Indigenous organizations to provide an avenue through which Native people could express their views. The NIB was preceded by the National Indian Council (NIC) which represented the concerns of both Status Indians and Métis concerns. With the origin of the NIB to represent Status Indians, the Canadian Métis Society was formed to represent Métis and nonStatus interests. These and other, newer organizations experienced some success through lobbying, organizing, and protesting. In response to these pressures, in 1970 the federal government decided not to proceed with implementing the White Paper (Purich, 1986: 187). Thus the veiled campaign to assimilate First Nations was compelled to continue in another vein.

The NIB response to the White Paper had a silver lining in terms of an implied educational policy. The background to the proposal included a series of quite unique events in northeastern Alberta. A group of Native parents at St. Paul, Alberta, some of them educated in residential schools themselves, had grown increasingly involved in the education of their children. Not content merely to act in an advisory capacity, and then only regarding such matters as school lunch programs and bussing, these parents intensified their campaign for greater involvement. Things came to a head in 1970 when nearly 300 Native people conducted a sit-in at the Blue Quills School in St. Paul Alberta. Reluctantly, the government gave in to the demands of participants in what became a three-month long event, and the first locally-controlled school in Canada came to be (Persson, 1986; Bashford and Heinzerling, 1987). By 1975 ten Indian band councils in Canada were operating their own schools and by 1985 two-thirds of reserve schools across the nation were either partly or completely managed by Aboriginal school boards.

In 1972 the NIB followed up on the Blue Quills event by issuing a suggested education policy dealing with four broad concerns. The first concern identified by the NIB was to wrest control of Indian schools away from external agencies and manage them locally. Second, the NIB raised the matter of curriculum relevancy, arguing that local education should make reference to local historical events and happenings. The NIB wanted the curriculum to reflect elements of Aboriginal history, beliefs, and culture. The organization requested that all future curricular innovations, teaching methods, and the nature of pupil-teacher relationships should have parental approval.

A third concern of the NIB pertained to the nature of teacher training in institutions of higher learning. The NIB argued that it was difficult to procure knowledgable, culturally sensitive teachers because relevant training was not available in Canadian university and colleges. Fourth, and finally, the NIB pointed out that educational facilities in most Native communities were well below standard when compared to those in nonNative communities, and the government should seek to address these concerns (Kirkness, 1981).

Several encouraging changes came about as a result of the NIB's policy paper, and the future began to look more promising for the First Nations of Canada. Increased Aboriginal input had a positive effect. School dropout rates and absenteeism generally decreased and a greater number of Aboriginal children were enrolled in public school systems. Parental involvement in school affairs increased and additional Indian band councils took charge of their local schools. The federal government appeared sympathetic to these developments and dozens of new schools were built in Native communities. The matter of teacher preparation was still a concern because teacher training institutions were slow to develop needed programs.

Second Response

In 1988 the Assembly of First Nations conducted a comprehensive community based review of the status of Aboriginal education in Canada. The result was a four volume report, *Tradition and Education: Towards a Vision of Our Future,* containing 54 recommendations. The report called on Canadians to recognize the inherent right of First Nations to maintain their unique cultural identity and to exercise control over their local educational systems. The AFN unanimously passed a resolution to back the intent of the report which outlined the need for local jurisdiction over education in Indigenous communities.

The foundational plank of the AFN report had to do with Aboriginal self-government. First Nations were demanding a return to the days when they governed all of their affairs, including education. Their argument was that governance over only one segment of community life (education) begged the question of Aboriginal self-government. Until the federal government and Native leaders came to an agreement as to the definition of Aboriginal self-government, First Nations would continue to be frustrated in their attempt to exercise control over their operations. Allocation of resources was a major concern because if purse strings were continued to be held by the federal Department of Indian Affairs, band control did not really exist.

Change does occur, however, and at the present time, most Native bands in Canada do exercise jurisdiction over educational policy, management methods and approaches, curriculum standards, program quality, and delivery service. Aboriginal bands can even determine total education resource requirements, including capital and operational requirements, but only in the field of education (Tremblay, 2001: 17). This is still a far way from realizing complete Aboriginal self-government, but it does show that some progress has been made in the last decade. In 1993 First Nations had only three options open to them. First, they could maintain the status quo; second, they could try to have access to funding by which to run their own schools (which they have attained), or third, they could attempt to establish closer links with provincial systems (Goddard, 1992: 165).

The DIAND responded to the AFN report by appointing James Macpherson to review *Traditional and Education: Towards a Vision of Our Future* and make recommendations. Macpherson immediately discovered that the exercise of authority over education by First Nations had no independent constitutional foundation and recommended that one be included in the Constitution of Canada. He pointed out First Nations jurisdiction over Indian education should comprise the pivotal point of negotiations about reform in Aboriginal education. This observation was premised on the reality that the Canadian government should accept and move ahead on First Nations self-government in Canada. Macpherson proposed that a constitutional amendment be made with regard to the fundamental relationship between Canada and First Nations. Following that, a national education statute should be installed that would improve the structure of education delivery systems and the quality of education for Native students in Canada (Tremblay, 2001: 30). Macpherson outlined four possible models by which reform in the field of Native education could be realized and he outlined specific steps for the government to take in this regard.

The Macpherson report recommended that First Nations devise and submit their own definition of Aboriginal self-government so that after negotiation, the definition could be included in the Canadian Constitution. Consequently the Aboriginal people would be able to establish educational policies that would be more compatible with their philosophy and beliefs. The report also recommended that the government increase funding for Indian education and establish in-service programs for nonAboriginal teachers wishing to work in Aboriginal communities.

The Royal Commission on Aboriginal Affairs

In 1991 the federal government established the Royal Commission on Aboriginal Peoples (RCAP), something which Prime Minister Brian Mulroney had offered Elijah Harper and his supporters in June 1990, when the Meech Lake Accord was struck down in the Manitoba Legislature. Chaired by former AFN Chief George Erasmus and Quebec Judge René Dussault, the Commission included both Native and nonNative member commissioners. A number of public meetings were held, transcripts were analyzed and a great deal of research was undertaken. Both the structure of the report and public hearings showed that the commissioners regarded their task as an exercise in public education as well as a government investigation (Miller, 2000: 385).

The RCAP completed its report in 1996. The report consisted of five volumes, over 3 500 pages and 400 recommendations. The report took over five years to prepare at a cost of over 50 million dollars. In response to the Report's recommendations, in 1998, the Liberal government, under the leadership of Prime Minister Jean Chrétien, set up a special healing fund in the amount of 350 million dollars as a token of the government's apology for the treatment of Aboriginals in residential schools. The fund was to be used over a four year period. In addition, the government approved an increase of 250 million dollars in the next year's budget as a means of supporting the Aboriginal cause.

The essence of the RCAP Report was to recommend a major reconstruction of Canadian society so that justice and equality would be better assured for Aboriginal Canadians. Two urgent concerns of the report had to do with the number of suicides in Native communities and the assurance of fair criminal justice. The Commission recommended swift action in these areas, starting with meetings of the various bars, law societies, and law associations. It urged increased government expenditures in preventative programs.

Constitutionally speaking, the RCAP recommended rewriting the principles of the Royal Proclamation to reflect the new nation-to-nation concept of negotiation as well as a new foundation by which to perceive the past treaty-making process. The commission also proposed the formation of an Aboriginal parliament as a first step towards creating a House of First peoples as the third chamber of the Parliament of Canada. This parliament would be primarily advisory and would have no law-making authority. The Commission also recommended the abolition of the Department of Indian Affairs and Northern Development to be replaced by two departments, that is, the Department of Aboriginal Relations and the Department of Indian and Inuit Services.

A number of other structures were also recommended by the RCAP. These included an Aboriginal Peoples' International University along with Aboriginal student unions and Aboriginal residential colleges. An Aboriginal Languages Foundation would parallel the work of the international university and supplement its efforts to maintain Aboriginal languages and culture.

Clearly the RCAP Report represents the most comprehensive effort to date undertaken by government on behalf of the Indigenous community. Only time will tell which of the many recommendations will see fruition. As Ponting (1997: 470) notes, "The rebalancing of political and economic power between Aboriginal nations and the Canadian governments represents the core of the hundreds of recommendations contained in this report."

Most Métis, Inuit, and nonStatus Indians were critical of the RCAP Report because most government action recommended in the report favored Status Indians. Phil Fontaine, Grand Chief of the AFN at that time, generally approved of the government's actions suggesting that they were the best one could hope for at the time.

Thomas Flanagan (2000), Professor of Political Science at the University of Calgary has been an outspoken critic of the RCAP

Report taking issue with its foundational assumptions. Flanagan refuses to accept the premise that Aboriginals differ from other Canadians because they have the right of first occupancy. He argues that before the European invasion of North America, Aboriginal peoples were almost in constant motion and in perpetual competition with one another for land. He also contests the notion that First Nations possessed sovereignty before European contact.. He bases his argument on a definition of statehood that includes sovereignty only as a corollary attribute. Flanagan argues that Aboriginal Peoples cannot be considered nations in the sense that they are subordinate communities within the nation of Canada. In addition, statements about self-government usually assume community. Any argument about permanent Indian communities that predate the arrival of Europeans has to assume that the various Aboriginal communities have been living in the same locations under the same governments for thousands of years. In fact, Indian tribes moved around a lot and their arrival on this continent probably stems from at least three migrations at three different times (Flanagan, 2000: 23).

Flanagan also attacks a fundamental premise of current land claim proponents who argue that Aboriginal property rights should be recognized as full ownership rights in Canadian law. He points out that the language of contemporary land claims needs to be modernized and reinterpreted to recognize the reality of an ongoing relationship between two parties. His solution for Aboriginal economic prosperity is for full integration of First Peoples into the modern economy. This implies a willingness to leave the reserves, if necessary, and relocate to where jobs and investment opportunities exist (Flanagan, 2000: 7).

Proposals on Education

The Royal Commission on Aboriginal Affairs reviewed many aspects of Native education including wholistic learning, teacher education, elder involvement, education for self-government, and new partnerships in First Nations education. Leaning heavily on the premise of education for self-government, the report proposed a two-phased model of a First Nations education system. In the first phase the government would acknowledge that education would be a primary channel through which to achieve self-government jurisdiction. In this phase local Native communities would be motivated to undertake initiatives to achieve self-government.

The second phase of the RCAP report recommended a reconstitution of Indian bands to put them in a better position to assume administration of local education. In some instances, for example, this might require the merger of smaller Indian bands. While reconstitution was going on the government would provide extra funds for the process and conduct an ongoing dialogue with Native communities to insure ideational compatibility.

Senate Response

A further response by the federal government to the proposals of the RCAP came in the form of a study undertaken by the Standing Senate Committee on Aboriginal Peoples (SSCAP). The purpose of the study was to provide opportunity for public reaction and formulate specific recommendations. The committee was particularly concerned that unresolved jurisdictional issues could seriously hamper a full realization of Aboriginal educational self-government. To this end the committee recommended the establishment of an Office of Aboriginal Relations with two main divisions—a Treaty and Agreements Negotiation Division, and a Treaty and Agreements Implementation Secretariat. The office would operate outside of the DIAND, with the hope that the DIAND could eventually be dissolved. The DIAND would then be replaced with a more streamlined government agency responsible for discharging the legal, fiduciary, and constitutional obligations of the Crown arising from the treaties and other agreements with Aboriginal peoples. The Standing Senate Committee on Aboriginal Peoples appropriately, recommended that judges, senior officials, and lawyers working with various levels of the judiciary in Canada be given opportunities for cross-cultural training to enable them to enhance their awareness of the various facets of the Aboriginal milieu. The training would include emphasis on Native history and culture, Aboriginal rights and treaty law, as well as First Nations' perspectives on related matters (Tremblay, 2001: 42-43).

Encouraging agreements that reflect the intent of the federal government to implement Aboriginal education self-government include the Framework Agreement on Indian Education in Manitoba (1990), the Umbrella Final Agreement with the Council for Yukon Indians (1993), the Nisga's Final Agreement (1993), and the Mik'maq Education Act (1998). In August, 2004, Phil Fontaine, Grand Chief of the AFN voiced his enthusiasm for renewed interest in Aboriginal affairs on the part of the federal government. Newly-appointed Minister of Indian Affairs and Northern Development and Federal Enterlocutor for Métis and Non-Status Indians, Andy Scott, was praised by Fontaine.

> Minister Scott very clearly demonstrated his understanding of our concerns about his dual appointment ... He knows that while there are common concerns among Canada's Aboriginal peoples, our histories, communities, traditions, and rights are different and must be recognized and treated as such. We need a First Nations agenda for First Nations citizens. (*Alberta Native News*, August, 2004: 3)

There are several challenges to be worked out in initiating necessary reforms in Aboriginal policy. *First* and foremost is the fact that a working definition of Aboriginal self-government has never been agreed upon by government and Native leaders. Progress has been made with regard to Indian educational jurisdiction and there is now unanimity. A *second* concern is the reality that the federal government alone has jurisdiction over funding. Severe curtailing of needed funds to any component of the proposed program could delay or derail important developments. *Third*, is the matter of achieving unanimity in the Aboriginal constituency particularly in regards to such complex issues as defining Aboriginal self-government. A united First Nations front could work towards convincing the federal government to negotiate conscientiously with Native organizations. Although it has always been the intent of the Assembly of First Nations to represent the various Indigenous communities across Canada, many bands still refuse to acknowledge this representation.

Any discussion of Aboriginal self-government must include reference to Aboriginal lands and Aboriginal land claims. While Indigenous lands are currently being held in trust by the federal government, and no individual band can initiate any action with regards to management sale thereof, it is sometimes frustrating for Indian bands to influence government decisions pertaining to use of lands. The key issue with regard to Native land claims is a subjective one, namely the political intent of the federal government. This is strongly influenced by the will of the Canadian people and the reaction by government to what they perceive is public opinion. There is no doubt that a better informed public would incline a more sincere attitude on the part of government to do right by the Indigenous Peoples of Canada. This challenge needs to be taken up by Aboriginal people themselves. No party is better qualified to define their needs and represent their interests, and no one stands to gain more by the process.

The following chapters outline a series of important educational frontiers representative of the kind of challenges faced by the Aboriginal people of Canada in other cultural sectors. These issues cannot be faced in isolation, but are related to the larger process of spiritual renaissance and cultural maintenance.

References

Ashworth, Mary. (1979). *The Forces Which Shaped Them: A History of Minority Group Children in British Columbia.* Vancouver, BC: New Star Books.

Barman, Jean. (1986). Separate and Unequal: Indian and White Girls at All Hallows School, 1884-1920. *Indian Education in Canada, Volume 1: The Legacy.* Jean Barman, Yvonne Hébert, and Don McCaskill, eds. Vancouver, BC: University of British Columbia Press, 110-131.

Bashford, Lucy and Hands Heinzerling. (1987). Blue Quills Native Education Centre: *A Case Study. Indian Education in Canada:, Volume 2: The Challenge.* Jean Barman, Yvonne Hébert, and Don McCaskill, eds. Vancouver, BC: University of BrItish Columbia Press, 126-141.

Boldt, Menno. (1993). *Surviving as Indians: The Challenge of Self-Government.* Toronto, ON: University of Toronto Press.

Brookes, Sonia. (1991). The Persistence of Native Educational Policy in Canada. *The Cultural Maze: Complex Questions on Native Destiny in Western Canada.* John W. Friesen, ed. Calgary, AB: Detselig Enterprises, 163-180.

Burns, George E. (1998). Factors and Themes in Native Education and School Boards/First Nations Tuiition Negotiaitons and Tuition Agreement Schooling. *Canadian Journal of Native Education,* 22:1, 53-66.

Cardinal, Harold. (1969). *The Unjust Society: The Tragedy of Canada's Indians.* Edmonton, AB: M.G. Hurtig Press.

Chalmers, John W. (1974). Marguerite Bourgeoys: Preceptress of New France. *Profiles of Canadian Educators*. Robert S. Patterson, John W. Chalmers and John W. Friesen, eds. Toronto, ON: D. C. Heath, 4-20.

Churchill, Ward. (1998). *A little Matter of Genocide: Holocaust and Denial in the Americas 1492 to the Present*. Winnipeg, MB: Arbeiter Ring.

Cornish, George H. (1881). *Encyclopedia of Methodism in Canada*. Toronto, ON: Methodist Book.

Duff, Wilson. (1997). *The Indian History of British Columbia: The Impact of the White Man*. Victoria, BC: The Royal British Columbia Museum.

Dyck, Noel. (1997). *Differing Visions: Administering Indian Residential Schooling in Prince Albert, 1867-1995*. Halifax, NS: Fernwood Publishing.

Fisher, Robin. (1978).*Contact and Conflict: Indian-European Relations in British Columbia, 1774-1890*. Vancouver, BC: University of British Columbia.

Flanagan, Thomas. (2000). *First Nations? Second Thoughts*. Montreal QC: McGill-Queen's University.

Frideres, James S. (1988). *Native Peoples in Canada: Contemporary Conflicts*. Scarborough, ON: Prentice-Hall.

Frideres, James S., and René R. Gadacz. (2001). *Native Peoples in Canada: Contemporary Conflicts*. Sixth edition. Scarborough, ON: Prentice-Hall.

Friesen, John W. (1974). John McDougall, Educator of Indians. *Profiles of Canadian Educators*. Robert S. Patterson, John W. Chalmers and John W. Friesen, eds. Toronto: D.C. Heath, 57-76.

Friesen, John W. (1983). *Schools With A Purpose*. Calgary, AB: Detselig Enterprises.

Friesen, John W. (1991). Highlights of Western Canadian Indian History. *The Cultural Maze: Complex Questions on Native Destiny in Western Canada*. John W. Friesen, ed. Calgary, AB: Detselig Enterprises, 1-22.

Friesen, John W. (1993). *When Cultures Clash: Case Studies in Multiculturalism*. Second edition. Calgary, AB: Detselig Enterprises.

Furniss, Elizabeth. (1995). *Victims of Benevolence: The Dark Legacy of the Williams Lake Residential School*. Vancouver, BC: Arsenal Pulp Press.

Goddard, John. (1992). *Last Stand of the Lubicon Cree*. Vancouver, BC: Douglas and McIntyre.

Gresko, Jacqueline. (1986). Creating Little Dominions Within the Dominion: Early Catholic Indian Schools in Saskatchewan and British Columbia. *Indian Education in Canada, Volume 1: The Legacy*. Jean Barman, Yvonne Hébert, and Don McCaskill, eds. Vancouver, BC: University of British Columbia Press, 88-109.

Haig-Brown, Celia. (1993). *Resistance and Renewal: Surviving the Indian Residential School.* Vancouver, BC: Tillacum Library.

Hawthorn, H. B., ed. (1967). *Survey of Contemporary Indians of Canada.* Vol. 2, Ottawa, ON: Indian Affairs Branch.

Jaenen, Cornelius. (1986). Education for Francization: The Case of New France in the Seventeenth Century. *Indian Education in Canada, Vol. I: The Legacy.* Jean Barman, Don McCaskill, and Yvonne Hébert, eds. Vancouver, BC: University of British Columbia, 45-63.

Johnson, F. Henry. (1968). *A Brief History of Canadian Education.* Toronto, ON: McGraw-Hill.

King, A. Richard. (1967). *The School At Mopass: A Problem of Identity.* New York, NY: Holt, Rinehart & Winston.

Kirkness, Verna J. (July/August, 1981). The Education of Canadian Indian *Children. Child Welfare,* LX:7, 446-455.

Lupul, Manoly, R. (1970). Education in Western Canada Before 1873. *Canadian Education: A History.* J. Donald Wilson, Robert M. Stamp. and Louis Philippe Audet, eds. Scarborough, ON: Prentice-Hall, 241-264.

McDonald, N.G. (1974). David J. Goggin: Promoter of National Schools. *Profiles of Canadian Educators.* Robert S. Patterson, John W. Chalmers and John W. Friesen, eds. Toronto, ON: D. C. Heath, 167-191.

McDougall, John. (1903). *In the Days of the Red River Rebellion.* Toronto, ON: William Briggs.

Miller, J. R. (1987). The Irony of Residential Schooling. *Canadian Journal of Native Education.* 14:2, 3-14.

Miller, J. R. (2000). *Skyscrapers Hide the Heavens: A History of Indian-White Relations in Canada.* Third edition. Toronto, ON: University of Toronto Press.

Persson, Diane. (1986). The Changing Experience of Indian Residential Schooling: Blue Quills, *1931-1970. Indian Education in Canada, Vol. I, The Legacy.* Jean Barman, Yvonne Hébert, and Don McCaskill, eds. Vancouver, BC: University of British Columbia Press, 150-168.

Ponting, J. Rick. (1997). Getting a Handle on Recommendations of the Royal Commission on Aboriginal Peoples. *First Nations in Canada: Perspectives on Opportunity, Empowerment, and Self-Determination* J. Rick Ponting, ed. Toronto, ON: McGraw-Hill Ryerson, 445-472.

Purich, Donald. (1986). *Our Land: Native Rights in Canada.* Toronto, ON: James Lorimer.

Purich, Donald. (1988). *The Métis.* Toronto, ON: James Lorimer.

Scott, Andrew. (1997). *The Promise of Paradise: Utopian Communities in B.C.* Vancouver, BC: Whitecap Books.

Titley, E. Brian. (1992). Red Deer Indian Industrial School: A Case Study in the History of Native Education. *Exploring Our Educational Past.* Nick Kach and Kas Mazurek, eds. Calgary, AB: Detselig Enterprises, 55-72.

Tremblay, Paulette C. (2001). First Nations Educational Jurisdiction: National Background Paper. Ottawa, ON: Educational Sector,

Wolcott, Harry F. (1967). *A Kwakiutl Village and School.* New York, NY: Holt, Rinehart and Winston.

Wuttunee, William. (1971). *Ruffled Feathers: Indians in Canadian Society.* Calgary, AB: Bell Books.

Four

The Frontier of Spirituality

We also have a religion which was given to our forefathers, and has been handed down to our children. It teaches us to be thankful, to be united, to love one another. We never quarrel about religion — Seneca Chief Red Jacket. (Weaver, 1998: xi)

The most fundamental feature of traditional Aboriginal culture is spirituality, but it is also one of the least understood. Observers of the Indigenous lifestyle are often attracted to the unique rituals of Aboriginal culture, as well as their colorful costumes, and intricate dances, unaware that these cultural enactments have important underlying spiritual implications. Teaching their young has always been a spiritual process for First Nations because of their concern that each individual, old or young must be given the opportunity to find the path that the Creator has designed for them. It is only recently that this truth has become known to nonNative educators who are busily trying to backtrack on past erroneous approaches. This revamped approach, however healthy, has deep unfortunate roots.

One of the most disconcerting religious tragedies of modern times may be traced back to the first contact between Europeans and First Nations. The explorers who initially came to North America adhered to a religious value system they believed had been handed to them by the Creator. They were convinced that their way of believing was superior to everyone else's. This perspective mandated them to investigate, analyze, and evaluate any religious system they might encounter in the new land, and if they felt like it, justify or condemn it. Any system they encountered different than their own would most certainly have to be revamped, enriched, or stamped out altogether and replaced with either Roman Catholic or Protestant forms of organized Christianity. European contact with the First Peoples of this continent, therefore, resulted in an inevitable theological clash.

95

The religious emissaries who represented France, Spain, and England took little time to learn about or compare resident theological systems with their own convictions. Instead, they devoted their energies to disabusing local Aboriginals of their belief system and substituting Europeans models. To avoid duplication and achieve maximum success, Catholic religious orders like Jesuits, Oblates, and Recollets devoted themselves to specific missions. As early as 1615, the Hurons of Georgian Bay were being educated by the Recollets. A school for Mik'maq children was opened in 1632, and by 1635 Father Paul LeJeune had begun a school for both French and Native children at Quebec. Initial efforts such as these were quite unsuccessful because the missionaries insisted on using classical languages for instruction. They also found it difficult to minister to people who adhered to a nomadic lifestyle.

Foundations of Faith

No one knows just how the Indigenous peoples formulated their faith systems, how old they are, nor how many practices or rituals have been retained or lost through time. Perhaps this is as it should be because the essence of Native spirituality is to demonstrate one's faith through behavior, rather than by talking about it. The key premise is to seek peace through harmony with the universe. When Christianity was first introduced to the First Nations, many tribes integrated aspects of the Christian faith which they found similar to their own perspectives. To this day there are many First Nations who celebrate a religion born of two distinct origins, their own traditional spirituality, and that of imported Christianity (Friesen, 1991).

When the newly-arrived missionaries explicated their doctrines to their Aboriginal listeners, the latter listened politely but innocently perceived that by doing so they were not necessarily committing themselves to major changes in their lifestyle. The Black Robes (priests) and missionaries who followed the fur traders declared themselves to be "men of God," so the Indians took them at their word and paid careful attention to them (Snow, 1977). It was an Aboriginal custom to respect anyone making this kind of claim, so they listened intently to the newcomers' message and sought to gain new insights. Later they discovered that by being good hosts they ran the risk of endangering their traditional religious status.

Somehow the proprietorship of their hunting and fishing lands was also put in question.

It would be unfair to suggest that regard for the Aboriginal peoples by explorers, fur traders, and missionaries was always negative. Many of this country's first immigrants married Native women and "lived happily ever after," so to speak. There were also missionaries who developed a strong respect for Native cultures and described them as representatives of an honorable and religious civilization (Friesen, 1991: 36).

Cree Elder, the late Joe Cardinal, Cree First
Nation, Saddle Lake First Nations

Fundamentals of Faith

A key to sharing in the lament for a once badly battered religious system demands discernment of the difference between the oral tradition and allegiance to the written word. Many social scientists are convinced that the First Nations never developed much by way of written forms except for petroglyphs and pictograms which some tribes left behind. Naturally, their belief system and practiced rituals changed slightly from one generation to the next, partially reflecting an inbuilt design of adjusting to time and place. A good example would be the First Nations practice of telling stories and legends which comprised a valued form of moral teaching. Stories would vary slightly from storyteller to storyteller and from one occasion to another, but no one worried about this. The people were sure that the essence of the particular truth being imparted was still being preserved. Children used to spend hours with their grandparents and with tribal elders, listening to them relate stories while acquiring valued beliefs in informal settings.

Deloria (1995: 52) suggests that;

> In the old days . . . religious ceremonials generally involved the recitation of the origin and migration stories, and most of the accumulated wisdom of the tribe was familiar to everyone. Special knowledge regarding other forms of life, if revealed in visions or dreams, was made available to the larger community on a "need-to-know" basis, since it was generally regarded as personal knowledge.

Even today, traditional Aboriginal societies tend to view the totality of nature through the same lens with which they view themselves, namely the bonds of kinship (Knudtson and Suzuki, 1992). Each living thing, animal, human or plant, and even inanimate objects, are perceived to have spirits, and contact might be made with that spirit. This contact might be undertaken in response to a dream or vision. In some societies the combined total of the people's spiritual powers is believed to be the unseen force that manages the world (Josephy, 1968). The belief goes even deeper, and extends to the arena of governance. Basically, the primary law of Aboriginal government is spiritual law. Spirituality is the highest form of politics and spirituality is directly involved in government. The responsibilities of Indigenous leaders is to see that the spiritual ceremonies are carried out because without ceremonies one does not have a basis on which to conduct government for the welfare of the people. It is important that ceremonies be conducted in the proper manner before the band council convenes to deliberate the welfare of the people (Lyons, 1984).

By contrast, adherence to the written tradition is premised on the notion that nothing can be proven, nor have any epistemological value, unless it can be identified in some written form. As it turns out, in retrospect, both forms have a measure of validity, and both stand in need of a degree of healthy scepticism in terms of comprising absolute knowledge forms. If some degree of compromise could have been worked out at the time of first contact, perhaps both systems could have benefitted a great deal. Alternately, if the incoming emissaries had been trained to show at least a modicum of respect for spiritual systems other then their own, a great deal of unnecessary stress and recapitulation might have been avoided.

Another factor that explains the gap between the two ways of mental deliberation is that EuroCanadian thinking relies on the presupposition that the universe can be understood and controlled through atomism. The intellectual tendency in western science is the acquisition and synthesis of total human knowledge from the perspective of a worldview that seeks to understand every entity from the immediate to those in outer space (Ermine, 1995). To an Aboriginal person, such intent is almost sacrilegious. Complicating things even more is the possibility that the nonNative value system may not even incorporate the necessary mental structural forms by which to understand the Aboriginal tradition (Friesen, 1995). An enlightened grasp of the reality contained in the oral tradition is usually thought to require the business of a lifetime. Traditionally elders have had access to this knowledge but they have been reticent and discreet about sharing and teaching this knowledge. Today the scene is changing, and elders are openly pointing to an unfolding prophecy which postulates that "the time has come to share the secrets" (Couture, 1991: 54). If writings by First Nations individuals are any indication, there is presently converging in North America and abundance of literature containing the message of hundreds of tribal voices who form one pluralistic body of diverse peoples newly-voiced in contemporary history. These peoples are sending a voice with the "power to move us" (Lincoln, 1985). Perhaps enlightenment about Native spiritual knowledge will include insights as well about the structural forms by which it can be understood and appreciated by nonAboriginals.

Relations

It is difficult for nonNatives to comprehend the implications of an holistic view of the universe. The Indigenous people have always believed that all phenomena, including material and nonmaterial elements, are connected and interconnected. Every living entity is related. AmerIndian peoples do not adhere to any "scientific" breakdown of how people function or how the universe operates. By contrast, the modern scientific view further allows and encourages the development of separate definitively different core academic disciplines which seek to ferret out and explain the basic components of varied phenomena. For example, when such fields as geography, physics and biology are further broken down into even finer distinctions, they comprise elements of interdisciplinary crossover, for example, astrophysics, biophysics, and so on. The social sciences feature similar distinctions such as anthropology, sociology, and psychology with further cross fertilizations, such as biopsychology, athro-archaeology or social psychology, with even more subdivisions in the making as these field continue to develop. Although proponents of each of these areas of expertise may make sophisticated claims about interdisciplinary parallels and concerns, there is always an element of academic ethnocentrism involved in their professional deliberations.

The delineation of disciplinary specialties is quite foreign to the Indigenous way of thinking. First Nations view the world as an interconnected series of only sometimes distinguishable or understandable elements. They experience no uneasiness at the thought of multiple realities simultaneously operant in the universe, and they do not differentiate among the varieties or qualities of entities, that is, between physical and spiritual elements. Their worldview allows for the possibility that a variety of "structurally different" elements may simultaneously be active, for example, in the process of holistic healing. This also explains why dreams and visions comprise as welcome a source of knowledge as scientifically derived truths or personal experience. Seekers can never be sure where they might gain valuable experience or acquire new knowledge.

In the traditional Indigenous world there was only one universal and absolute truth; the universe exists. Often described in terms such as respect for nature or working in harmony with nature, the underlying truth requires much more consideration, but not necessarily additional analysis. Coupled with the concept of connectedness, for Indigenous people the universe remains the object of reverence albeit its workings are veiled in mystery. There are no satisfying scientific explanations in this approach, and the deeper mysteries are only partially understood and then only through an intensive lifelong spiritual search.

The mystique of the universe suggests a deep respect for the universe. Pelletier (1974), describes the difference between a Native and nonNative approach to the universe in a scene that places him on the top of a mountain in British Columbia. There he imagines he has been assigned the awesome responsibility of improving his natural environment. His first inclination is to stock the sky with a few more birds or perhaps move some clouds around to provide balance. Then his eye falls on an old plank lying on the ground at his feet and he decides to relocate it to a more appropriate place. As he lifts the plank he notices that the underside of it contains a whole colony of insect life. Ants are scrambling to move their eggs to safety, woodlice are digging to get down into the ground, earthworms are coiled up like snakes, and a spider is staring him straight in the face demanding, "What have you done to my world?" Pelletier immediately puts the board down as close to the original location as possible, and apologizes to the insects for disturbing their society. Then he thanks them for the lesson they have taught him not to interfere with the doings of the universe nor view other societies with curiosity or disrespect.

Pelletier's experience may be compared with that of the staff of a construction company charged with digging basements to prepare the ground for new homes in an urban development project. The crew's mandate is to rearrange the earth in a pattern that is virtually indistinguishable when compared with the previous format; nothing in the way will remain untouched, if not completely destroyed – the terrain, trees, and any and all forms of other vegetation. This, after all, is progress.

The Indigenous handsoff approach to the universe generates several spin offs which, from the dominant North American perspective, have varying implications. The positive aspect has to do with providing the would be learner with a more open attitude towards personal growth. By placing oneself at the disposal of the inner workings of the universe, its every component and process become potential teaching/learning situations in the manner that Pelletier's experience demonstrates. There may be some resistance to the nature of these potential teaching opportunities on the part of more scientific minded observers, since the essence of the experience will necessarily be intuitive and/or spiritual. Seldom is even the most committed scientist prepared for or open to learn about any or all of Nature's inexplicable mysteries (Knudtson and Suzuki, 1992: xxx). In addition, the orientation and pace of everyday human ongoings in dominant society virtually dictate a total disregard for this sphere.

The down side of "universe reverence," if it may be so labelled, is that the resultant attitude towards the universe can take somewhat unusual forms. The strong penchant towards "maintenance," so strongly valued by many EuroCanadians, for example, might be viewed by Aboriginal peoples as comprising a form of tampering with the operations of the universe. Nowhere is there a better illustration of this than when formerly "developed" communities paralyzed by "progress" wither and fall into disuse. Abandoned townsites serve to substantiate the Indigenous view that nonNative people tend to build and destroy. Their engineers dig holes, erect buildings, lay paved roads, and develop streets, and then install elaborate underground wiring and plumbing systems.

When a settlement is abandoned, however, in many cases the modern trappings of convenience are simply left to decay, often inflicting permanent damage to the earth as well as comprising an eyesore (even by nonNative standards). Traditionally-minded Native people find this state of affairs quite intolerable. In their view, in time, the earth will return to find its own form—provided that in the meantime the damage inflicted by "civilization" is not irreparable.

The vision of permanence, particularly the notion of building a bigger, better future for one's successors or, better still, in heaven, is not a vital plank in Aboriginal philosophy, and in light of today's happenings, it does seem somewhat pointless to value such ends. And towards what purpose? First Nations continually see nonNatives using up all their energies "building for the future" and then end up dying any way. Perhaps a better way would be to adjust one's energies towards fulfilling the Creator's immediate and long-range plan for one's life.

Comparisons

One Sunday morning, members of an Indigenous Christian congregation in Alberta were leaving the church when someone remarked what a beautiful day it was. As the people glanced up to view the clear sky they saw an eagle circling high above the grounds. "This is good," said one of the elders present. "This is a good day. The Creator is smiling on us. We are being blessed!"

The implications of this simple scene cannot easily be elaborated. Implicit in the elder's observation is the assumption that all of nature is interconnected and all living things are potentially capable of relating Divine messages. The eagle is viewed as a particularly special creature because it speaks of strength and wisdom. The fact that this special bird was visible on a day of worship, and circling above the congregation, definitely meant Divine good will was being showered upon the people. It is situations like this that continue to affirm the traditional Indigenous view of the universe. Spiritual lessons and blessings can indeed be received in many varied and often unexpected forms.

When first forced up against the European perspective, with its penchant for philosophical dissection and analysis, the First Nations were baffled by the newcomers' enamour with wanting to explain and control every element of the universe. There was apparently no respite from this assignment. The Europeans even gave the impression that this was the main purpose for which humankind was put on earth. Interestingly, this fixation persistently dogs EuroCanadian descendants to this day and appears to be embedded in every philosophical, cultural, and religious institution.

The Aboriginal perspective towards openness augured well for the European invaders. When their philosophical captors indicated that the traditional First Nations lifestyle was out of sync with the Creator's instructions and expectations many Indians believed them and attempted to change their ways. After that it was only an extension of logic to convince the AmerIndians also to give up their lands and transfer their control to their spiritual superiors. The Aboriginal orientation of respect for the universe logically blossomed into a resignation to work with the forces of the universe. The power of these forces was invisible, yet rhythmic, and by respecting these reliable patterns, it was possible to sustain a perpetual form of cultural life on earth. A further extension of this mind-set was an inherent warning not to seek to dominate or exploit nature, but to work in harmony with its various manifestations. Above all, the Aboriginals believed that they should never close the door to any possibility of learning spiritual truths. This made them a ready audience to anyone who claimed to be possession of Divine truth.

Porterfield (1990: 156) concurs that many Aboriginal tribes initially incorporated aspects of the Christian faith into the structures of their rituals because they seemed familiar to them. In fact, after gaining some familiarity with the rudiments of the Christian faith, one Seneca prophet, Handsome Lake, postulated that his people understood and followed the teachings of the Gospel to a greater degree than the newcomers who were importing the faith. He was particularly disconcerted to learn that the EuroChristians who considered themselves to be God's people had crucified their own prophet, Jesus, and still perceived their religious practices to be superior to those of the First Nations. Despite what he perceived to be a rather portentous deficiency Handsome Lake, like many other prophets, tried earnestly to endorse the Christian faith and adapt its teachings to everyday life. As Chief John Snow (1977: 17) notes;

> If one understands the native religion of my people, it is not difficult to understand why so many of us embraced the gospel of Christianity. There was simply not that much difference between what we already believed and what the missionaries preached to us. What differences there were did not seem very important.

The contemporary rise of interest in Native spirituality in North America is heartening. This curiosity has potential, but it must be directed by knowledgeable guides both familiar with and sensitive to a very complex way of believing. NonNative intrigue with Aboriginal spirituality is of recent origins; a few decades ago the pursuit was left to anthropologists. Then, during the 1960s a sudden interest in philosophical variations burst forth, attributable to many different factors. North American society appeared to be in a state of upheaval. The Vietnam War was in progress, hippies were conducting sit-ins at local parks, and students were smoking grass as they raised serious questions about "the establishment," including the utility of organized religion. As subsequent decades have unfolded, however, this sceptical perspective has been substituted by an interest in spiritual matters, oft-times motivated and symbolized by seekers with a bent towards inclusiveness and sympathy for the New Age movement. Although generally discredited by Christian theologians, these orientations have probably assisted in spawning a renewed interest in the otherworldly aspects of human existence.

On a very fundamental level it can be shown that there are many similarities in both structure and function between Christianity and Aboriginal spirituality. Spence (1994: 359) appropriately notes, "... such a resemblance cannot be advanced as a proof that the divergent races at some distant period possessed a common mythology." What this resemblance does illustrate, however, is that the first North American missionaries might have saved themselves a lot of effort if they had taken the time to learn about the fundamentals of AmerIndian spirituality if only to provide them with a more palatable and effective format by which to try to evangelize their new contacts. Christian evangelists like to stress that an effective starting point in any such effort is to "know your target community." Unfortunately, the first missionaries did not have enough of this kind of regard for Aboriginal rituals even to study their meanings, much less appreciate them. Tooker (1979: 31) observes that Aboriginal religious narratives have often been labelled "myths" by outsiders probably in order to demean them, but they are based on no less astute observations of nature than their European-derived counterparts, nor do they reflect any less intellectual effort than do the sacred and secular texts of the "high" civilizations of the Old World.

Creator Concepts

In contrasting Christianity and Aboriginal theology, the most obvious question to ponder is, "Did North American Native peoples traditionally believe in God?" The answer is a qualified "yes." Smith (1995: 242) suggests that the First Peoples have always believed in the existence of a Superior Divine Being, but not in the sense that theologians do who adhere to EuroCanadian interpretations. At its core the EuroCanadian perspective focuses on individuality and conjectures that God is a separate, unique Creator Being who exists against the particular created universe. God is perceived in a "parent" role, and is usually elaborated in male form, that is, God, the Father. According to Smith, First Nations believe in the Creator as a great Prevailing Force who resides in the sky. All brightness emanates from the firmament above mankind and people's eyes are dazzled by its splendor. Mankind therefore concludes that the abode of the Creator, the "Great Mystery," is the source of all life and of all spiritual excellence (Spence, 1994: 101-102).

Native North Americans in precontact days described God in terms of a Universal Principle instead of a determinate Being one might call "God." This God may be perceived as an eternal spiritual Force characterized by presence and unity. This Force exists as a vital, energizing part of every living entity. Native Americans have always believed that by honoring the spirits of animals, for example, they are acknowledging the universal presence of the Eternal Spirit, not any particular form or separate entity. The concept of interconnectedness is also significant in this context because it implies responsibility to all living things. Traditionally, when an animal was killed for food it was the plains Indian tradition to offer a prayer of thanks to the spirit of the animal for sustenance. A portion of meat was then buried in the ground to honor the interconnectedness of all things. The Sioux believed, "We are all related to all things" or "we are all related – we are all relatives" (McGaa, 1995: 9). Prayers were often ended with the phrase, "And all my relations," referring to the interconnectedness of all living phenomena. Since a very fundamental plank in Indian philosophy mandates caring for one's relatives, and sharing with them whatever resources one has, by parallel argument it also means that one has a responsibility to the earth and to every living thing, animate or inanimate.

One key difference between Indigenous theology and EuroCanadian-originated creeds may be illustrated with reference to the interpretation of John 3:16a, "For God so loved the world that He gave . . ." To First Nations this simply means that God (the Force) created and provides for the earth in all facets as a complete entity. EuroCanadian Christians, on the other hand, will interpret this passage to mean that God loves and gives to people, but not necessarily to other living entities He has created – at least not in the same sense. As Tinker (1996: 156) notes;

> The danger of such privileging of human beings should be obvious. It runs the risk of generating human arrogance, which too easily sees the world in terms of hierarchies of existence, all of which are ultimately subservient to the needs and whims of humans.

Earmarking nonhuman forms of life as inferior minimizes responsibility towards other life forms and often justifies the abuse of animal life as well as abuse of the earth's resources. In this context it is easier to appreciate the implied universe stewardship inherent in Aboriginal theology.

As an addendum, it might be mentioned that some Aboriginal observers conceptualize the workings of Mother Earth as a unity. The esteemed Sioux leader, Black Elk, perhaps because of Christian influence, identified the Great Spirit as a governing force with authority over everything and synonymous with the God of the white man. Porterfield, (1990: 159) suggests that Black Elk ascribed to the workings of the Great Spirit parameters that included all things: the trees, the grasses, the rivers, the mountains, all four-legged animals, and the winged people. Black Elk's God, therefore, was perceived as more than a governing force; He is the Creator and Life Force within all things.

Until recently, most Christian theologians viewed the ecological concerns of Indigenous Peoples as corollary to the Christian obligation to stewardship. For the Indigenous people, however, belief in God mandates an inherent admonition to respect the earth, which may be perceived as our natural "mother" (Cajete, 1994). The "parents" of mankind, the Great Spirit and Mother Earth (who are essentially a unity), have provided their children with all of the resources needed to sustain and perpetuate life. If properly guarded, respected and cared for, Mother Earth will provide plenty of food, water, shelter and resources for other needs for all generations to come. In light of the many recent incursions into sacred territory for destructive purposes, that is, the abuse of the earth, Native leaders are deeply concerned that the corruptions of western society will permanently harm Mother Earth. Ironically, this abuse clearly violates Christian responsibility and displeases the Creator.

Personal Faith?

Stolzman (1998: 182f), a Roman Catholic pastor and theologian has observed that some AmerIndian spiritual leaders object to the EuroCanadian tendency to describe God in anthropomorphisms. Stolzman claims that Native elders prefer to depict God in strictly abstract, philosophical, and theological terms which he calls "third-order abstractions from reality" in the sense that they are always deficient in some reality. Stolzman suggests that First Nations theologians deliberate on the assumption that the more simple and abstract a term is, the more spiritual it is. He disagrees with this assumption, arguing that cognitive distinctions examine the materiality of phenomena, rather than their spirituality. This is why cognitive examinations of God always end up in paradoxes. True to his Roman Catholic attachments, Stolzman postulates Jesus Christ as the total, real anthropomorphization of God and the model for all Christians. This belief mandates evangelistic efforts among peoples who possess only a shadow of the Gospel truth, that is, anyone whose experience of the Almighty varies with this interpretation.

Stolzman may be correct that Aboriginal conceptualizations of God are abstract and fuzzy, but this perspective apparently does not diminish the feasibility of belief in the reality of incarnation. The Blackfeet, for example, have a legend of Poïa, who was sent to earth as Star Boy by the Sun God for the purpose of instructing the Blackfeet in worship. After establishing the ceremonial of the Sundance, Poïa returned to the home of the sun and became a morning star (McClintock, 1992: 491). Similarly, the Mik'maq believe in an incarnate being named Glooscap who reportedly came to earth to transform animals into their present shapes and teach his people how to make a living. Glooscap travelled a great deal while he was on earth, spoke all languages, and made friends with the animals. He had control of the elements and could make the sun shine or the rains fall at will, much in the manner that Christ stilled the storm (Mark 6:51). When Glooscap's work was done, he left the earth but promised to return whenever the people had need of his guidance (Friesen, 1997: 54).

Most plains Indian tribes traditionally postulated a similar concept of a "middle kind of god" like Glooscap. Confusingly, he was also called the trickster, a half-god, half-man who had the ability to do good or mischief. The Ojibway called him "Nanabush" and believed that he came to earth to arrange things in order, that is, the shape of animals and the landscape of the earth. Like the parallel postulated by many other tribes, in the form of the trickster, Nanabush served a somewhat ambiguous function both as benefactor to people and as a self-indulgent and rather aimless wanderer (Miller, 1995: 108).

Aboriginal notions of incarnation basically parallel the Christian concept of Jesus Christ as the sent Son of God who was to interpret God's will to mankind. If the Native perception of God (the Great Mystery) was vague, there was less doubt about the role of their envisaged intermediary figure. Perhaps these similarities explain why so many Indian tribes so readily accepted elements of the Christian Gospel when it was first presented to them.

While much of traditional AmerIndian religious life was community-oriented, a special place for the individual was set aside in the system—particularly in the context of religion. The notion that the Great Spirit was traditionally perceived by First Nations theologians as a universal Force or Presence may lead some observers to conclude that any form of individual contact with the "Grand Force of Being" would be impracticable. On the contrary, there is ample evidence that in Aboriginal thinking individual human contact with the Divine was not only considered a legitimate pursuit, but was both sought after and often realized.

One of the ways in which individual spirituality was affirmed in traditional Aboriginal society was through the vision quest. When young Indian men reached a certain age, depending on their tribal affiliation, they volunteered or were selected to isolate themselves from their communities (usually for four days), during which time they would seek contact with the Great Spirit. There were also tribes who selected both men and women for this assignment. The possibility of the success of the process was enhanced by the participant refraining from any form of nourishment and maintaining an attitude of prayer. The vision seeker was also carefully tutored by an elder who oversaw the process. Among plains tribes the practice was that a young man would travel alone to a hillside or canyon top and pray that a guardian spirit would be revealed to him. Should the experience prove to be successful, the youth might experience a visit by the spirit of an animal or bird and, if so, could later consult with that spirit whenever he felt the need to do so. Such visitations were seen as an awarding of spiritual power, insight or gift which was respected by members of the community who were also expected to be beneficiaries of that vision.

The perception of dreams as valid forms of Divine message is crucial to an understanding of Aboriginal theology. Chief Red Crow of the Blood First Nation once had a dream in which a gopher spirit came to him and told him that if he put a blade of grass in his hair every time he went to battle he would never be hurt. Red Crow did as he was advised and although he was engaged in 19 battles during his lifetime, he was never harmed.

Ecclesiastical Structures

Traditionally, the plains First Nations of North America had neither formal church congregations nor permanently-designated worship centres. Wherever they travelled in search of buffalo, however, their portable temples went with them. When the Sundance was sponsored, the teepee at the centre of the camp was designated as the high place of worship while the ceremony was being held. When the Sundance was over, religious rites and rituals were again entrusted to elders who governed the spiritual welfare of the people.

Today ample literature is available about formalized religious enactments among the First Peoples in most parts of North America before and immediately after first contact. The fundamental spiritual purpose and meaning of many of these ceremonies and rituals, however, have only recently been brought to light, thanks largely to Aboriginal writers. Early North American scholars who spent time in First Nations communities made numerous observations about aspects of their lifestyle have been helpful in passing along rudimentary knowledge of Indigenous religious structures. These have recently been supplemented (as well as corrected) by Aboriginal writers. In eastern Canada, for example, inside knowledge about the Midewiwin has recently been made available thanks to two principal works by Ojibway scholar, Basil Johnston (1988 and 1995).

Essentially the Midewiwin comprised a group of esteemed spiritual leaders who were in charge of maintaining and developing all aspects of Ojibway medicinal religious practices, and it took years of instruction for an initiate to master four calibrated levels of knowledge. The plains tribes also featured formal societies known as sodalities whose responsibility it was to preserve and pass along revered knowledge that was translated into songs, rituals, and ceremonies (Friesen, 1997: 132).

Moving away from the plains region per se it is possible to affirm the establishment of formalized religious edifices among North America's First Nations, particularly among moundbuilding cultures of the southeastern states. Before Christopher Columbus' arrival in North America in 1492, moundbuilders in this region amassed thousands of piles of earth into effigy formations and as temple foundations or burial sites. These earthen edifices were plentiful in regions from the Great Lakes in the north to the Gulf of Mexico in the south; from the eastern portions of the Great Plains to the Appalachian Mountains. These were impressive structures, and constituted the most conspicuous record of prehistoric American Indian culture to be found on the landscape of eastern North America (Woodward and McDonald, 1986). The first European viewers naturally assumed that a people other than the First Nations had built them, but gradually archaeological proof emerged to show that the builders were native to the area. Central to their culture was a form of orally-based, but organized religion, epitomized in the form of elaborate temples built on carefully-constructed mounds.

Spiritual Practices

It is difficult to formulate a catalog of the varied spiritual rituals of Aboriginal peoples because of tribal and regional differences within their communities. It helps to keep in mind that there are probably more significant cultural differences among North American Native groups than there are among transplanted European cultures. Compiling a list of Aboriginal beliefs and practices would be quite an extensive undertaking. Traditionally, among some First Nations, religious leaders spent the majority of their waking hours in religious activities of some type.

Sundance

The complexity of Aboriginal ceremonies and rituals are illustrative of a highly developed religious system, each of which is rife with meanings and submeanings. For example, note Underhill's (1965: 108) description of one aspect of the Sundance, the most revered ceremony celebrated by Plains Indians:

> At a Plains Sun Dance, the priest is to lay a rabbit skin at the centre pole in memory of a vow. It is a flimsy, grayish, little skin but he holds it in both hands as reverently as a different priest might hold a golden chalice. Three times he gestures towards the centre pole and withdraws. The uninstructed visitor grows impatient, for there is no pageantry to mark the importance of this event. But the Indian spectators know that the number four symbolizes perfection.

Celebrating the Sundance is something like a modern church conference. Although explanations regarding the origin and nature of the Sundance vary slightly among its descriptors, most authorities agree that it is essentially a four-day event comprising an expression of joy and ecstasy (Snow, 1977: 111). Blood tribal members of the Blackfoot Confederacy celebrate their Sundance as a joyful renewal of acquaintances featuring feasting, playing games, and the exchange of properties. At least one day is devoted to spiritual activities. Some viewers also suggest that the Sundance is a form of petition with the Almighty to guard the people from possible disaster (Hanks and Hanks, 1950).

Explanations regarding the origins and nature of the Sundance vary among its descriptors. Snow suggests that the purpose of the ceremony was "an expression of the joy and ecstasy of a religious life, of being thankful for life, the beautiful creation, the rain, the sun, and the changing seasons" (Snow, 1977: 111). The ritual comprised an expression to the Great Spirit with a prayer for a good future, health, strength, and prosperity for the tribe. Hanks and Hanks (1950: 25) interpreted the Sundance ceremony as an occasion for joyful renewing of acquaintance, exchanging property, and feasting as well as a form of insurance to guard the people against disaster (Hanks and Hanks, 1950: 25). Hoebel (1965: 11) postulated that for most plains tribes, the objective of the Sundance was world renewal, even though its corollary aims varied from one tribe to another.

For the nonNative and unsympathetic observer elements of the Sundance enacted in some tribes were considered cruel. This part of the event was the piercing component which some male participants inflicted on themselves as part of the procedure (Erdoes, 1972: 105-6). Some anthropologists promoted this interpretation; Jenness observed that the sensational element of the Sundance was unessential and labelled the participants, "misguided devotees" (Jenness, 1986: 316). For this reason, beginning in 1890, the Canadian Government outlawed the ceremony pressured by missionaries who interpreted the practice as barbaric (Friesen, 1983). In symbolic terms when the missionaries came, the sacred Sundance tree was torn down and replaced by the cross and a flagpole (Lincoln, 1985: 173). Then, without any attempt to understand the background to Indian rituals, the Christian church service and chapel services of the residential school were touted as desirable spiritual festivities for First Nations children. This attitude discouraged an objective understanding of the Sundance and its basic features survived mainly through secretive practice and reliance on the oral tradition. A number of North American tribes omitted the torture element from their Sundance, namely the Kiowa, the Ute, and the Shoshone. Other tribes included it as a voluntary component while the Dakota and the Ponca tribes celebrated it as a theme (Lowie, 1963: 199).

The traditional commencement of the Sundance in the Blackfoot Nation was announced by a well-respected woman (Lincoln, 1985: 115), and generally consisted of a formal three or four day ceremony. Jenness (1986: 316) described the event as consisting of the following program: the first day was for dancing, the second for spiritual activities, and the third for feasting. The initial step for celebrating a Sundance involved the building of a sacred lodge at the centre of the camp where the main activities would take place. The call for a Sundance was based on dedication to a specific prayer request identified by a respected woman. The request might be for the recovery of a sick loved one or for the return of someone who had undertaken a dangerous mission. The woman would offer her thanks in the form of the Sundance in which the whole tribe would participate. The event also gave opportunity for socializing; old warriors could recount their deeds of bravery and young people could learn the sacred ways of their people (Dempsey, 1976: 66).

Elements of the Sundance ceremony were quite structured. Among the Blackfoot the cutting down of the tree for the centre pole of the sacred lodge at the centre of the camp followed very specific dictates. Once cut, the tree could not touch the ground again until it was carried to the lodge site. In the Stoney tribe one or more men were selected by the medicine man or woman to make the centre lodge ready for the ceremony. When the structure was completed the medicine man or woman would start the sacred fire. On the fire they would burn sweetgrass, cedar branch needles, and boughs, or other forms of incense dedicated to the Great Spirit. Like all sacred events the Sacred Pipe would be smoked, its participants seated in a circle, always holding the stem of the pipe in a northerly direction (Snow, 1977: 11).

Medicine Bundles

A special feature of the Sundance is the opening and/or exchange of medicine bundles known as the pipe bundle ceremony. Medicine bundles are leather pouches containing such articles as feathers, special rocks, skins, or bones, and put together by the originator who experienced the special message contained in the bundle in a vision or dream. Medicine bundles are deemed sacred articles and they are not to be handled just by anyone. If they are touched by someone other than a designated guardian, a purification ceremony may need to be conducted. Medicine bundles are viewed as possessing special powers or insights which accompanied the original vision. Bundles may be bought and sold, and the price may be set by recognized elders. The new owner may then access the power of the bundle. A closely-related artifact is the medicine pouch which may be worn by an individual seeking spiritual direction and protection, or Divine mercy for the healing from a certain ailment. A medicine pouch may contain plant material prescribed by an elder.

In specifically describing the use of pipe bundles among the Blackfeet, Harrod (1992: 71) states;

> The material objects in the pipe bundle may typically include the following: At the centre is the sacred pipe, often accompanied by the white buffalo headdress, both of which may be wrapped in red flannel. A number of other items may also be present, such as a smaller pipe for smoking during the ritual, as well as the skins of certain animals and birds, such as the owl, loon, swan, crane, muskrat, otter, fawn, and prairie dog. Tobacco will often be placed in the bird skins, and a rattle may be wrapped in the prairie dog skin. In addition, there are pouches containing paints, incense materials, and other items for use in the ritual.

Medicine bundles were traditionally viewed as representative of the vision which the original creator of the bundle experienced before assembling it. Subsequent owners may have added items based on their own experiences. Making the bundle and using it in the sense of "enquiring of it" made its message vital to the spiritual life of the tribe. Among the Blackfoot Indians medicine bundles could be purchased by other members of the tribe but only if the transfer of the bundle and its representative power or gift was approved by elders who traditionally opened it on occasion, particularly when a transfer of ownership occurred. In such cases protocol was quite specific. The centre teepee at the Sundance camp was the location for such a ritual, and only people specifically invited to attend were allowed to observe or participate. The ritual of opening a bundle began with the recitation of the origin narrative, preparing the participants for the ceremony to follow. Essentially, the ritual consisted of a complex of songs, prayers, dance, and symbolic behavior intended to evoke horizons of transcendental meaning. Four major sequences governed the ceremony, each introduced by a set of seven songs, and if ownership of the bundle was transferred, the prospective owner's face was painted during the ceremony, marking him off from the everyday world and identifying him with meaning structures evoked symbolically in the ritual (Harrod, 1992: 75).

Closely related to the pipe bundle ceremony among the Blackfoot, albeit more complex in protocol, is the beaver bundle ceremony. Beaver bundles are much older than pipe bundles and go back to the time when the Blackfeet were a stone age people. Rituals connected with beaver bundles per se were always preceded by participation in a sweat-lodge ceremony so that purification would be realized. A smudge was prepared within the sacred teepee for additional cleansing; this involved the placing of sweetgrass on a hot coal and the fragrance of the sacred smoke filled the teepee during which the first set of songs were performed.

The Pipe

A variety of specially regarded physical items are included in the inventory of Aboriginal spiritual ceremonies. Pipes, for example, may be used during private and group ceremonies in connection with fasting or cleansing ceremonies. Pipes are used exclusively by specially recognized men and women. Not all Native sweat-lodge ceremonies involve the pipe, but in the Lakota tradition, it is essential. The pipe is smoked within the sweat-lodge each time the door-flap is opened, and it is kept on the altar outside the lodge when the doorflap is closed. The pipe is very sacred to the Lakota people and its origins are steeped in the legend of White Buffalo Calf Woman.

Sweetgrass or herbs are used as incense in connection with the pipe ceremony or as a purification ritual. Sweetgrass is often braided and burned because it symbolizes positive energy, good thoughts, and purification. Tobacco is similarly considered, because it is the first plant given by the Creator; thus it is used in ceremonies for prayer requests and in thanksgiving. Rattles are used during pipe ceremonies and are believed to help "shake up the spirit of life." They may also be used by elders during healing ceremonies. Drums represent the heartbeat of the nation, the pulse of the universe. Eagle whistles are blown to honor the drums. Eagle feathers are used to adorn costumes and for other purposes. These feathers are special because the eagle is considered a Divine messenger; its feathers represent power, protection, and solar majesty.

Sweatlodge

Many First Nations erect sweatlodges that are used for ceremonial purposes. Sweatlodges are structures about a metre and a half in height (about five feet), made of willow branches, and covered with hides. Functioning much like a sauna, sweatlodges are used mainly for communal cleansing purposes and include a series of songs and prayers (Stolzman, 1998: Waldram, 1997).

A sweatlodge is a tiny, airtight hut, once primarily used for steambaths in areas where there were no streams for bathing. For the Native North Americans the sweatlodge is viewed as a microcosm of the universe, and all living things are represented in its makeup – plants, birds, stones, air, water, and fire. Each part of creation has special powers and these are available to the individual participating in the sweat-lodge ceremony. Among most plains tribes each of the four endurances of the ceremony lasts about ten minutes, and each represents a particular color, direction, and inherent theme.

A sweatlodge is constructed by securing willow branches in the ground, tying them together at the top, then covering the dome shaped structure thickly with brush, skins, or old blankets (Underhill, 1965: 109). The principal parts of the sweatlodge include the poles, the covering, the stones and the pipe. Each part of the preparation of the sweat-lodge has special meaning, and the sweatlodge itself represents a spiritual womb. The willow poles form the structure of the device. Willow is perceived as representative of plant life and has a special relationship with water since it grows best next to a water source. Willow is also deemed to have the power of resurrection which is motivated by the fact that it dies and is reborn by the process of losing leaves each year and growing new ones the following spring. Symbolic death is enacted by individuals who enter the sweat-lodge, and symbolically bury old unclean thoughts and are reborn by the regeneration of the ceremony.

Coverings of the sweatlodge were traditionally made of buffalo hides and today other materials are used. Once inside, the covering serves as the night sky, and when the opening to the sweat-lodge is closed, the inside becomes a living being. Within the lodge the individual becomes part of the body of something alive and very powerful. Another important component of the interior is the selection of stones placed at the centre of the structure. Bruchac (1993: 36) emphasizes that the stones are treated with the utmost respect because each of them represents a unique characteristic. In some cases the number of stones and their arrangement may have occurred to the originator in a vision. Thus the stones are never thrown or dropped, and if one falls accidently while it is being carried from the fire to the inside of the lodge, it is replaced by another.

Future Outlook

The spirituality of the First Nations has always incorporated fasts, prayers, and dances, often enacted in connection with such themes as the cycles of life including birth, adolescence, marriage, old age, and death. For instance, a family celebrating a member's formal entry into the dance circle, or wishing to commemorate the death of a loved one, could host a giveaway dance during a pow-wow. These are social events staged to celebrate a special happening or to honor an individual (Horse Capture, 1989). Gifts such as blankets, beadwork, or crafts may be given to friends or visitors followed by appropriate songs and dances. Pow-wows consist of dancing, feasting, and having fun; old ways are remembered, friendships are

Personal Friends, Fred and Beatrice Powder and Family.
Stoney (Nakoda Sioux) First Nation, Morley, Alberta

renewed, and unity is highlighted. These are times to share the sense of oneness with one another and Mother Earth, a sense of interdependence with all living creatures. Visitors who attend a pow-wow will always be welcomed and accepted as part of the circle.

As time goes on, the renewed intensity of Aboriginal spirituality is becoming more evident in all facets of their cultural life. Doige

(2003: 144) cautions that Aboriginal spirituality alone is the basis upon which Native students can be empowered to formulate appropriate attitudes toward others, toward learning, and towards the formulation of a workable philosophy and pedagogy. There is hope that its power will not only strengthen the outlook of the Indigenous peoples of Canada, but elements of it will eventually be appropriated or at least appreciated by earnest, seeking nonNatives as well.

References

Bruchac, Joseph. (1993). *The Native American Sweat-lodge: History and Legends.* Freedom, CA: The Crossing Press.

Cajete, Gregory. (1994). *Look to the Mountains: An Ecology of Indigenous Education.* Durango, CO: Kivaki Press.

Couture, Joseph E. (1991). The Role of Native Elders: Emergent Issues. *The Cultural Maze: Complex Questions on Native Destiny in Western Canada,* John W. Friesen, ed. Calgary, AB: Detselig Enterprises, 201-218.

Deloria, Jr., Vine. (1995). *Red Earth, White Lies: Native Americans and the Myth of Scientific Fact.* New York, NY: Scribner.

Dempsey, Hugh A. (1976). *Crowfoot: Chief of the Blackfoot.* Edmonton, AB: Hurtig Publishers.

Doige, Lynda A. Curwen. (2003). A Missing link Between Traditional Aboriginal Education and the Western System of Education. *Canadian Journal of Native Education,* 27:2, 144-160.

Erdoes, Richard. (1972). *The Sun Dance People: The Plains Indians, Their Past and Present.* New York, NY: Random House.

Ermine, Willie. (1995). Aboriginal Epistemology. *First Nations Education in Canada: The Circle Unfolds.* Marie Battiste and Jean Barman, eds. Vancouver, BC: University of British Columbia Press, 101-112.

Friesen, John W. (1983). *Schools With A Purpose.* Calgary, AB: Detselig Enterprises.

Friesen, John W. (1991). Native Cultures in a Cultural Clash. *The Cultural Maze: Complex Questions on Native Destiny in Western Canada.* John W. Friesen, ed. Calgary, AB: Detselig Enterprises, 23-38.

Friesen, John W. (1994). *The Riel (Real) Story: An Interpretive History of the Métis People of Canada.* Ottawa, ON: Borealis Press.

Friesen, John W. (1995). *You Can't Get There From Here: The Mystique of North American Plains Indians Culture & Philosophy.* Dubuque, IA: Kendall/Hunt.

Friesen, John W. (1997). *Rediscovering the First Nations of Canada.* Calgary, AB: Detselig Enterprises.

Hanks, Lucien M. Jr., and Jane Richardson Hanks. (1950). *Tribe Under Trust: A Study of the Blackfoot Reserve of Alberta.* Toronto, ON: University of Toronto.

Harrod, Howard L. (1992). *Renewing the World: Plains Indians Religion and Morality.* Tucson, AZ: University of Arizona Press.

Hoebel, E. Adamson. (1965). *The Cheyennes: Indians of the Great Plains.* New York, NY: Holt, Rinehart and Winston.

Horse Capture, George P. (1989). *Pow Wow.* Cody, WY: Buffalo Bill Historical Center.

Jenness, Diamond. (1986). *The Indians of Canada.* Seventh edition. Ottawa, ON: National Museum of Man.

Johnston, Basil. (1988). *Ojibway Heritage: The Ceremonies, Rituals, Songs, Dances, Prayers, and Legends of the Ojibway.* Toronto, ON: McClelland and Stewart.

Johnston, Basil. (1995). *The Manitous: The Spiritual World of the Ojibway.* Vancouver, BC: Key Porter Books.

Josephy, Jr., Alvin M. (1968). *The Indian Heritage of America.* New York: Alfred A. Knopf.

Knudtson, Peter and David Suzuki. (1992). *Wisdom of the Elders.* Toronto, ON: Stoddart.

Lincoln, Kenneth. (1985). *Native American Renaissance.* Berkeley, CA: University of Berkeley Press.

Lowie, Robert M. (1963). *Indians of the Plains.* New York, NY: The Natural History Press.

Lyons, Oren. (1984). Spirituality, Equality, and Natural Law. *Pathways to Self-Determination: Canadian Indians and the Canadian State.* Leroy LittleBear, Menno Boldt, and J. Anthony Long, eds Toronto, ON: University of Toronto, 5-13.

McClintock, Walter. (1992). *The Old North Trail.* Lincoln, NB: University of Nebraska Press.

McGaa, Ed Eagle Man. (1995). *Native Wisdom: Perceptions of the Natural Way:* Minneapolis, MN: Four Directions.

Miller, Alan D. (1995). *Native Peoples and Cultures of Canada.* Revised edition. Vancouver, BC: Douglas and McIntyre.

Pelletier, Wilfred. (n.d.) Two articles. Toronto, ON: Neewin Publishing Co., quoted in J. S. Frideres. (1974). *Canada's Indians: Contemporary Conflicts.* Scarborough, ON: Prentice-Hall, 105-106.

Porterfield, Amanda. (1990. *American Indian Spirituality as a Countercultural Movement. Religion in North America.* Christopher Vecsey, ed. Moscow, ID: University of Idaho Press, 136-151.

Smith, W. Alan. (Spring, 1995). A Cherokee Way of Knowing:Can Native American Spirituality Impact Religious Education? *Religious Education,* 90:2, 241-253.

Snow, Chief John. (1977) *These Mountains Are Our Sacred Places: The Story of the Stoney Indians.* Toronto, ON: Samuel Stevens.

Spence, Lewis. (1994). *North American Indians: Myths and Legends..* London, UK: Senate.

Stolzman, William. (1998). *The Pipe and Christ.* Sixth edition. Chamberlain, SD: Tipi Press.

Tinker, George. (1996). An American Indian Theological Response to Ecojustice. *Defending Mother Earth: Native American Perspectives on Environmental Justice.* Jace Weaver, ed. New York, NY: Orbis Books, 153-176.

Tooker, Elizabeth. (1979). *Native North American Spirituality of the Eastern Woodlands.* New York, NY: Paulist.

Underhill, Ruth. (1965). *Red Man's Religion.* Chicago, IL: University of Chicago Press.

Waldram, James B. (1997). *The Way of the Pipe: Aboriginal Spirituality and Symbolic Healing in Canadian Prisons.* Peterborough, ON: Broadview Press.

Weaver, Jace, ed. (1998) *Native Religious Identity: Unforgotten Gods.* Maryknoll, NY: Orbis Books.

Woodward, Susan L., and Jerry N. McDonald. (1986). *Indian Mounds of the Middle Ohio Valley: A Guide to Adena and Ohio Hopewell Sites.* Blacksburg: VA: McDonald & Woodward.

Five

The Frontier of Eldership

I am of the opinion that Elders are the superb embodiments of highly developed human potential. They exemplify the kind of person which a traditional, culturally-based learning environment can and does form and mould. Elders are also evidence that Natives know a way to a new high in human development, to a degree greater than generally suspected. (Couture, 1991a: 207-208)

Guide showing bowl made of tree knot,
Old Fort William, Thunder Bay, Ontario

When the European explorers arrived in North America they encountered a people with a well-developed culture who had been local residents for centuries. During that time the Indigenous people had developed finely tuned political institutions that were quite successful in keeping order and promoting social harmony. The arrival of the Europeans posed a new kind of challenge and greatly affected their formulated social structures and organization. Like most Indigenous cultures in other lands the Canadian First Nations had in place a system of hereditary leadership with built-in checks and balances to provide for any glitch in operation. Training for leadership positions, like most other important roles, was done by elders, men and women who were respected by local bands for their wisdom and knowledge, or who had handed down to them the right to perform special ceremonies via an apprentice system.

Stoney Elders, Lazarus and Lily Wesley, Stoney (Nakoda Sioux) First Nation, Morley, Alberta

As McFarlane (1998: 50) observes;

Like other Native political institutions, the process of anointing leaders drew much of its strength from its flexibility. If the youth showed that he did not have the mettle for the job, he could be passed over and someone else would be found to fill the role.

Traditionally, elders predominantly filled the role of teacher because of their experience and knowledge and their symbolic link to the past. This role has never been abandoned, but when the Europeans arrived the pressures of yielding to imported institutional practices and value systems compelled the elders to go underground. Some public rituals and ceremonies traditionally presided over by elders were banned by governments and forced these leaders to practice their skills in secret. Today the scene has changed, and both Aboriginals and nonAboriginals are seeking out ways to reactivate and access Indigenous wisdom. Couture (1991a: 202) notes that elders are making a comeback and are being "hammered back into the woodwork" of Native spiritual life. The good news is that;

> It is true that Elders who "know" have been reticent, most discreet about sharing and teaching their "knowledge." However, those same Elders now point to an unfolding prophecy, which states that ". . . the time has come to share the secrets." Couture (1991a: 202)

Joe Crowshoe, an elder from the Peigan First Nation, concurs;

> Some tribes say they don't want white people at ceremonies. Well, that's not sharing or communicating. The world is changing, and now is the time to reveal much of what was once considered secret. (Meili, 1991:100)

Some Aboriginal spokespersons, like Pam Colorado (a Wisconsin Oneida of the Iroquois Confederacy), are actively promoting a synthesis of Indigenous and scientific knowledge (Colorado, 1988: 57). Success in this pursuit could provide science with a much needed spiritual base. According to the Indigenous tradition, the search for truth and learning is essentially a spiritual relationship between an individual and the Great Spirit. Not everyone is so generous. Marie Battiste, a Mik'maq educator, and James Henderson, a Chickasaw educator, (2000: 70), argue that indigenous knowledge is intellectual property and belongs to the Aboriginal community. They suggest that;

> . . . the first concern of Indigenous peoples is their right not to sell, commoditize, or have expropriated from them certain domains of knowledge and certain sacred places, plants, animals, and objects. The protected Indigenous knowledge is described as knowledge of current use, previous use, and/or potential use of plant and animal species, as well as soil and minerals; knowledge of preparation, processing, or storage of useful species . . .

Perhaps Battiste and Henderson are overly cautious about exclusive ownership of spiritual knowledge since that concept was never entrenched in traditional Aboriginal societies. Historically, if anyone had access to resources, they would be expected to share them with their neighbors. This was particularly true of the resources and benefits of Mother Earth. The resources of Mother Earth could not be owned and her bestowals were for everyone to enjoy. As Nez Perce Chief Joseph stated

> All men were made by the same Great Spirit Chief. They are all brothers. The earth is the mother of us all, and all people should have equal rights upon it (Friesen, 1998: 45).

The Elder Phenomenon

Every religious configuration features a leadership stratum and role for individuals who possess vital knowledge of the faith and have authorization to perform related rituals and ceremonies. In certain contexts these individuals are also considered experts on life. Generally known as elders (or priests or shamans) these individuals were traditionally charged with the responsibility of carrying forth to the next generation the valued beliefs, traditions, and practices of their respective tribes. Further analysis of the office reveals that the role of elder was actually much more complex than that. Elders were often regarded as specialists in ceremonial knowledge and performance, traditional teachings, language, and heritage. Many Indian bands were historically quite specific in their regard for those who possessed revered knowledge, those who were authorized to perform certain rituals and ceremonies, and those who had valued medicinal knowledge. In some bands the term "elder" could even be used to refer to an older person who would not necessarily possess any of the gifts usually assigned to that office.

In recent times a kind of "circus elder" has emerged in the form of individuals who "look elderly" and who are willing to perform minor rituals publicly for a price. These individuals are not usually recognized nor respected in their local communities and they do not generally function in that capacity at home. NonAboriginals need to be aware that not every short sentence uttered by an elderly Indigenous individual in broken English is worthy of being categorized as an elder saying.

For the most part the elderly are treated with respect in First Nations communities, but not all are regarded as spiritual elders. Native cultures fully realize that all elderly people have valuable knowledge to share about their life experiences, but only a few have specialized knowledge about the workings of the cosmos that uniquely equips them to provide counsel to their communities (Knudtson and Suzuki, 1992: 179-180). These individuals usually have a deep abiding humility and a reverence for life and the natural world. They generally fulfil their teaching role as facilitators and guides. Today, as historically, these individuals see their mandate as one of guiding their people toward a better knowledge of their rituals and growth processes that might help them become more aware of themselves as well as the natural world and their place within it.

Medicine (1987: 143) cautions that elders who have "lost their way" are not true representatives of authentic Native ways of knowing. Unfortunately, although these individuals may have lost their Aboriginal cultural focus, they may still attempt to serve in the role of elder. The status of elder may appeal to such individuals as a means of trying to get back some of the authenticity they have lost, or never were party to. By acting as elders they may hope to redeem themselves. Organizations interested in having Indian representation on their boards often engage circus or seeking elders because they appear to be interested in serving in that capacity. Too often their role is merely that of figurehead or tokenism (Stiegelbauer, 1996: 40).

Indigenous rituals of spirituality are presided over by elders, that is, men and women who have demonstrated to their communities their appropriateness for that office over time. They have also received a kind of formalized community approval. Consistent with the "vagueness" or elusiveness of the oral tradition, spiritual elders are not elected nor appointed, nor do they have special training for their task. They simply "emerge over time" and their wisdom is informally recognized by their community, particularly their talent for giving guidance when it is sought.

There is observable a definite process by which certain individuals become elders in some tribes. The individual's motivation to take up that role could have been sparked by a personal, spiritual, or political event or events that turned them back to the traditional way. As Stiegelbauer (1996: 47) points out, such experiences may motivate individuals to take up the task of learning tribal teachings and ceremonies in an active and involved way by practising them. They in turn may be called upon by the community to "give those teachings back" and through that process become "recognized" as teachers and elders. However, their corollary experiences outside of learning those teachings may also contribute to their ability to help others find their culture and regain the "good life of health."

The proof of the pudding or verification of eldership is the local Aboriginal community. Elders develop their stature through interaction with their neighbors. Their statuses and gifts are reinforced by the people who respect them and come to them for guidance. The current resurgence of interest in seeking direction from these spiritual advisors is evident among many North American tribes today and comprises a strong indication of the increasing importance of their role and the vitality of the Aboriginal ways (Lincoln, 1985; Couture, 1991b). In recent years elders have been invited to participate in Aboriginal organizational structures while continuing to consult with troubled youth on an individual basis (Medicine, 1987: 148). It might be too much to hope, but it would be encouraging to discover a genuine intrigue on the part of both Native and nonNative observers to share in this revival.

When the Europeans first became acquainted with the various cultural configurations of the North American First Nations, they did not appreciate the nuances of the office of shaman, particularly the belief that some shamans were perceived as having strong supernatural powers. Commonly dubbed "medicine men" or "medicine women" by the newcomers, locals believed that elders' powers went far beyond the arena of healing. They were seen as being able to establish direct contact with the spirit world or themselves be possessed by the spirit. They were approached by individuals in the tribe about such matters as success on a hunt, the time for planting crops, or seeking good fortune in war. A related position in some tribes was the office of counsellor elder held by certain senior members of the community. These individuals had lived long, full lives, learned the way of Mother Earth, and survived a myriad of experiences valued by the tribe. They were viewed as repositories of tribal knowledge and wisdom. They were consulted for advice on matters, listened to, and usually heeded, even though their wisdom was not imposed on anyone. In some tribes elders held memberships in what have been called sacred (or secret) societies, dedicated to specific spiritual purposes within the tribe. These operated much like the religious orders committed to specific purposes within certain Christian denominations. Members of sacred societies, like the Horn Society in the Blood (Kainai) tribe, were believed to have special spiritual powers and they were feared and respected by their compatriots. Even today, for example, people are not to walk in front of a Horn member, even other elders, lest the power of the Horn members affect them (Taylor, 1989).

At one point in the mid nineteenth century the Blackfoot had seven age-graded men's societies in their religious structure, the youngest being called the "Mosquitos," and the oldest, the "Buffalo Bulls" (Ewers, 1989: 105). When the older members of the latter group passed away their secrets died with them and a new society, the "Pigeons" (or Doves) was organized. As a new society, however, it held the lowest rank among the seven. To make things more complicated, the members of these societies also belonged to different hunting bands which were only active during the summer months. At times the head chief of the summer camp would call on one or two of the societies to police the camp and the summer hunt. Each society performed its unique ceremony during the Sundance, which was practiced during this time.

Many Woodland First Nations also operated sodalities or secret societies whose members (elders) were holders of special spiritual knowledge including charms, rituals, prayers, and songs. The Great Lakes Ojibway region was home to one such organization known as the "Midewiwin" (Underhill, 1965: 92). The society was apparently started by Nanabush (the trickster) by order of the Great Spirit. It was somewhat unique to the Ojibway, the Menomini, and the Winnibego. The Midewiwin was a society of wonder workers and an individual could be admitted to membership only if he had been recipient to a vision. After being apprenticed the initiate would be instructed by a chosen member in herbal lore and spiritual traditions.

The Midewiwin was organized in eight ranked levels. The higher an individual ascended in the ranks, the greater the cost of membership. Few individuals ever achieved the highest rank, but if they did they were seen to possess very special spiritual powers and were greatly respected. A special function of the Midewiwin was to sponsor healing services. If an individual became ill, he or she might request help from the society (Taylor, 1994: 332-33). At that point the individual became a member of the society and paid fees for the privilege.

The formal societies of the First Nations played an important role in preserving and passing on spiritual knowledge. During the years when governments banned certain religious practices, the societies took them underground until it was safe to reveal them again. Today a revival of these practices has spread throughout out most of North American Native communities.

Role of Elders

There are self proclaimed prophets who claim that the Native Way holds a key, if not the key to the future survival of mankind

(Couture, 1991a). Elders are definitely the most important link in this formula because they alone have access to the knowledge that may save Mother Earth from being extinguished. Fortunately, elders are currently being sought out for healing and inspiration, and inter- pretation of past and present events. Battiste (2000: 201) emphasizes that elders are a critical link to Aboriginal epistemology through their knowledge of Indigenous languages. The last vestiges of Aboriginal languages exist in the hearts and minds of Indigenous elders.

In the days before European contact an individual's role in the community had to be recognized and affirmed by elders. Indian males, for example, were often recognized for their talents as hunters, warriors, or guides, but before they could be formally exe- cuted these enterprises required a form of spiritual confirmation. This enactment was the responsibility of the shaman or elder, whose office was not one of appointment but of informal recognition. As Beatrice Medicine (1987: 141), herself a Lakota Sioux elder, explains ; elders are ". . . those people who have earned the respect of their own community and who are looked upon as elders in their own society."

As previously stated, it is important to differentiate several kinds of functions fulfilled by elders in the traditional First Nations context. A wide range of gifts were recognized for that office. Elders were perceived as individuals who had special insights pertaining to medicines, leadership, spiritual knowledge, or other areas. In order to maintain cultural and spiritual continuity, elders might apprentice to themselves young people who would hopefully incul- cate this special knowledge over an unspecified period of time, on a one-to-one basis. That way the unique gift of knowledge held by the elder would safely be transmitted to the next generation. The elders referred to by Medicine (1987) were men and women of wis- dom, so designated because they demonstrated unique insights, and perhaps offer relevant, insightful prophetic utterances. Meili (1992: xi) describes her experiences in consulting with such elders:

> I was impressed by their prophetic vision. They taught me that I am part of God, so I could stop my search in trying to find Him/Her in someone else . . .the Great Spirit, or life, or God (what- ever you consider to be the highest), is love and always says yes if we seek it and try to live good lives. The elders collectively taught me that all things have a spirit and gently influenced me to give up

the search for personal enlightenment and gain. I need to love, trust, and learn from all my relations.

Since the office of elder has been revived and strengthened in recent decades, the functions of the office have been magnified and expanded. Today elders are being called upon to help communities with decisions regarding everything from education and health issues to community development and self-government. Others are involved in developing "culture-based" programs, language instruction, and curriculum-making. Still others have become active planners and decision-makers in education (Castellano, Davis, and Lahache, 2000: 98). It has been concluded that elders can offer input that takes the minds of their apprentices beyond the walls of the classroom. "Such strategy provides the community with contact with tradition, traditional beliefs, ceremonies and experiences, and a philosophy unique to First Nations cultures" (Stiegelbauer, 1996: 40).

Several years ago the community of Bear Lake/Stevenson at Island Lake, Manitoba, initiated a program to absorb participants in traditional Aboriginal philosophy and practice using elders as teachers (Grant, 1995). The main purpose of the program was for participants to learn firsthand about trapping, hunting, and fishing from those who knew. The program was made available to students at Brandon University in Manitoba for academic credit and the content of the course consisted of field experiences with elders. Students were expected to keep a daily log and this form of feedback was used to provide an evaluation of the project. The teaching elders insisted that the criteria for measuring success be individualized. Significant sex differences emerged from the study. Not surprisingly, it seemed that male participants were more comfortable with traditional activities since these were historically the purview of men. Female students, however, developed a higher level of Native language skills, but both males and females indicated that a significant degree of learning about traditional Indigenous ways had transpired.

More recently the University of British Columbia experimented with a language course in Kaska territory in Yukon, using elders as consultants and language teachers (Moore, 2003). Kaska is a member of the Athapaskan language family, and the course involved both oral and written use of the language. Thirteen elders participated in the course and were a major factor in its success. The elders functioned as linguistic tradition-bearers and authoritative sources of information on the Kaska language and its many dialects. Their familiarity with the language served to encourage others to attain a sophisticated level of language acquisition. As instruction continued, it became clear that the elders were being called upon to function as cultural and spiritual advisors. It seems that knowledge of Aboriginal languages cannot easily be separated from its cultural and spiritual content.

Today, rapid changes are affecting the role of elders as large numbers of Indigenous people leave their reserves and move to urban areas. Many elders have moved to cities and towns along with their families. There they have carved out a unique niche for themselves as ritualists, consultants, and counsellors. Some elders even make house calls in response to individual or family requests for counselling or prayers. Once again, as is so typical of their history, they have demonstrated an ingenious ability to change with the times. These changes, however, have only affected their geographic location, not their spirituality. Perhaps the time will come when the nonNative world seeks out the kind of advice that Aboriginal elders can offer to a needy world.

Elder Sayings

Psychologist and Cree elder, Joseph Couture (1991a: 205), points out that elders often serve as mediaries or spiritual therapists in assisting seekers to grasp the Divinely-designated roles they should play in this life. For example, consider the following elder sayings;

> Don't worry. Take it easy. Do your best. It will all work out. Respect life. Respect your elders. It's up to you. You have all the answers within you.

> Listen to what Mother Earth tells you. Speak with her. She will speak to you.

Native elders often also play an interpretive role as the following recommendation by the late Charlie Blackman, an elder of the Chipewyan Nation, reveals (Couture: 1991a: 205).

> On a given day, if you ask me where you might go to find a moose, I will say, "If you go that way you won't find a moose. But, if you go that way, you will." So now, you younger ones, think about that. Come back once in a while and show us what you've got. And we'll tell you if what you think you have found is a moose.

In pondering this saying, it becomes evident that the pursuit of the "moose" metaphorically represents the individual's search for personal meaning, purpose and destiny. Initially, an individual may seek out an elder for guidance regarding a potential direction to undertake in seeking personal fulfilment regarding a life goal. The elder invites seekers to check in from time to time in order to help them evaluate whether or not they are indeed "on the moose's trail."

In some capacities and appropriate contexts elders today engage in humor or metaphor as a means of getting their point across. Consider these examples (Friesen, 1998);

It just seems to a lot of Indians that this continent was a lot better off when we were running it. – Vine Deloria, Jr., Sioux First Nation.

And then we started to learn about money. People kill for that. A lot of Indians spend money the day they get it . . . it makes us do things we're not supposed to do. I always say, Indians were not born with money. We were born with animals. —Maggie Black Kettle, Siksika First Nation.

I am proud to be an Eskimo, but I think we can improve on the igloo as a permanent dwelling. —Abraham Okip, Inuit First Nation).

Believe it or not, the Indian had to learn the white man's language to break the first commandment. In the Indian language we have no profane words. —Chief Dan Kennedy (Ochankuhahe), Assiniboine First Nation.

I am not as American as those whose ancestors came over on the Mayflower, but we met them at the boat when they landed. —Will Rogers, Cherokee First Nation.

If the Great Spirit wanted man to stay in one place he would have made the world stand still. —Chief Flying Hawk, Oglala Sioux First Nation.

Perhaps the most appropriate way to end this chapter is with an elder saying by Chief John Snow outlining the potentiality of Native wisdom;

And so I say to you EuroCanadians; you have discovered our land and its resources, but you have not yet discovered my people, nor our teachings, not the spiritual basis of our teachings. (Friesen, 1998: 60)

Welcome to Carry-the-Kettle (Assiniboine) First
Nations Reserve, Sintaluta, Saskatchewan

References

Battiste, Marie. (2000). Maintaining Aboriginal Identity, Language, and
Culture. *Reclaiming Indigenous Voice and Vision.* Marie Battiste, ed.
Vancouver, BC: University of British Columbia, 192-208.

Battiste, Marie, and James (Sa'ke'j) Youngblood Henderson. (2000).
Protecting Indigenous Knowledge and Heritage. Saskatoon, SK: Purich
Publishing.

Castellano, Marlene Brant, Lynne Davis, and Louise Lahache. (2000).
Innovations in Education Practice. *Aboriginal Education: Fulfilling the
Promise.* Castellano, Marlene Brant, Lynne Davis, and Louise Lahache,
eds. Vancouver, BC: University of British Columbia, 97-100.

Colorado, Pam. (1988). Bridging Native and Western Science. *Convergence*,
21:2-3, 57.

Couture, Joseph E. (1991a). The Role of Native Elders: Emergent Issues. *The
Cultural Maze: Complex Questions on Native Destiny in Western Canada.*
John W. Friesen, ed. Calgary, AB: Detselig Enterprises, 181-200.

Couture, Joseph E. (1991b). Explorations in Native Knowing. *The Cultural
Maze: Complex Questions on Native Destiny in Western Canada.* John W.
Friesen, ed. Calgary, AB: Detselig Enterprises, 53-73.

Ewers, John C. (1989). *The Blackfeet: Raiders on the Northwestern Plains.* Norman, OK: University of Oklahoma.

Friesen, John W. (1998). *Sayings of the Elders: An Anthology of First Nations Wisdom.* Calgary, AB: Detselig Enterprises.

Grant, Agnes. (1995). The Challenge for Universities. *First Nations Education in Canada: The Circle Unfolds.* Marie Battiste and Jean Barman, eds. Vancouver, BC: University of British Columbia, 208-223.

Knudtson, Peter, and David Suzuki. (1992). *Wisdom of the Elders.* Toronto, ON: Stoddart.

Lincoln, Kenneth. (1985). *Native American Renaissance.* Berkeley, CA: University of California Press.

McFarlane, Peter. (1998). Aboriginal Leadership. *Visions of the Heart: Canadian Aboriginal Issues.* David Long and Olive Patricia Dickason, eds. Second edition. Scarborough, ON: Nelson Canada, 49-80.

Medicine, Beatrice. (1987). My Elders Tell Me. *Indian Education in Canada: The Challenge,* Volume Two: The Challenge. Jane Barman, Yvonne Hébert, and Don McCaskill, eds. Vancouver, BC: University of British Columbia.

Meili, Dianne. (1991). *Those Who Know: Profiles of Alberta's Elders.* Edmonton, AB: NeWest.

Moore, Patrick J. (2003). Lessons on the Land: The Role of Kaska Elders in a University Course. *Canadian Journal of Native Education,* 27:1, 127-139.

Steigelbauer, S. M. (1996). What is an Elder? What Do Elders Do? First Nation Elders as Teachers in Culture-based Urban Organizations. *The Canadian Journal of Native Studies,* XVI:1, 37-66.

Taylor, Fraser. (1989). *Standing Alone: A Contemporary Blackfoot Indian.* Halfmoon Bay, BC: Arbutus Bay Publications.

Taylor, J. Garth. (1994). North Algonquians on the Frontiers of "New Ontario, 1890-1945." *Aboriginal Ontario: Historical Perspectives on the First Nations.* Edward S. Rogers and Donald B. Smith, eds. Toronto, ON: Dundurn Press, 307-343.

Underhill, Ruth. (1965). *Red Man's Religion.* Chicago, IL: University of Chicago.

Six

The Frontier of Language

The critical state of Aboriginal languages in Canada is causing confusion and uncertainty among academics, both Aboriginal and nonAboriginal, elders, parents and youth. (Verna J. Kirkness, 1998: 93)

Language learning is currently big business in Canada and for good reason. Without language, communication would be virtually impossible, except for sign language, body language, and perhaps the "universal language of love!" Through language we express ourselves and we share meanings with one other. It is the means by which we voice our concerns, our loves, our joys, and our sadness (Pattanayak, 1987: 28). Language is also a means of expressing one's feelings and inner thoughts. It is a symbol of who people are, and for Aboriginal people this is a most significant fact (Dorias, 1995).

Aboriginal elders and educators point out that the process of ongoing EuroCanadian colonialism is hitting Indigenous languages very hard. They argue that colonialism did not only exist at the time when Canada was a colony of either Britain or France, but rather it has been perpetuated in one way or another to the present. Its various manifestations include the destruction of Indigenous languages which are seen as central to the maintenance of Indian culture and spirituality. Colonization is viewed as the primary ideology underlying the education of Aboriginal people in Canada today. Unless it is stifled or changed, there is little hope that many First Nations languages will survive this century (Nicholas, 2001: 10).

Language Learning

There are still people in various sectors of society who need to be convinced about the beneficial aspects of language learning and language maintenance. These individuals have little sympathy for Aboriginals who lament the passing of their historic linguistic roots.

135

The reality is that although a great many languages are being taught in Canada as second languages, Aboriginal languages are greatly under represented. This situation has caused great consternation in the Native community.

Research is desperately needed to determine what happens to people who lose their language, but it is also of interest to determine what happens when individuals become fluent in a second language. Has learning a new language broadened their outlook? If they do use the newly acquired language, in what contexts, and with what frequency do they use it? Gamlin (2003: 19) shows that meaningful literacy development requires reflective thinking as well as learning new sounds and new words. Learning to be literate is always an act of resymbolizing and reinterpreting previous experiences in relation to present and projected experience. Critical thinking cannot occur in a vacuum, but must be grounded in personal experience. That experience can be enriched when individuals reflect on it and analyze the implications of it in terms of everyday usage. Some linguistic authorities state that in order to be taught effectively, the teaching scenario of language learning must be grounded in the underlying value system of the language being taught. Fortunately, today much linguistic work is applied, rather than purely academic so underlying belief systems become quite important. Today linguists are working with First Nations communities all across Canada in developing writing systems and assisting in preparing materials for Native language instruction (McMillan, 1995: 13). A lot of their work is contextual, with ample input from community leaders and elders.

Literacy is the means by which individuals articulate the expression of their consciousness and experience. Literacy depends on an existent form of interpretive representations of words, either alphabetic or symbolic. Those learners whose original language is at risk should be taught that language along with implicit cultural concepts in order for them to obtain a definition and understanding of their culture. The link between literacy, language, and identity is that literacy and language are the symbolic representations of concepts, and thereby language becomes the vital means of expressing one's beliefs, knowledge, and values (Paulsen, 2003: 25). Learning a language by itself will not revitalize the culture to which it belongs. As Native elders have long emphasized, the two must be absorbed and appreciated hand in hand.

Language Appreciation

There are still some Canadians in various walks of life who remain unconvinced about the benefits of learning a second language. It is difficult to convince them otherwise, and it is equally difficult to teach reluctant young learners who may be enrolled in language courses simply because their parents want to please their grandmothers who still "long for the old days" (Glazer, 1980; Friesen, 1985). Such a situation is little better than hopeless, because motivation is the most crucial ingredient to a successful literacy program. Swanson (2003: 72) suggests that a key factor to successful language learning is the approach of the language teacher. By focussing on cultural awareness, cultural teaching practices, and a sense of community, language teachers can motivate learners to be successful. Being able to provide such a learning environment implies that teachers will need to be sufficiently acquainted with the community milieu of the language they are teaching.

Several decades ago it was popularly believed that there was only so much neurological space in the brain for language learning, and if it was overtaxed, other aptitudes might suffer. Educators of some time not long ago pointed out that second language learners could jumble up concepts that they had already learned in their major language. Recent studies have shown, however, that second language study actually assists learning in other sectors. Acquiring another language enables individuals to think more globally, holistically, and creatively (Lambert, 1983; Lambert and Tucker, 1972). Rather than being a deterrent, second language learning actually enhances the ability to learn in other areas.

Specific objections to second language learning have historically included three arguments, each of them intended to deter educators from pursuing second language instruction. It has been asserted that: (i) it is the task of the school to assimilate minority children, and they should therefore be taught only the official languages of society; (ii) if minority children have deficiencies in learning the language of dominant society language, there is no point in their receiving instruction in their mother tongue; and (iii) children can only absorb so much linguistic information so why not stick to teaching a singular language (Ashworth: 1988, 187).

It is encouraging to note that when individuals are afforded the opportunity to engage in new and meaningful language learning experiences, under appropriate conditions, many do learn to enjoy the experience. By comparison, when parents strongly encourage their children to pursue instrumental music lessons regardless of approach, some children do learn to enjoy the experience. The day comes when the child "catches on" to the joys of performing music and undertakes to practice an instrument even without much parental encouragement. It may be an underrated occurrence, but sometimes learning is its own reward. Aboriginal youth who gain appreciation for their heritage are often eager to acquire knowledge of their Native langauge as well.

Effective language learning must meet certain specific criteria. It is not enough to be satisfied with minimal language learning because meagre familiarity with language simply will not prevail. Three conditions must be met if language learning is to be meaningful. First, there must be a high rate of acquisition, not the mere memorization of a series of primary monosyllables. Second, the language learner must have a strong support system to back the undertaking, namely family, peer groups, close friends, or significant others who actively encourage the pursuit. Third, language students must be positively motivated, and they must have ample practice time using the newly acquired language in real life situations. There is little lasting value in mastering a language if its usage is limited to artificial or contrived situations. This fairly well implies that the newly-learned language must be spoken in the home.

What we know about the value of language learning has deep historical roots. Johann Amos Comenius (1592-1670), a sixteenth century educator, outlined four major advantages of learning another language, namely: (i) cultural reasons, to enable individuals to learn about others in the nation; (ii) political reasons, to assist one to be of value to the nation; (iii) practical reasons, meaning that through the knowledge of additional languages it would be possible to communicate with a wider range of peoples; and (iv) educational reasons; learning a language sharpens the mind. In keeping with Comenius' diagnosis, more contemporary sources indicate that learning the rules and configuration of another language provides one with the ability to organize different perceptions of reality. This skill contributes toward meeting and resolving complex linguistic and cultural challenges.

Language for Cultural Learning

Learning to function effectively in a cultural setting through the vehicle of a language, other than one's own, can greatly enhance one's perspective. Such knowledge builds understanding and sensitivity. A deeper understanding of someone else's lifestyle fosters tolerance and promotes acceptance. Many potential social conflict situations can be alleviated through enhanced understanding; for example, the events of Oka could have probably been avoided if there had been better communication between Aboriginals and nonAboriginals living in that area. Enough interest in Iroquois culture to the extent of learning the language might have been a factor in encouraging that understanding. Even a cursory study of Aboriginal spirituality, culture, and language could help develop the perspective that First Nations religious symbols are as important to them as other religious symbols are to members of another faith (the cross for Christians, for example). Intolerance is often simply the result of a lack of sufficient knowledge, and inadequate knowledge is often due to insensitivity and lack of interest.

Knowing a second language can enable one to think in a different dimension, conceptually speaking. Some students of language actually develop new cultural practices after having widened their linguistic repertoire. Research indicates that second language learning can lead to changes in attitude, often resulting in a more global, accepting mode of orientation (Mollica, 1989). Often second language learning produces a new dimension in social convergence, conceptually bringing peoples together as members of one human family (Cummins and Swain, 1986).

Mastering a second language has personal advantages as well as cultural advantages. Contrary to some fears, second language learners actually perform better in their "main" language than individuals who are familiar with only one language. The former manifest a higher degree of creativity and self-esteem; they feel better about themselves and their attitudes towards others are more accepting. It becomes almost impossible to think negatively about individuals living in other cultural configurations when their ways of behaving, language, and culture have been comprehended and appreciated. What were once strangers are now seen as fellow human beings with feelings, desires, and wants.

A national survey (O'Keefe, 1990: 9) probed the question, "Do you think that learning both official languages is necessary in order to succeed financially? A breakdown, by province showed that affirmative answers to the question were as follows: British Columbia, 36%; Alberta, 37%; Saskatchewan, 50%; and Manitoba, 48%. Newfoundland led the provinces with 66% in favor. The real proof, however, was "in the pudding." Seventy-two percent of Anglophones living in Quebec said that both official languages were essential to financial success. And small wonder; a bilingual challenge requires bilingual familiarity! Living in a province where dualistic language usage exists reduces the tendency to rest on one's learning laurels. There is too much to be gained by appropriating the advantages of an additional linguistic world.

Child at Play, Morley United Church, Stoney (Nakoda
Sioux) First Nation Reserve, Morley, Alberta

The assurance that a second language will be learned and maintained is, at best, guaranteed under slightly "atypical" circumstances. For example, learning a second language is a tough challenge when one's parents originate from the same cultural and linguistic setting. However, when cultures mix (as they often do through intermarriage), statistics change. In Canada, if one has an English-speaking father and a French-speaking mother, there is a 22 percent chance that the children of that union will learn French. When both parents are French chances are that their children are almost certain to learn the language, *even if the family lives in an English-speaking setting*. Thus any proposal to back a program of language maintenance for all of Canada's heritage languages has strong research support. All that remains is the will to put it this knowledge into policy and practice.

Maintaining Aboriginal Languages

Social scientists have known for a long time that language conveys cultural content. The language of any cultural configuration incorporates all aspects of its implicit and explicit structures including social, cognitive, linguistic, material, and spiritual elements. Leavitt (1995) notes that the most significant aspect of language is found in its ways of conceptualizing, preserving, and transmitting knowledge. Indigenous languages, for example, tend to exemplify awareness of happenings, eventuating change, flow, and interrelationships. This is because of a dominance of verbs. If these linguistic characteristics are to be appreciated, Aboriginal languages must be kept alive. When a language disappears its implicit ways of conceptualization vanish and society is that much poorer for it.

When the various European groups, French, English, and Spanish, arrived in North America they made a number of erroneous assumptions about Native literacy. First of all, they surmised that Aboriginal languages were not composed of many words. After all, the Indigenous peoples adhered to what appeared to be rather uncomplicated lifestyles and it was deduced that they probably had no need for abstractions. The Europeans who supplied the first written forms of Aboriginal languages tended to describe them in terms of what they did not like. This attitude undoubtedly biased their descriptions. Father Francis Talbot, who worked among the Hurons, was puzzled to discover that his Aboriginal informants were able to express spiritual and abstract concepts when he had not expected them to do so (Steckley, and Cummins, 2001: 26-27). After all, Indigenous people learned and lived according to their senses. Why would they require complex language forms?

Time proved that Father Talbot and his colleagues had sold the Hurons short. Later research showed that they had grossly underestimated the complex nature of the Huron language. As a devoted Roman Catholic priest, Talbot failed to recognize the spiritual validity of Aboriginal religion, and so ignored the fact that spiritually-oriented cultures naturally require highly complex terms. In fact, even simple lifestyles, such as the Native people were purported to foster, utilized a great many terms to describe what appeared to be the same phenomenon. The northern Inuit people had a wide variety of words for ice and snow, each with a slightly unique emphasis. This practice would completely escape the uninitiated observer.

A second false assumption made by incoming European nations was that the First Peoples had not developed literacy forms of any kind. After all, theirs was an oral culture. Doige (2001) suggests that the case of the Mik'maq (also spelled Micmac) people disputes this claim. The Mik'maq, in fact, had well developed literacy forms in their pictographs, petroglyphs, notched sticks, and wampums, all of which existed long before the arrival of the first French settlers. What counted as literacy in Aboriginal society before the arrival of the colonists was to be able to read and write symbolic representations of ideas and events that communicated both practical and spiritual understandings of the environment and how society should function. Even if the European newcomers had been able to acknowledge Mik'maq accomplishments in literacy, they were apparently too short-sighted to recognize its validity in its own right. Apparently only reading and writing in French or English counted as literacy.

It is a well-supported fact that the foisting of English and French languages on the Indigenous community has been culturally costly. Indigenous myths and legends, even though translated into English or French, are seldom told in those languages, and when they are the lessons they contain are not as clear as they might be if told in an Aboriginal language. When revered customs, rituals, and ceremonies are translated into foreign languages, their essence is often diminished or takes on new meaning. This development affects the social life of the people as well. As new words, new meanings, and new emphases enter the domain of daily discourse, the very geist (spirit) of a culture can also change. This is not a necessarily a negative happening, however, because all cultures change through time. If cultural and/or linguistic changes are not satisfactory to those who stand to lose by it, it will be up to those who most value a given language to use any and all means at their disposal to preserve it.

All is not lost, of course. Cultures can survive even if their members replace their traditional tongue with a new language. The reality is that such an occurrence is part of the normal process of cultural change. Indigenous cultures, probably more than any other cultures in the world, have demonstrated that they can make far-reaching structural and linguistic changes and still survive. Their history underscores this fact. The migrations of many First Nations across the North American continent before first contact, tribal mergers, and subsequent shifts in economy have proven this. Centuries ago many eastern Woodlands people migrated west and traded their agricultural economies for dependence on the buffalo. The mound-builders of the southeast migrated to the northwest and their means of livelihood changed dramatically. Their language also changed to incorporate new realities. Still, despite these changes, they retained the spiritual rudiments of their culture. These examples illustrate that cultures can change economies and even language composition without undue effect on their spirituality. Couture (1991a: 206) quotes Aboriginal elders to say that to be bilingual is always be "better" and "richer." However, the elders also confirmed that bilingualism is not essential for a core-sense of self as Native, keeping open thereby the possibility of authentic Nativeness to those large number of Aboriginals who, for whatever reason, do not speak an Indigenous language.

Generally speaking, when languages are lost or wiped out, it is cause for lament. Not only do language losses represent cultural changes, they imply cultural losses. Those losses not only affect the respective community, but they affect the greater makeup of the nation. Any kind of knowledge loss is unfortunate, to say nothing of the hidden structural forms that also disappear. Fortunately, many Aboriginal peoples have not taken this debilitating situation sitting down. Since 1970, a variety of language instruction courses have been established in First Nations communities across the nation. These programs were first established on a bilingual basis using Native languages as a foundation. The methodology included a transitory process to English so that the procedure would not strip children of their own languages. Students received 100 percent instruction in their Native language in kindergarten, 80 percent in grade one, 60 percent in grade two, 50 percent in grade three and so on. By junior high school, all instruction was in English.

The 1980s witnessed a continuing effort on the part of Aboriginal leaders to increase opportunities for instruction in Native languages. Universities were a favored target including a campaign to develop teacher training courses for language instruction. The University of Manitoba, for example, initiated an undergraduate degree in Indigenous languages in conjunction with the Manitoba Association for Native languages (Norton, 1989; Manitoba Association for Native Languages, 1986). By 1986 a total of 14 607 students in Manitoba public schools were enrolled in courses offering Aboriginal languages as subject matter, and 25 443 were enrolled in classes where Native languages were used as the language of instruction.

The Province of Saskatchewan initiated a similar language program and enrolled 6 317 students in Native language courses in the 1986-87 school year. Languages offered included Cree, Saulteaux, Dene, and Dakota. The majority of students were taught their language as a school subject with a specific slot in the timetable. Although Aboriginal languages were taught in every grade from kindergarten to grade 12, most students served were in grades 1-6 (Littlejohn and Fredeen, 1993: 78).

In 1986 the Province of Ontario established the Ontario Community Literacy Grants Program to deliver adult literacy programs to three communities, Anglophone, Francophone, and Aboriginal. The following year the three streams coalesced to form the Ontario Native Literacy Coalition charged with providing advocacy, training, information, cultural awareness, and sensitivity in all materials developed and program approaches. The effort was criticized for operating with an underlying goal of providing means by which individuals could join the Canadian mainstream lifestyle. Aboriginal critics pointed out that the program did not support the Indigenous way of life, and was assimilative in focus (Antone, 2003: 10).

Nicholas (2001: 10) estimates that at least 50 of the some 58 languages indigenous to Canada will disappear in the next century. In order to reduce this trend, many schools in or near Aboriginal communities have established Native language classes. Paupanekis and Westfall (2001: 101) warn that schools cannot rejuvenate Native languages, and when such programs are introduced, it is mandatory that Aboriginal parents be supportive. Parents need to realize how an adequate Aboriginal language program will add to a child's total learning process. In the past this kind of support has not always been forthcoming. Sadly, there have been a few cases where parents have requested that their children be removed from Native language classes with no reason provided.

One of the most of the taken for granted facts about Aboriginal languages is the complexity of their identification. Linguists estimate that there are 11 Aboriginal language families in Canada which make up for some 58 languages, each of which varies slightly from the others. The existence of six distinct Indigenous culture areas in Canada also affects language composition, complexity, and accent thereby contributing to greater linguistic variation (Morrison and Wilson, 1995). As it is, a startling reality about language loss exists in the Indigenous community; there are only three languages, Cree, Inuktitut, and Ojibway that have more than 5 000 speakers. Many Native languages have less than 100 speakers including Chinook, North and South Haida, Haisla, Musee (Delaware), Onondaga, Tsuu T'ina, Sechelt, Seneca, Squamish, Tagish, Tahltan, Tanana, and Tuscarora. Extinct languages include Beothuk, Laurentian, Pentlatch, Tsetsaut, and Wyandot. Kirkness (1998: 95) observes that 13 Aboriginal languages have less than 40 speakers and 23 languages are seriously endangered. Kirkness projects that at the current rate of decline only four languages, Cree, Ojibway, Inuktitut, and Dakota have a chance of surviving over the next century.

According to the 1996 census, only a small proportion (26 percent) of Aboriginal people speak their mother tongue and another 30 percent claim to have a working knowledge of their mother tongue. These individuals apparently speak and understand the language well enough to carry on a conversation, but only 18 percent admit that they speak their mother tongue in their home (Norris, 1998: 217). Linguists have known for a long time that unless a language is used daily in a meaningful environment like the home, its perpetuity is seriously threatened. Individuals and institutions that design programs to increase familiarity with Aboriginal languages must be aware of this reality.

The reasons for Aboriginal language losses may be correlated with assimilative efforts by educational agencies, and insensitive religious attitudes. Administrators of organizations that do not support the maintenance of Native languages sometimes perceive that mainline societal acculturation is hindered by the maintenance of Aboriginal languages (or any second language, for that matter), and hence discourage their use. Strong federal support for Canada's two official languages may also have taken its toll of Indigenous language maintenance by insistence that a thorough knowledge of an official language is more important than proficiency in a nonofficial language. A reverse action of the federal government has been to establish a national Aboriginal Language Institute, but its effectiveness in terms of First Nations language preservation has yet to be determined.

Language Programs

The last three decades have witnessed an increasing number of language maintenance programs initiated by Aboriginal organizations and communities themselves. Several important steps must be followed in this quest if it is to be successful. The first step is to make certain that the language form in question has sufficient acceptability in the community in which it is to be promoted. Community members, particularly elders, must be on board if the program is to work. Next, it is important to establish that the various sounds of key words are validated as distinct sounds by recognized speakers of that language. This is especially difficult in communities where related dialects exist. Third, is the challenge of choosing an alphabet and writing conventions for the language.

Preparing a language form includes a myriad of responsibilities not readily appreciated by nonlinguists. These include dealing with alternate pronunciations, alphabet symbols, word divisions, and punctuation. Extralingual issues include literacy training, publication of reference materials, second language teaching, linguistic research, place names, and promotion of language-related literature. Once these details have been handled it becomes necessary to solicit feedback and support from local interest groups and form a writing committee charged with the responsibility of preparing and publishing materials. The final step will be to concentrate on a literacy campaign and promote public awareness. That being accomplished, it needs to be kept in mind that establishing a standard language form and building a program around it will not necessarily eliminate the need to update established forms from time to time. An active language, like any other cultural component, is perpetually subject to change.

Language framers will need to struggle with the challenge of deciding on language format and content without yielding to the subtle assimilative forces inherent in modern language preservation. The structures of contemporary language preservation programs are essentially nonNative, arising as they do from nonNative academic sources. It stands to reason that some influence regarding content and format will be evident. Although no one can be certain to what extent these forces will be active in any given language preserving program, the cause is probably still greater than the concern.

Dorais (1995) emphasizes that the mere process of bringing literacy and formal education to a given society is a political activity. Native language rejuvenation programs that utilize nonAboriginal processes are strongly in danger of being affected by contaminating influences. A case in point is the Ojibway language which absorbed a multiplicity of Christian concepts when European missionaries first introduced the Gospel to them (Matthews and Roulette, 1998: 354). Some of the most useful old Ojibway language categories were expanded to include new Christian meanings. For example, the notion of incarnation, that is, the relationship of Jesus to God the Father, so central to Christianity was introduced to the Ojibway under the concept of apprenticeship. The translation was apt, but the introduction of the concept changed meanings in the Ojibway language and contributed to a breakdown in communication between the generations.

A reverse example is that of the Mik'maq First Nation who were taught to read and write in English by incoming missionaries. By the latter part of the nineteenth century, however, the Mik'maq refused to adopt the practice of Bible reading and resisted attempts to make Catholics of them. As Battiste (1986: 34) states;

> Mik'maqs became consumers of English and colonial-made goods and vices, partly to convince the English that they were not different from them and they therefore need not be feared or oppressed. But the Mik'maq never cognitively assimilated English knowledge or values. They did not forget the tribal knowledge, history or language, nor did they change their tribal rituals or lifestyle. Mik'maq society continually rejected the English language, the Protestant worldview, and its individualistic society as demonic in nature.

Mik'maq literacy was at its height in 1920 when the federal government instituted a policy that only English be used in all Aboriginal schools, and schooling was made compulsory for all Aboriginal children aged six to 16. In 1930 the compulsory age was raised to 18. Using education as a tool of cognitive manipulation, coupled with disclaimers about the validity of Mik'maq tribal knowledge, the government process took its toll. Use of the Mik'maq language gradually dwindled until 1974 when the

Mik'maq Association of Cultural Studies developed their own script using both Native and nonNative linguists. Today half of a Mik'maq population of over 14 000 are fluent in their Native tongue.

Any success in Aboriginal language maintenance will depend on two main elements, chief of which is the will of First Nations themselves. Second, the cause may be furthered by the entrench- ment of Aboriginal language rights in appropriate legislation by the nation's federal and provincial governments. Both elements have a somewhat unpredictable and emotional side to them, the former in the heart of the members of the Indigenous community in the inter- ests of cultural maintenance, and the second from within the hearts of the Canadian people in the interests of national pluralism. When these two elements mesh, Native language perpetuation will be assured.

There is growing concern voiced by those Indigenous elders who cling tenaciously to the idea that if their traditional languages are replaced with other forms, their culture will die out. This is rather a harsh perspective and should perhaps be tempered with the observation that their culture will not likely die out, but it will change to meet the times. This happened in the past when the economies and social/political constructs of Aboriginal cultures changed, and it will likely happen again. More importantly, not all cultural changes in First Nations country can be blamed on the infu- sion of European ideas. Many tribes significantly altered their lifestyle long before European contact, due to such factors as inter- tribal wars, geographic shifts, migrations, new spiritual insights, and climactic changes.

Many cultural groups in Canada other than Aboriginals have experienced the necessity to alter or change language structures and meaning but have survived in a transformed state. Dozens of ethno- cultural groups who immigrated to Canada over the past century have virtually abandoned their heritage languages and adopted French or English as their primary means of communication. This is particularly true of second and third generation immigrants. These individuals still treasure the values of their homeland and continue to practice significant elements of their heritage lifestyle. Canada, as a multicultural country not only permits this kind of adjustment, but encourages it. The reality is that the responsibility for cultural main- tenance is primarily in the hands of each cultural group. Speakers of a particular language (and some linguists and anthropologists) are the only ones who value it sufficiently enough to maintain it. Even if Aboriginal groups obtain governmental support and funding for extensive Indian language programs, there is no assurance that they will be effective. Too many Aboriginal youth today prefer to speak one of the nation's official languages. These youth daily subject themselves to all manners of media influence, the bulk of which are transmitted in either English or French. Despite this trend, many Native youth believe themselves to be full members of their respective First Nation society. They insist that they are Aboriginals, but they differ slightly in thought and practice from their parents and grandparents, just as the ancestors of their parents and grandparents differed from their predecessors.

Some Indigenous languages are currently being taught in public schools as heritage languages. Saskatchewan has become the lead province in developing a centralized Aboriginal language curriculum for primary and secondary schools (Fettes and Norton, 2000: 47). This is a positive step because it will, hopefully, give opportunity for nonNatives to expand the repertoire of their potential language learning. At that point they may be able to appreciate some of the nuances of traditional Native thought and perhaps even adopt some of the values implicit in Aboriginal language. Such a development may lead to a deeper level of appreciation for the ancient ways of Canada's First Peoples.

The inclusion of Indigenous languages in public school curricula will only happen if the First Nations' lobby actively promotes it. These are, after all, Aboriginal languages, not EuroCanadian languages. No one can appreciate that fact more than Indigenous people themselves, and no one can do a better selling job of it than they. Native language promotion is a vital plank in the program of Aboriginal integration defined in this discussion, and the challenge to support such an undertaking lies uniquely within the Native community itself.

Future Outlook

A growing crescendo of Aboriginal voices has sounded in recent years to emphasize the importance of a renewal of Indigenous knowledge and spirituality (Meili, 1992; Cajete, 1994; McGaa, 1995; Johnston, 1995; Bear Heart, 1998; Weaver, 1998;

Battiste, 2000; Battiste and Henderson, 2000). These writers have been accompanied by the voices of First Nations elders in attempting to explain Indigenous metaphysical systems. The good news is that unlike a century or two ago, nonNatives are beginning to show interest in what they have to say (Couture, 1991b).

Yazzie (2000) maintains that if First Nations are to throw off the yoke of epistemological colonialism, they must commence the process within themselves. This requires a revitalization of all Indigenous cultural aspects including language. Political self-determination begins with internal sovereignty which means taking control of one's personal, family, clan, and community life. Essentially this means a return to tradition and a relegation of modern EuroCanadian value systems to second place. The latter will not be easy, as Findley (2000: x) notes;

> The task of opposing the dominant orthodoxies of modernity from a position at their ever-extending margins, or from a strategically primitivist place outside, is crucial and dangerous work . . . Significant numbers of EuroCanadian scholars have become remarkably good at critiquing the pretensions and practices of modernity and defending marginalized groups, but they do so within institutions among whose faculties Aboriginal people are minimally represented.

Battiste (2000: 199-200) insists that Aboriginal languages must be viewed as the basic media for the transmission and survival of Indigenous knowledge. It is Battiste's contention that unless the revival of Aboriginal languages becomes a principal government undertaking, many of them will be lost along with the distinctive Aboriginal orientation to understanding the world from an holistic perspective. Kirkness (1998: 96) suggests that the protection of Aboriginal languages is an inherent right, a treaty right, a constitutional right, and an Aboriginal right. Unfortunately, neither the people of Canada nor their government particularly share his concern. They have other things to do, but this sad reality does not diminish the fact that the primary responsibility for maintaining Indigenous language and culture must be assumed by First Nations themselves. It cannot be safeguarded by government policies, school programs, or university degrees (Goulet, Dressyman-Lavallee, and McCleod, 2001: 45).

The maintenance of Indigenous languages must first of all be a demonstrated priority in Indigenous communities. The First

Nations must know their languages in order to teach them. They must value them enough to put aside less important pursuits in the scheme of things and get on with the business of language teaching. This statement may not be welcomed by more politically-inclined Aboriginal leaders, but it is reality.

References

Antone, Eileen. (2003). Culturally Framing Aboriginal Literacy and Learning. *Canadian Journal of Native Education,* 27:1, 7-15.

Ashworth, Mary. (1988). *Blessed With Bilingual Brains: Education of Immigrant Children With English as a Second Language.* Vancouver, BC: Pacific Educational Press.

Battiste, Marie. (1986). Mik'maq Literacy and Cognitive Assimilation. *Indian Education in Canada, Volume 1: The Legacy.* Jean Barman, Yvonne Hébert, and Don McCaskill, eds. Vancouver, BC: University of British Columbia, 23-44.

Battiste. Marie. (2000). Maintaining Aboriginal Identity, Language, and Culture in Modern Society. *Reclaiming Indigenous Voice and Vision.* Battiste. Marie, ed Vancouver, BC: University of British Columbia, 192-208.

Battiste, Marie, and James (Sa'ke'j) Youngblood Henderson. (2000). *Protecting Indigenous Knowledge and Heritage.* Saskatoon, SK: Purich Publishing.

Bear Heart. (1998). *The Wind Is My Mother: The Life and Teachings of a Native American Shaman.* New York, NY: Berkley Books.

Cajete, Gregory. (1994). *Look to the Mountain: An Ecology of Indigenous Education.* Durango, CO: Kivakí Press.

Couture, Joseph E. (1991a). The Role of Native Elders. *The Cultural Maze: Complex Questions on Native Destiny in Western Canada.* John W. Friesen, ed. Calgary, AB: Detselig Enterprises, 201-215.

Couture, Joseph E. (1991b). Explorations in Native Knowing.*The Cultural Maze: Complex Questions on Native Destiny in Western Canada.* John W. Friesen, ed. Calgary, AB: Detselig Enterprises, 53-76.

Cummins, J. and M. Swain. (1986). *Bilingualism in Education.* London, UK: Longman.

Doige, Lynda A. Curwen. (2001). Literacy in Aboriginal Education: An Historical Perspective. *The Canadian Journal of Native Studies*, 25:2, 117-128.

Dorais, Louis-Jacques. (1995). Language, Culture and Identity: Some Inuit Examples. *The Canadian Journal of Native Studies*, XV:2, 293-308.

Fettes, Mark, and Ruth Norton. (2000). Voices of Winter: Aboriginal Languages and Public Policy in Canada. *Aboriginal Education: Fulfilling the Promise*. Marlene Brant Castellano, Lynne Davis, and Louise Lahache, eds. Vancouver, BC: University of British Columbia, 29-54.

Findley, L. M. (2000). Foreword. *Reclaiming Indigenous Voice and Vision*. Battiste. Marie, ed Vancouver, BC: University of British Columbia, ix-xiii.

Friesen, John W. (1985). *When Cultures clash: Case Studies in Multiculturalism*. Calgary, AB: Detselig Enterprises.

Gamlin, Peter. (2003). Transformation and Aboriginal Literacy. *Canadian Journal of Native Education*, 27:1, 16-22.

Glazer, Nathan. (1980). Toward a Sociology of Small Ethnic Groups, a Discourse and Discussion. *Canadian Ethnic Studies*, XII:2, 1-16.

Goulet, Linda, Marjorie Dressyman-Lavalee, and Yvonne McLeod. (2001). *Aboriginal Education in Canada: A Study in Decolonization*. K. P. Binda and Sharilyn Calliou, eds. Mississauga, ON: Canadian Educators' Press, 137-153.

Johnston, Basil. (1995). *The Manitous: The Spiritual World of the Ojibway*. Vancouver, BC: Key Porter Books.

Kirkness, Verna J. (1998). The Critical State of Aboriginal Languages in Canada. *Canadian Journal of Native Education*, 22:1, 93-107.

Lambert, W.E. (1983). Deciding on Languages of Instruction: Psychological and Social Considerations. *Multicultural and Multilingual Education in Immigrant Countries*. by Torsten Husen and Susan Oppe, eds. Oxford, UK: Pergamon, 93-104.

Lambert, W. E., and G. R. Tucker. (1972). *Bilingual Education of Children: The St. Lambert Experiment*. Rowley, MA: Newbury House.

Leavitt, Robert. (1995). Language and Cultural Content in Native Education. *First Nations in Canada: The Circle Unfolds*. Marie Battiste and Jean Barman, eds. Vancouver, BC: University of British Columbia, 124-138.

Littlejohn, Catharine, and Shirley Fredeen. (1993). Indian Language Programs in Saskatchewan: A Survey. *Aboriginal Languages and Education: The Canadian Experience*. Sonia Morris, Keith McLeod, and Marcel Danesi, eds. Oakville, ON: Mosaic Press, 57-84.

Manitoba Association for Native Languages. (1986). Report of the Native Education Concerns Group on the Native Language Enrichment Project. Winnipeg, MB: MANL Annual Report, April 1985 to March 1986.

Matthews, Maureen, and Roger Roulette. (1998). Fair Wind's Dream: *Naamiwan Obawaajigewin/. Reading Beyond Words: Contexts for Native History.* Jennifer S. H. Brown and Elizabeth Vibert, eds. Peterborough, ON: Broadview, 330-363.

McGaa, Ed Eagle Man. (1995). *Native Wisdom: Perceptions of the Natural Way.* Minneapolis, MN: Four Directions.

McMillan, Alan B. (1995). *Native Peoples and Cultures of Canada: An Anthropological Overview.* Vancouver, BC: Douglas & McIntyre.

Meili, Dianne. (1992). *Those Who Know: Profiles of Alberta's Native Elders.* Edmonton, AB: NeWest.

Mollica, Anthony. (1989). Language Learning: the Key to Understanding and Harmony. *Language and Society.* 26: 40-41.

Morrison, R. Bruce, and C. Roderick Wilson. (1995). *Native Peoples: The Canadian Experience.* Second edition. Toronto, ON: McClelland and Stewart.

Nicholas, Andrea Bear (2001). Canada's Colonial Mission: The Great White Bird. *Aboriginal Education in Canada: A Study in Decolonization.* K P. Binda, and Sharilyn Calliou, eds. Mississauga, ON: Canadian Educator's Press, 9-34.

Norris, Mary Jane. (1998). Aboriginal Peoples in Canada: Demographic and Linguistic Perspectives. *Visions of the Heart: Canadian Aboriginal Issues.* Second edition. David Long and Olive Patricia Dickason, eds. Toronto, ON: Nelson Canada, 167-236.

Norton, Ruth W. (1989). Analysis of Policy on Native Languages: A Comparison of Government Policy and Native Preferences for a Native Language Policy. Unpublished paper. Calgary, AB: University of Calgary, 35pp.

O'Keefe, Michael. (1990). *An Analysis of Attitudes Towards Official Languages Policy Among Anglophones.* Ottawa, ON: Office of the Commissioner of Official Languages.

Pattanayak, D. P. (1987). *Multilingualism and Multiculturalism: Britain and India.* Occasional Paper No. 1, London, UK: International Association for Intercultural Education.

Paulsen, Rhonda. (2003). Native Literacy: A Living Language. *Canadian Journal of Native Education,* 27:1, 23-28.

Paupanekis, Kenneth, and David Westfall. (2001). Teaching Native language Programs: Survival Strategies. *Aboriginal Education in Canada: A Study in Decolonization.* K. P. Binda and Sharilyn Calliou, eds. Mississauga, ON: Canadian Educators' Press, 89-104.

Steckley, John L., and Bryan D. Cummins. (2001). *Full Circle: Canada's First Nations.* Toronto, ON: Pearson Canada.

Swanson, Sharon. (2003). Motivating Learners in Northern Communities. *Canadian Journal of Native Education,* 27:1, 61-73.

Weaver, Jace, ed. (1998) *Native Religious Identity: Unforgotten Gods.* Maryknoll, NY: Orbis Books.

Yazzie, Robert. (2002). Indigenous Peoples and Postcolonial Colonialism. *Reclaiming Indigenous Voice and Vision.* Battiste. Marie Battiste, ed Vancouver, BC: University of British Columbia, 39-49.

Seven

The Frontier of Self-identity

> ... a number of us were discussing issues concerning Aboriginal identity. We talked about how our parents had tried to hide any semblance of their Aboriginal identity and how in our experience today it was not only acceptable, but indeed desirable to be Aboriginal. In our experience dream catchers were everywhere and Aboriginal plays and events in the city were sold out. (Restoule, 2000: 102)

Although it is perhaps a bit optimistic, the above quotation is indicative of the trend toward acceptance of Aboriginal culture in Canada. There is a great deal more "Indianness" about, particularly in the commercial market, but this does not mean that people of Aboriginal background are much closer to experiencing social equity than they were a few decades ago. There are still many situations and communities in which Indigenous people find themselves victims of racism, prejudice and discrimination. The increasing sale of Indigenous artifacts will not change that; a public will to enact appropriate legislation and positive social action can.

It is generally accepted that individuals who feel good about themselves perform better in virtually any kind of situation. Students who have a good handle on who they are—culturally, physically, socially, and psychologically, always do better on tests and get higher grades. The resulting challenge, therefore is to develop learning conditions that will enhance student self-identity as a means of maximizing student learning.

National statistics indicate that the majority of Canadian youth will graduate from high school. Despite this encouraging trend, this is not the case with Aboriginal youth. Part of the difficulty is that accurate statistics about Aboriginal academic success are not readily available. Research evaluating factors that prevent or contribute to dropout of First Nations students are also virtually nonexistent (Poonwassie, and Charter, 2001: 124). We know that retention rates of Aboriginal students in both high schools and postsecondary institutions are rising, but it is difficult to determine just how successful these students are.

Defining Self-Identity

The term "self-concept" may be defined as what an individual knows or believes about oneself. Oakdale (2002): 159) calls this "the experience of a human's own someoneness." The notion of identity is closely linked; basically it is the way in which one identifies oneself in terms of social attachments since self-identity usually denotes attachment to a particular group or community. Part of individual self-concept, therefore, derives from one's knowledge of one's membership in a social group together with the value and emotional significance attached to that membership. To show how complicated such a definition can be, note Berry's (1999: 6) description of self-identity in Aboriginals;

> A positive Aboriginal cultural identity is viewed here as an internal (symbolic) state (made up of cognitive, affective and motivational components) and external (behavioral) expression of being an Aboriginal person (individual emphasis) and a member of an Aboriginal community (social emphasis).

The degree of attachment to a cultural community exhibited by individuals varies widely. Schultz and Kroeger (1996) point out that in the case of North American Aboriginals there are at least five options. These are provided in a model for understanding cultural group identity and behavior patterns. Each of the five categories is a reaction to the pressure brought about by being a minority in a majority setting.

The first response group might be called *traditionalists.* These are individuals who have a strong tie to their cultural background. They know which tribe, band, linguistic group, and clan they belong to and although proud of their attachment, they are not unduly so. Members of this group were raised within their particular community; they are ecology-oriented and in tune with the environment. They possess a fair amount of cultural knowledge and are appreciative of Indigenous spirituality. They have strong peer support, they know their history, and they are aware that they will have a role in passing along revered cultural traditions.

The second response to threatened marginality is exhibited by *assimilated* Aboriginals. These individuals may or may not have been raised in a Native setting, but if they have, they have abandoned their cultural roots. They have willingly and knowingly adopted new norms and made new social attachments. They are competitive and materialistic and essentially middle class oriented. They accept the notion of social stratification and hierarchical power existent in dominant society, and they do not value Indigenous beliefs. Hence, they are unable to be role models for traditional lifestyles.

The third response group are *lost identity* Indians. These are individuals who are powerless due to transitional stress; they are psychologically and culturally in limbo. They possess a mixture of traditional Indigenous knowledge and spirituality and that which they have gained has been in connection to religious institutions within dominant society. They suffer from social and cultural break-down and tend to vacillate between extremes. They have a confused identity and often exhibit characteristics of deprived syndrome, grief, and dependency. They generally occupy the lower socioeconomic levels of society and are frequently prone to substance addiction.

The fourth group are *new traditionalists* or "born again" Indians. These individuals may have little knowledge of traditional Indigenous beliefs and practices so they generally take great pains to emphasize their blood ties to specific Aboriginal cultures (Restoule, 2000: 105). Because of their lack of knowledge, they will likely appear to be interested in bringing back the hunting, gathering, and fishing mentality of centuries ago. For them, everything old is good and everything new is bad; this, despite the fact that they are often active in academic circles where they espouse a kind of discrepancy. Most of the members of this group are young, articulate, and stridently moving in an upward mobile direction. They openly display their braids, ribbon shirts, and items of bead-work. They espouse the theme of going back to the land while they continue to live in urban forms of accommodations in keeping with their middle class incomes. They are often unwilling to put in the time needed to learn Indigenous knowledge, and they are poor role models of traditional values and behaviors. Much of their time is spent in attempting to recruit others to their cause.

The fifth and final group may be labelled *international human beings* in that they appreciate the gifts of both Aboriginal and nonAboriginal worlds. These individuals are accommodating and adaptable. They are antiracists and socially-conscious. They have a healthy spirit and a vision for the future. They value their own cultural background without finding it necessary to belittle that of others. Often recognized as "movers and shakers," they work hard to stay in tune with the environment and with their peers in an increasingly culturally crowded world.

Berry (1999: 10) suggests that studies with Indigenous people over the period from 1970-1988 revealed three distinct cultural options. The majority of Aboriginal youth involved in these studies preferred to be bicultural along with a dual identity. They saw themselves as "Cree-Canadians, Blackfoot-Canadians," or "Ojibway-Canadians, with a sense of attachment to both Aboriginal and mainstream cultures." The second most often chosen option featured a form of separatism whereby the values and lifestyles of dominant society were rejected and a traditional Aboriginal lifestyle was idealized. The third and not very frequently chosen option was that of assimilation with its threat of marginalization. Few young AmerIndians indicated that they preferred to live that way.

Decolonization

A virtual buzzword that appears regularly in Indigenous literature today is decolonization. Governments, religious orders, and educational systems are constantly accused of continuing a campaign to debilitate or annihilate Aboriginal culture, sometimes as an excuse for lack of progress. This may be true. Adams (1999: 54) and Flanagan (2000: 90-92), however, maintain that the process of colonization has adopted another turn, this time undertaken by Aboriginal leaders against their own people. The yoke of colonization has not been thrown off; only the cultural affiliations of the bureaucrats have changed. Indigenous leaders now colonize their own people in the same manner that they claim to have been colonized, while at the same time complaining that governments, religious orders, and schools are still "doing it to them."

Does this charge have merit? If so, can the situation be changed? Would a fundamental shift in dominant societal structure to more traditional models alleviate this situation? Such a change is not likely to happen in the near future, so what is the alternative? Few observers would disagree with the view that dominant society is here to stay even though a handful of radicals might wish otherwise. Most Canadians, regardless of cultural affiliation, either enjoy or can realistically aspire to a fairly high standard of living complete with a home mortgage, good schools and health facilities, and a comfortable retirement lifestyle. To achieve these objectives, however, means either inheriting a great deal of money and status, or buying into the system and pursuing the "Canadian dream." Rare are individuals who can minimally play by the rules and still accomplish the "good life." Self-management and self-direction are directly related to making good life choices (Jones, 2003: 46).

The Inuit community of Nunavut is a unique example of having chosen the option of cultural separatism with a degree of success. Perhaps geographic isolation is a positive factor in this regard. The Inuit see their culture as existing quite apart from the rest of Canada. Geographically and climatically, this is certainly true. Although all Inuit under 40 years of age in Nunavut speak English, they view the language as a tool, necessary to compete efficiently in the modern world, but not good enough for an adequate expression of their feelings (Dorais, 1995: 297). They believe that speaking Inuktitut, their mother tongue, is where its at. A knowledge of English is directly tied to schooling and economic institutions, not life. Neither biculturalism nor assimilation are viable options because in Nunavut, life goes on pretty much as usual. Upward mobility, if it exists at all, flows along traditional lines.

Meanwhile, back in dominant society, life is not so simple. Every day and in virtually every situation, youth of many different cultural backgrounds are bombarded with seductive messages from a multiplicity of media forms including internet, television, CDs, videos, movies, and advertisements. Every young female is supposed to want to be a Britney Spears or Jennifer Lopez, and every young man a sports hero. Canadian youth adopt the dress styles of their idols, sing their songs, and change their hair colors to match those individuals who are popular in the media. But how can these youth possibly enter the race to achieve these goals if they do not possess the needed knowledge and skills?

The procedure for full societal endorsement can virtually be standardized. Individuals who know who they are, personally, culturally, and spiritually, and know what they want out of life will likely opt for socioeconomic conformity. If this is the case, there has to be a way of assuring that the great majority of Canadians will have opportunity to develop positive self-evaluations that will enable them to achieve such a measure of success. The standard response to this challenge has been to address the institution most often charged with delivering on that kind of mandate. This is where the school comes in.

Witt (1998: 269) points out that Aboriginal people face a unique contradiction by being defined as a minority group in their own country. Aboriginal people did not have to immigrate to a different cultural context thinking they might have to change their ways in order to fit into the new environment. In fact, the very country in which they originated suddenly became foreign to them. Poonwassie and Charter (2001): 125) argue that mental health issues for Aboriginal people, such as adequate self-concept, are therefore different than the general Canadian population due to their histori-cal experience of colonization. The cultures from which the First Nations originate has experienced a loss of viable economic activity and loss of language and self-government, and forced the members to endure a life of poverty, prejudice, and discrimination. While many Indigenous people have managed to cope and even overcome these obstacles, many are still struggling with them. The key concept to overcoming the past is empowerment, particularly its interper-sonal and structural dimensions. Empowerment is also a process through which individuals can obtain personal, organizational, and community resources that enable them to gain greater control over their environment and their aspirations.

Before a people can be empowered, however, they must be able to throw off the yoke of colonization. Laenui (2000: 155f) identifies five steps to decolonizing the human mind, the *first* of which is rediscovery and recovery. Individuals whose culture, language and heritage has been suppressed or eradicated will first need to be given an opportunity to become familiar with it again. Today many locally controlled reserve schools are meeting this challenge by turn-ing to an Indigenous emphasis in language and curriculum content (see next chapter). Urban schools enrolling Aboriginal children are similarly attempting to include Indigenous content but teachers (Native and nonNative), are not always sufficiently acquainted with the nature of the content nor do they necessarily appreciate the need for its inclusion. Universities can go a long ways towards meeting this need by developing more courses in First Nations history and culture, particularly in faculties of education.

A *second* step in the decolonization process is mourning. Laenui (2000: 150) suggests that when Aboriginals realize how much they have been missing in terms of heritage loss, they inevitably experience tremendous personal loss; they begin to mourn. The needed approach to accomplish this for this is to develop an atmosphere of openness and healing, and encourage victims to express their loss. They must be assured that steps will be taken to alleviate their pain so mourning is followed by the *third* step, "dreaming." This is a time when possibilities are voiced and explored, but little will come of these dreams, however, unless the individuals involved will also realize that they can fulfil those dreams. They must believe that they have the ability and talent to achieve them. This is empowerment in its best form. It is at once personal and spiritual.

When AmerIndians finally reach the conclusion that they are capable of fulfilling their dreams, a *fourth* step is required, namely the development of a sense of commitment to inaugurate necessary changes. At this point it will be very important for individuals to have strong peer and community support, particularly if the envisaged goals involve the situations of others. Strong, healthy relationships built on trust and mutual respect contribute to the educational success of Aboriginal students. The nature of teacher-student relationships often determine the level of success students achieve in school. The teacher-student relationship is a prerequisite to a positive classroom environment and to the development of positive student outlooks (Bazylak, 2002: 145).

The development of a sense of commitment will be followed by a *fifth* and final step, action. Actions undertaken by previously disempowered individuals cannot be isolated from the milieu in which they have been conceptualized. Breton (1994) suggests that five distinct elements must be realized if empowerment is to realized. These include: (i) group social action motivated by individuals aimed at bringing about socioeconomic and structural changes; (ii) political awareness; (iii) individual equity in addressing oppressing issues; (iv) recognizing oneself and being recognized as having something of value to contribute; and, (v) being individually empowered to make decisions by supporting or withholding support when the situation appears to call for such action.

Role of the School

> We need to consider the role that schools and society in general play in creating self-esteem in children. That is, students do not simply develop poor self-concepts out of the blue. Rather they are the result of policies and practices of schools and society that respect and affirm some groups while devaluing and rejecting others (Sonia Nieto in Siccone, 1995: xv).

Always on the firing line when it comes to resolving social dilemmas, schools can be important agents of social change. Virtually everyone goes to a school of some kind, except for home schoolers, of course, and individuals first frequent this institution at a very young age. The impact of the early years of schooling often lasts well into adulthood (there is much talk of lifelong learning, these days), so it is important that proper attitudes, effective skills, and important knowledge be developed in school. Most importantly, it is essential that students be prepared to learn, partly by having the fact stressed that every student can learn and every student should succeed in school.

Although a myriad of changes have been effected within the parameters of schooling over the past few decades, the impact of most of them have remained within the confines of school walls. Examples include curriculum changes (core curriculum), team teaching, magnet schools, open area schools, year round schooling, cooperative education, and others. Schooling has also been the target of reforms originated outside of its walls such as the campaign to educate for nationalism (Wiggin, 1962), proposals to deschool society (Illich, 1971), the accountability craze (Callahan, 1964; Sciara and Jantz, 1972), and the plea to develop an enhanced vocational bent in the nation's schools (Stamp, 1974). While all of this is going on school personnel are expected to facilitate personal autonomy and self-actualization on the part of students (Lucas, 1984).

A few decades ago, for example, Canada's neighbor to the south left it to their schools to take on the challenge of racial integration at a time when the rest of the populace was unwilling to tackle it. The willingness to work towards an alleviation of a major social deficiency illustrates the importance of schooling as an avenue by which to resolve important societal needs. By default, schools are also left on the frontline to deal with most other social adjustments necessitated by changing morals and new technology. Other less academic challenges left to the school would include driver education, consumer education, sex education, and substance abuse education, all of which have somehow become responsibilities of the school.

Canada's commitment to free public education rests upon a conviction that the political and social institutions of a free people cannot flourish without a literate and informed electorate. Growth and development of the nation's education system reflects deep convictions about the nature of the good life in an increasingly affluent country and the rights of all citizens to participate fully in that configuration. Unfortunately, for many minority groups in Canada, access to the good life has been severely restricted.

Future Outlook

In October, 2003, the Alberta Commission on Learning released a report entitled, *Every Child Learns: Every Child Succeeds* (2003: 5). In part the report reads;

> To achieve the vision we set, the Commission believes that concerted and deliberate actions are needed.... Success for every child [means] adapting programs and providing support so that all children, including Aboriginal children, children with special needs, children new to Canada, and children who have special gifts and talents, get every opportunity to succeed in school.

Educators have known for a long time about the significance of self-esteem to learning and the importance of helping students develop positive outlooks on life. Tiedt and Tiedt (1995: 34-35) report on a six-year watershed project by Virginia Shipman in 1975 which discovered that schools can have a great effect on self-esteem. Three decades ago Shipman discovered that disadvantaged and middle class children entered school with about the same average level of self-esteem and range of abilities as children of any other background. After three years of schooling, however, children from lower income families experienced a significant drop in self-esteem compared with their middle class peers. Encouragingly, although there was a loss of self-confidence, children from low income homes still felt positive rather than negative at this stage about their ability to take care of themselves.

Decades later, educators became much more aware of how to build self-esteem among students. A fundamental premise to developing a self-esteem building program is to recognize that everyone wants to belong. Because we are born and nurtured in social communities, human beings as a species have a need to belong. To belong in the context of self-esteem means that an individual is part of a group and is accepted and valued by the group. For self-esteem to be operative, it is not only necessary that the group accept individuals but that individuals experience a sense of belonging in the group. In order to develop a healthy sense of self, individuals need to experience themselves as unique individuals who are accepted for who they are. They also need to feel they belong, that they are important members of their circle of friends, their families, and their communities. This can only occur in a truly multicultural environment, one that is bias-free and accepting of diversity.

One of the most effective approaches to building self-esteem has been to validate the world of the individual student in the classroom. This can be done by allowing each student's peers to become familiar with the background and culture of their classmates. Bennett (1995: 301) elaborates several important components in strengthening cultural consciousness. These include helping students to develop multiple historical realities, build social action skills, strengthen cultural competence, and increase their awareness of the state of the planet and global dynamics. The underlying goal of such a mode is to help students accept and appreciate cultural diversity and gain a respect for human dignity and universal human rights. Hopefully, they will develop a sense of responsibility to the world community, beginning with their classmates, and take an active role in combatting racism, sexism, and other forms of prejudice and discrimination.

When students see their life configurations reflected around them, whether in art, music, cooking, books, or other ways, they feel that sense of belonging which is such a fundamental condition of positive self-esteem (Roberts-Faiti, 1997: 97). This approach demands that teachers be acquainted with and sensitive to the varying cultures represented in the classroom. The implications of including Aboriginal content in school curricula is addressed in the next chapter. It should be mentioned that teacher training institutions have a vital role to play in this regard and administrators must take great care to provide courses in First Nations education and multiculturalism.

Berry (1999: 31) identifies government policies, residential school experiences, prejudice, schooling, church beliefs and practices, and media as mainly negative past influences on Aboriginal development of self-concepts. Positive factors include traditional Indigenous culture, reverence for the land, family connections, language, spirituality, and a recognized role of elders. The clash of these factors for many has resulted in various forms of debilitating behavior including abuse, additions, incarceration, marginalization, and loss of cultural identity. The positive side of the ledger also lists few items including individual and group resilience, social support, Native institutional political affiliations, cultural reaffirmation, consolidation, and renewal of cultural identity.

(Clarke, 1978: 5) echoes this paradigm, pointing out that;

> We build our own brands of self-esteem from four ingredients: fate, the positive things life offers, the negative things life offers, and our own decisions about how to respond to fate, the positives, and the negatives.

Positive self-esteem may be nurtured in positive learning environments. Classroom climates are set by teachers, who are undoubtedly the key element in promoting learning. The way teachers talk, they way they treat students, and the way they evaluate individual student achievement all demonstrate attitudes of the profession. Teachers who respect students select their teaching approaches accordingly. Respect for students is best demonstrated by expecting success from each student and accepting each student. The behavior of teachers influences to a great extent the way students regard one another. Communication is the most essential element in the development of effective teacher-student partnerships. Communication styles vary among cultures, of course, and multiculturally-aware teachers try to be sensitive to subtle differences such as gestures, facial expressions, personal space, wait time, and touching.

Although it is not always possible for teachers to be acquainted with all of the cultural orientations represented in their classrooms, there are several aspects of ethnicity that teachers can readily cue into. These are include effective verbal communication, understanding the subtlety of nonverbal communication, and the ability to utilize a variety of intellectual modes in dealing with subject matter. As the field of education continues to advance, the gap between its expertise and that of unrelated disciplines will no doubt be diminished. This development will substantiate the claim that the endeavor to promote positive learning experiences for all students is most effectively championed by educators.

References

Adams, Howard. (1999). *Tortured People: the Politics of Colonization.* Revised edition. Penticton, BC: Theytus Books.

Bazylak, Darryl. (2002). Journeys to Success: Perceptions of Five Female Aboriginal High School Graduates. *Canadian Journal of Native Education,* 26:2, 134-151.

Bennett, Christian I. (1995). *Comprehensive Multicultural Education: Theory and Practice.* Third edition. Boston, MA: Allyn and Bacon.

Berry, J. W. (1999). Aboriginal Cultural Identity. *The Canadian Journal of Native Studies,* XIX:1, 1-36.

Breton, M. (1994). On the Meaning of Empowerment and Empowerment-Oriented Social Work Practice. *Social Work With Groups,* 17:3, 23-37.

Callahan, Raymond E. (1964). *Education and the Cult of Efficiency: A Study of the Social Forces that have Shaped the Administration of the Public Schools.* Chicago, IL: University of Chicago Press.

Clarke, Jean Illsley. (1978). *Self-esteem: A Family Affair.* Minneapolis, MN: Winston Press.

Dorais, Louis-Jacques. (1995). Language, Culture and Identity: Some Inuit Examples. *The Canadian Journal of Native Studies,* XV:2, 293-308.

Flanagan, Thomas. (2000). *First Nations? Second Thoughts.* Montreal, PQ: McGill-Queen's University Press.

Illich, Ivan. (1971). *The DeSchooling of Society. Alternatives in Education.* Bruce Rusk, ed. Toronto, ON: General Publishing, 105-106.

Jones, Christianna. (2003). Self-Management and Self-Direction in the Success of Native Literacy Learners. *Canadian Journal of Native Education,* 27:1, 45-54.

Laenui, Poka. (2000). *Processes of Decolonization. Reclaiming Indigenous Voice and Vision.* Marie Battiste, ed. Vancouver, BC: University of British Columbia, 150-160.

Lucas, Christopher. (1984). *Foundations of Education: Schooling and the Social Order.* Englewood Cliffs, NJ: Prentice-Hall.

Okadale, Suzanne. (May/June, 2002). Creating Continuity Between Self and the Other: First Person Narration in an Amazonian Ritual Context. *Ethos*, 30:1-2, 158-175.

Restoule, Jean-Paul. (2000). Aboriginal Identity: The Need for Historical and Contextual Perspectives. *Canadian Journal of Native Education*, 24:2, 102-112.

Roberts-Faiti, Gloria. (1997). Encouraging Self-Esteem in Early Childhood. *Include Me Too! Human Diversity in Early Childhood*. Kenise Murphy Kilbride, ed. Toronto, ON: Harcourt Brace & Company, Canada. 83-105.

Schultz, Marylou, and Miriam Kroeger, eds. (June, 1996). *Teaching and Learning with Native Americans: A Handbook for Non-Native American Adult Educators*. Phoenix, AZ: Arizona Adult Literacy and Technology Resource Center.

Sciara, Frank J., and Richard K. Jantz. (1972). *Accountability in American Education*. Boston, MA: Allyn and Bacon.

Siccone, Frank. (1995). *Celebrating Diversity: Building Self-esteem in Today's Multicultural Classrooms*. Boston, MA: Allyn and Bacon.

Stamp, Robert M. (1974). John Seath, Advocate of Vocational Preparation. *Profiles of Canadian Educators*. Robert S. Patterson, John W. Chalmers, and John W. Friesen, eds. Toronto, ON: D. C. Heath, 233-252.

Tiedt, Pamela L., and Iris M. Tiedt. (1995). *Multicultural Teaching: A Handbook of Activities, Information, and Resources*. Boston, MA: Allyn and Bacon.

Wiggin, Gladys A. (1962). *Education and Nationalism: An Historical Interpretation of American Education*. New York, NY: McGraw-Hill.

Witt, Norbert. (1998). Promoting Self-esteem: Defining *Culture*. *Canadian Journal of Native Education*, 22:2, 260-27

Eight

The Frontier of Curriculum

It must be straightforwardly realized that education, as currently practiced is cultural genocide. It seek to brainwash the Native child, substituting non-Native for Native knowledge, values and identity. (Hampton (1995: 35)

The current backlash against perceived European colonization incorporates a variety of pedagogical targets including curriculum revisions and substitutions. Aboriginal educators are concerned that schools have been employed as mechanisms of social control for generations. They view education in general and everyday meanings of school curriculum as guilty of promoting the values of those who enjoy social privilege in Canada. This implies that the interests and knowledge of one element of the population are being touted in schools at the expense of less powerful groups (Maina (1997: 301). The resultant mismatch of educational objectives forces minority students into positions of failure because they are evaluated with instruments developed and normed for children from mainstream culture. Minority children face inevitable economic disappointment because of their inability to obtain adequate employment.

Efforts to overthrow this form of colonization have included two major thrusts – curriculum revisions and curriculum substitutions, the latter primarily based on a revitalization of Aboriginal language learning. Revisions have been made to school curricula to include elements of Aboriginal history and cultural knowledge which has not always blended into existing subject matter, nor have teachers necessarily been trained to handle its inclusion. At best it has been maintained at addendum status rather than as a synthesized part of the overall school program.

A second response to colonization has been to devise alternative curricula based entirely on Aboriginal content, featuring Indigenous spirituality, history, cultural life, values and norms, knowledge about ceremonies and rituals, and teachings of the elders.

Essentially antithetical in nature, this approach tends to ignore the reality of contemporary society and downplays the idea that it would probably be in the best interests of Indigenous students if they could access elements of both cultures, Aboriginal and mainstream. This form of dualism is important if Native students are to appreciate their heritage as well as experience success in dominant society should they choose to do so.

Perhaps a more fruitful avenue to providing Aboriginal youth with a balanced perspective would be to formulate a curriculum with three foci: (i) traditional First Nations history and culture; (ii) contemporary, transitional First Nations culture and lifestyle; and, (iii) mainstream EuroCanadian knowledge. This would require a synthesized form of curricular integration so that students could conclude their studies with a wider base of knowledge. Integrating conceptual elements of traditional and contemporary First Nations culture validates Aboriginal cultures and languages as central to the curriculum. The challenge will be to complete the task with sensitivity and respect for all cultural perspectives. No one can afford to live in a world of cultural isolation.

Cultural Clash

Philosophers of education conceptualize educational systems as comprising a series of standard subsections including objectives, curriculum content, methodology, and personnel (Friesen, 1993: 56). Analysis of precontact Aboriginal cultures reveals a fairly explicit parallel with these components, but this reality was completely disregarded by the various groups of incoming European explorers, fur traders, colonizers, and missionaries. Instead the invaders superimposed their educational and religious system on the locals, thereby precipitating one of the most extensive cultural takeovers in North American history.

Aside from blatant negative labelling of Indigenous cultural beliefs and practices, incoming European educators developed extensive curricula that foisted their value systems on Native youngsters whom they often forcefully enrolled in educational institutions such as day schools, residential schools, and industrial schools. The latent function of curriculum materials used in these schools was obviously to transmit the myths, mores, traditions, legends, folkways, and superstitions of the culture that produced them.

Aboriginal children subjected to these materials quickly gain the impression that they ought to be ashamed of their heritage and shed themselves of it. In some instances, missionaries incorporated First Nations values and customs into their conversion methods as a means of trying to gain cooperation and support but these instances were rare. Native support for missionary efforts only increased when Aboriginal parents began to appreciate the assistance of missionaries in helping them to overcome the effects of disease and alcohol abuse (Archibald, 1995: 292).

The juxtaposed value systems between their home culture and that which they encountered in school environments caused great consternation among First Nations children, especially older students. The students discovered that many of their beliefs were diametrically opposed to those being taught them, and they were told that their ways were wrong. In contrast to Aboriginal value systems, for example, European philosophy could be described as linear and singular, static, and objective. The European concept of time was a good example of linear thinking. For Europeans, time began at some specific point in the past followed a linear progression from A to B to C to D. The linearity was constituted in terms of a hierarchical social organization with implicit inbuilt levels of power. Socially, it manifested itself in increased, higher, faster, and enlarged forms, which were preferred over smaller, older, lower or slower forms (Little Bear, 2000: 82).

There were radical differences between the way Aboriginal parents and elders traditionally taught their young and the way missionary schools operated. Before European contact, Indian children "learned on the job." with the emphasis on observation, modelling, and individual experience. Aboriginal children watched their parents and emulated them, much in the way that all rural families, Native and nonNative, once passed on their valued behaviors and skills in early Canada. The children participated in so-called adult activities at a relatively young age in order to get the feel of the activity. The specialty of the traditional First Nations' educational style was that it rested on entirely unique philosophical and spiritual grounds. The Indigenous peoples saw the universe as a whole; everything being connected, and all living things—people, animals, and plants—perceived as "all my relations." There were no separate subdivisions of thought such as biological, mental, spiritual, or psychological. The curriculum encountered by First Nations children brought everything together, encompassed within a spiritual blanket. Every act, every behavior, was seen as having spiritual implications in that it reflected on the individual's earthly journey. How the individual reacted to each momentary experience was an indication of his or her interpretation of why they had been placed on earth by the Creator.

When contrasted with imported European models of schooling, significant differences emerged. The newly-arrived missionary teachers were not so much interested in identifying individual interpretations of perceived phenomena as they were in instructing children in what they had to know and how they had to act. The missionaries did not view the universe as a unified whole but as a metaphysical laboratory with distinct subdivisions – biological, mental, psychological, and, to a lesser extent, spiritual.

The mentality that knowledge can analytically be dissected pervades educational systems to this day with the exception that all references to spiritual aspects of living have been eliminated. In many Canadian public schools today it is not even permissible to allude to Canada's Christian heritage (even at Christmas) lest someone emigrating from another country or faith be offended. Canada is now being portrayed as a multicultural country with no particular religious or spiritual history or previous philosophical allegiance. With the elimination of any references to the spiritual domain in school programs, small wonder that many First Nations students do not do well. According to what they learn in their home communities, spirituality is the primary foundation for all learning. In a truly modern Canadian school they are being told that spirituality is a "private" matter, if it even comes up at all. Discussions of spiritual matters are relegated to outside of school hours. Aboriginal students soon learn that the way some mainstream Canadians practice their spirituality is only for an hour or so one day a week, in a special building appropriately named.

The press for cultural assimilation of Indigenous children through schooling has gone on for generations. As late as the 1960s, Indigenous children were reading books that said very little about Indigenous culture, and when they did read about it, the content was quite negative and denigrating. As a result First Nations students found stories in school textbooks boring, bland, and unrealistic. Despite suggestions that Aboriginal students might learn better if curriculum materials contained content which they could comprehend and identify with, little was done to accommodate this suggestion (Reyhner, 1992: 98). The result was a passive and decreasing loss of interest in schooling and an increased dropout rate and diminished attendance.

Transitions

The inadequacy of federally and provincially-operated schools for Native children has gained significant attention in recent years, and a variety of fronts including curriculum, have been targeted for change. Native educators view the development of relevant curricula for students of Canada's First Nations background as fundamental to the maintenance of their culture, language, and worldview. First identified as an urgent need by the National Indian Brotherhood in 1972 in a report entitled, "Indian Control of Indian Education," the NIB report also identified a need for local control of Indian schools, enhanced school facilities, and appropriate teacher training. Efforts to improve these areas have continued since the release of the report.

One of the most obvious approaches to curricular improvement has been to add an Aboriginal emphasis to existing materials or simply substitute an Aboriginal-originated curriculum. This form of procedure may not be as simple as it at first appears because Indian bands generally vary somewhat in belief and practice even if they are part of the same culture area. For example, not all plains tribes believe or practice their cultural ceremonies in the same manner. There are further variations of similar habits among west coast Indigenous cultures, Plateau Indians, northern First Nations, Woodland peoples, and others. Even local Aboriginal communities or bands, who may be members of a larger First Nations cultural configuration, can differ slightly in lifestyle from their tribal counterparts. Teachers working in these respective areas need to keep their ears and eyes tuned to what is acceptable in each community. Increased awareness of the various elements of local community life can potentially lead to the development of more culturally appropriate teaching styles and materials.

Aboriginal educator, Verna Kirkness (1998) is blunt on the subject of cultural revitalization and places a great part of the responsibility for needed curriculum change on her own community.

Kirkness suggests the addition of a fourth "r" to the historical three "r's,' namely "rhetoric," and accuses her peers of having cold feet when it comes to cultural maintenance. In her words;

> We say that culture is language and language is culture . . . yet we continue to teach our languages for only a few minutes a day in our schools knowing that this approach is ineffective. We say that our education must respect our values and customs, yet we encourage competition rather than cooperation, the individual over the group, saving instead of sharing. (Kirkness, 1998: 13)

Kirkness laments the abundance of rhetoric in relation to cultural urgencies such as consulting with elders and parental involvement in local school activities. Kirkness emphasizes that a restoration of cultural knowledge, language, and values will require quality time spent with elders because they alone possess the wisdom and knowledge that must be the focus of all Aboriginal learning. Despite this insight, Kirkness contends that in many Indian communities only minimal consultation with elders occurs and elders are seldom included in a meaningful way.

Aboriginal rhetoric also includes acknowledgement of parents being involved in schooling, yet in many First Nations communities parents have no idea what goes on in their local school. They are rarely invited to meetings to decide on school matters and if they do attend they are seldom asked what their thoughts on any subject might be. School board meetings are closed meetings and, of course, few Aboriginal parents even sit on school boards.

When Native communities embark on local curriculum development, they face a set of complex challenges. The first step is typically to obtain funding for the project and attempt to influence constituents to appreciate the worthiness of the concept. Individuals representing the various community sectors will then be invited to an introductory meeting. When this happens it becomes necessary to outline the task and ascertain if consensus on objectives can be attained. An added challenge is that not everyone will readily buy into the process. There will also be some individuals who will participate in such activities strictly for the social benefits they offer. After all, it is good to get together with friends (Archibald, 1995: 297).

Obtaining community consensus on curriculum development is not necessarily an easy task. Because of the impact of assimilative influences in many communities, Native parents and leaders often have different perspectives on what constitutes appropriate subject content in school. There will also be differences in values and language usage. Some Indigenous parents will prefer to see their children taught strictly in the old ways while others will appreciate the need for their children to be able to function effectively in both Native and nonNative worlds. There may even be a few individuals who lean more toward a contemporary curriculum emphasis in their local school. The factor of language variation will also be present because differences of usage tend to emerge over time among the various bands within a given Native community. Obviously consensus on language form needs to be achieved if a standardized curriculum is to be developed (Morris and Price, 1991: 181f).

The primary objective for local curriculum development is to provide a means by which Aboriginal students can learn about their historical backgrounds within the school context. The concept is that a relevant curriculum will help students gain a more positive self-image and thus improve their academic achievement. It may also serve to develop an increased awareness and more positive attitude toward their cultural affiliation. At the same time, Aboriginal curriculum designers are well aware that any modifications they undertake cannot in any way deprive students of the opportunity to develop usable skills for today's job market. Generally speaking, local curriculum changes in First Nations' communities have served to bolster student confidence as well as enhance student marketable skills. Archibald (1995: 301) cites three remarkable and somewhat optimistic objectives for Aboriginal curriculum development: (i) to help students develop a more positive self-image; (ii) to assist nonNative students who may have access to the curriculum, to develop an increased awareness of and a more positive attitude toward Aboriginal people; and, (iii) to provide Indigenous students with the opportunity to become aware of the transition between tradition and contemporary forms of First Nations culture.

Curriculum revisions logically necessitate new forms of teacher training for elders who will participate in teaching as well as involved certified classroom teachers. For the latter group this may require two significant adjustments, one in regard to familiarizing themselves with new content, and the other with regard to restructuring teaching and learning procedures. The involvement of elders in the teaching process has proven to be one of the highlights of

Aboriginal curriculum development even though certain adjust-ments have been necessary. Elders are discovering that the contem-porary classroom is quite different from the traditional Aboriginal scene in which their predecessors used to gather children in a circle around them and tell them stories. This reality makes it essential that elders become part of the training process along with classroom teachers. There is reason to believe that an open attitude on the part of both parties toward such opportunity can be a mutually-benefi-cial, culturally-enriching experience.

While Native children are currently gaining exposure to the his-tory and culture of their ancestors, there is also a need for nonNative children to learn about traditional Indigenous ways. Public school curricula should incorporate First Nations-produced materials so that students can study the viewpoints of Aboriginal writers on vital subjects. Too much of Indian content produced by departments of education today is shallow, patronizing, and often erroneous, and tends to gloss over significant events and cultural themes from a EuroCanadian viewpoint. Aboriginal produced curricula can pro-vide a balance by demonstrating another perspective. After all, with the strong emphasis in schools today on studying all aspects of a given subject, and then making up one's own mind, it behooves school systems to provide alternative interpretations of all kinds of happenings and phenomena. Incorporating First Nations-produced materials could go a long ways toward such an end and place a stamp of approval on what has been praised as an admirable multi-cultural approach.

The development of Native curricula usually involves language because language reflects social structure, and reflects how people relate to one another. When a language disappears, relationships suffer. In an Aboriginal context, the relationships concerning peo-ple's connection to the Great Spirit (Creator), nature, and the order of things is affected (Smith, 2001: 81). Battiste (2000: 199) insists that Aboriginal languages must be viewed as the basic medium for the transmission and survival of Indigenous knowledge. Unless the revival of First Nations languages becomes a principal government undertaking, many of them will be lost along with the distinctive Aboriginal orientation to understanding the world from an holistic perspective. Most Aboriginal educators would agree, and be quick to point out that First Nations students cannot understand tradition-al ceremonies and rituals unless they comprehend them in their original language. Legends and storytelling also lose meaning when told in one of Canada's official languages. At one time youngsters could go to an elder and learn songs, stories, and rituals in the context of Native culture and language. Unfortunately too often today there is neither a cultural environment nor an opportunity for Aboriginal youth to be exposed to Indigenous traditions, let alone experience them in their Native language. Functional curriculum development, therefore, must almost certainly include language instruction (Kimura, 1998).

Obstacles

Aboriginal curriculum developers are currently at an intersection of several political, economic, and cultural boundaries. There is an underlying contradiction in trying to bring back traditional ways while at the same time preparing students for a successful lifestyle in the mainstream society are sometimes at loggerheads. There is obviously a need to develop educational initiatives that are autonomous from the institutions of the Canadian state, yet considered of value according to exclusively originated community criteria. Evans, McDonald, and Nyce (1999) recommend that participatory curriculum development is a preferred approach because it assures equitable representation to make certain that all sectors have adequate opportunity for input. It is crucial that elders, locally-recognized experts and other spokespersons be included in these ongoings in order to build community interest and develop ownership at the same time. In the meantime, certain national academic standards will need to be acknowledged. Both parties must view the other as having equal status in the process, otherwise a danger exists that institutional assimilation will be enhanced (Hare and Barman, 1998: 349; Hampton, 2000: 210). There are numerous examples of projects undertaken for First Nations schools that turned out to be for the benefit of dominant society, not local Aboriginal interests.

The challenge of balancing national interests with local specialities is immensely complicated, particularly when significant value differences are evident. Degrees of assimilation among Indian bands are often quite visible, with some of the communities quite tied to their old ways and others much entwined with mainstream institutional life. Curricula designed by mainstream educational institutions, even with input from Aboriginal educators and elders, are often criticised for their subtle assimilative objectives. Conversely, one of the criticisms lodged against a locally adapted curriculum is the charge that its content is often less intellectually constituted than the regular curriculum. Western knowledge is treated as the product of a depoliticized process of intellectual refinement, while Indigenous knowledge is treated as a product of local tribal politics. The result is the creation of an artificial divide between Indigenous knowledge and western thought (Goddard, 2002: 129).

Future Outlook

The process of developing a workable curriculum for First Nations students must of necessity incorporate two unique concepts—individual healing and cultural integration. Those who have been deprived or disabused of the right to know who they are in terms of their cultural past and affiliation are in need of healing. The sacred circle, called the medicine wheel in plains Indian culture, is a useful tool for the healing process. The medicine wheel contains four spokes—connectiveness, power, introspection, and models (Friesen, 1995: Regnier, 1995). It constitutes a functional model for individual healing when the four concepts are conceptualized and appropriated by individual students. The *first* spoke or concept (connectiveness), emphasizes the human link with the universe, with all living things. A consideration of this concept should foster the notion that individuals are not alone; they are or can be connected to their heritage, their culture, their community and indeed to the universe. This realization provides a good base for healing.

The *second* spoke represents the concept of power or empowerment, implying that the strength for individual healing emanates from within. An appreciation of the implications of this concept should produce the realization that each individual is special and has a unique role to play in the Creator's universe. The individual's obligation is to discover his or her unique station and stay in tune with the spiritual forces of the universe that will guide him or her in the related role, and not try to run ahead. There is no greater source of empowerment than to realize the Creator's plan for oneself.

The *third* spoke of the medicine wheel is introspection and its ground is a deep reverence for spiritual things. Elders emphasize that each individual, regardless of age must be encouraged to engage in spiritual meditation, to ask themselves what their purpose in life is. The principle of noninterference is vital in this connection because an individual's connection to the universe is ultimately personal. No two individuals are connected to the universe in exactly the same way because everyone can have a special connection to the Creator. Any gift or blessing to be derived from that unique connection will be recognized by the immediate community who should logically be the primary beneficiary of that connection.

Fourth and finally, is the spoke of models, implying that there are men and women in each cultural context whose exemplary

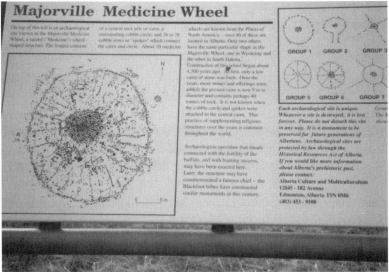

Majorville Medicine Wheel, east end of Siksika First Nations Reserve, Cluny, Alberta

behaviors can serve as patterns to emulate. Usually these people are elders, of course, and they reveal patience, wisdom, and respect in their dealings with all living things. Their experiences are deeply rooted in human experience and their knowledge is vital to all aspects of cultural revitalization and enrichment. A number of Native communities have rediscovered the value of eldership in recent years and have enlisted their assistance in a variety of crucial activities including curriculum building.

As the process of healing continues students will, hopefully, be able to study a relevant curriculum that integrates elements of Aboriginal history and culture with needed information and insights that will allow them eventually to attain functional and fulfilling places of their own choosing in contemporary society.

As Kirkness (1998: 15) notes;

> . . . how will you know when you are there? You will know when you have achieved your goal of quality education when your children are enjoying the challenge of school/learning, and when their self-esteem and self-confidence are evident, when your children are proud of who they are, when their links with the older generations are made. You will know you have achieved your goal when most children who enter your system graduate and go on to further education or get a job, when they are living happy and living fulfilled lives of their own making

References

Archibald, Jo-ann. (1995). Locally Developed Native Studies Curriculum: An Historical and Philosophical Rationale. *First Nations Education in Canada: The Circle Unfolds.* Marie Battiste and Jean Barman, eds. Vancouver, BC: University of British Columbia, 288-312.

Battiste, Marie. (2000). Maintaining Aboriginal Identity, Language, and Culture in Modern Society. *Reclaiming Indigenous Voice and Vision.* Marie Battiste, ed. Vancouver, BC: University of British Columbia, 192-208.

Battiste, Marie, and Jean Barman, eds. (1995). *First Nations Education in Canada: The Circle Unfolds.* Vancouver, BC: University of British Columbia.

Evans, Mike, James McDonald, and Deanna Nyce. (1999). Acting Across Boundaries in Aboriginal Curricuum Development: Examples from Northern British Columbia. *Canadian Journal of Native Edufcation,* 23:2, 190-205.

Friesen, John W. (1993). Formal Schooling Among the Ancient Ones: The Mystique of the Kiva. *American Indian Culture and Research Journal,* 17:4, 55-68.

Friesen, John W. (1995). *You Can't Get There From Here: The Mystique of North American Plains Indians Culture & Philosophy.* Dubuque, IA: Kendall/Hunt.

Goddard, J. Tim. (2002). Ethnoculturally Relevant Programming in Northern Schools. *Canadian Journal of Native Education,* 26:2, 124-133.

Hampton, Eber. (1995). Towards a Redefinition of Indian Education. *First Nations Education in Canada: The Circle Unfolds.* Marie Battiste and Jean Barman, eds. Vancouver, BC: University of British Columbia, 5-46.

Hampton, Eber. (2000). First Nations-Controlled University Education in Canada. *Aboriginal Education: Fulfilling the Promise.* Marlene Brant Castellano, Lynne Davis, and Louise Lahache, eds. Vancouver, BC: University of British Columbia, 208-223.

Hare, Jan, and Jean Barman. (1998). Aboriginal Education: Is There a Way Ahead? *Visions of the Heart: Canadian Aboriginal Issues.* Second edition. David Long and Olive Patricia Dickason, eds. Scarborough, ON: Nelson Canada, 331-360.

Kimura, Takeshi. (1998). The Cayuga Chief Jacob E. Thomas: Walking a Narrow Path Between Two Worlds. *The Canadian Journal of Native Studies,* XVII: 2, 313-333.

Kirkness, Verna J. (1998). Our Peoples' Education: Cut the Shackles; Cut the Crap; Cut the Mustard. *Canadian Journal of Native Education,* 22:1, 10-15.

Little Bear, Leroy. (2000). Jagged Worldviews Colliding. *Reclaiming Indigenous Voice and Vision.* Marie Battiste, ed. Vancouver, BC: University of British Columbia, 77-85.

Maina, Faith. (1997). Culturally Relevant Pedagogy: First Nations Education in Canada. *The Canadian Journal of Native Studies,* XVII:2, 293-314.

Morris, Joann Sebastian, and Richard T. Price. (1991). Community Control Issues and the Experience of Alexander's Kipohtakaw Education Centre. *The Cultural Maze: Complex Questions on Native Destiny in Western Canada.* John W. Friesen, ed. Calgary, AB: Detselig Enterprises, 181-198.

Regnier, Robert. (1995). The Sacred Circle: An Aboriginal Approach to Healing Education at an Urban High School. *First Nations Education in Canada: The Circle Unfolds.* Marie Battiste and Jean Barman, eds. Vancouver, BC: University of British Columbia, 313-329.

Reyhner, Jon. (1992). *Adapting Curriculum to Culture: Teaching American Indian Students.* Jon Reyhner, ed. Norman, OK: University of Oklahoma Press, 96-103.

Smith, Murray. (2001). Relevant Curricula and School Knowledge: New Horizons. *Aboriginal Education in Canada: A Study in Decolonization.* K. B. Binda and Sharilyn, eds. Mississauga, ON: Canadian Educators' Press, 77-88.

Nine

The Frontier of Teaching

The grandmothers are natural teachers because they take care of children . . .they laughed and worked and told stories to little children and rode up into the mountains, were kind, were strict, made twine out of plants, cut willow switches to make children behave, rocked babies to sleep (Sterling, 2002: 5).

Long before the Europeans arrived in North America the Indigenous people had in place an effective means of passing along their values and traditions to their children. Teaching was mainly done by grandparents and elders at no specified times, and the curriculum centred on the various tasks and responsibilities of daily life. Children learned on the job, so to speak, and instruction was both formal and informal, the former through spiritual institutions known as secret societies or sodalities, and the latter through everyday experience.

The qualifications of Aboriginal teachers in traditional times included patience, experience, and knowledge acquired through time. Trained by their own elders and grandparents, these instructors were careful to pass on what they had learned, subject of course, to the changes and vicissitudes of their cultural milieu. When the Europeans arrived everything changed, including schooling, which was soon overtaken by missionaries who viewed Indigenous cultures as constituting heathen ways and pagan beliefs. The objective of assimilating local First Peoples to European ways begun by the invaders has more or less continued in some form to this day (Maina, 1997: 296).

The process of European indoctrination from the beginning took various forms. Some missionaries gave a great deal of attention to "civilizing" the Indians, which meant giving instruction in manners, dress, and societal protocol, while others concentrated on spiritual instruction. French missionaries were particularly concerned that the First Nations change their method of livelihood to one of agronomy and forestry development. They wanted gradually to render the Indian "from a state of barbarism and introduce amongst them the industrious and peaceable habits of civilized life" (Maina, 1997: 297).

Today things are slowly changing because of Aboriginal cultural revitalization, and the evolution of Indigenous education in Canada has taken on the shape of an evolving state of Indigenous input and control. More First Nations young people are graduating from universities, specifically from teacher training programs. Many Aboriginal teachers are employed in schools situated in their home communities and although this has generally proven to be a positive move, there are still complex challenges to be confronted. First Nations teachers are struggling with the frontier of living in traditionally-oriented settings while trying to apply their urban-derived skills. Often Native teachers have to struggle with the mismatch that results between the educational objectives of a school system based on one culture, and the way of life, values, and goals of students attending it who come from a different cultural background. Aboriginal teachers have to deal with different forms of communication and learning styles from those they are taught to expect in teacher training institutions. They also face the challenge of integrating Indigenous cultural concepts into the teaching-learning process (Aikenhead and Huntley, 1999: 160).

Some First Nations educators (Kirkness, 1999: 57), believe that the availability of university-trained Aboriginal teachers is a real boon to Native education even though the evidence to make this assertion is scant. McAlpine (2001: 111) points out that despite the increasing number of individuals who graduate from Aboriginal teacher education programs and who are hired and stay in their positions, this trend has not impacted substantially on the nature of Aboriginal education, nor the experience of children attending them. Those who envisage that First Nations teachers will make a great difference need to take into account the burden of cultural brokering that Native teachers often have to undertake. They are many times called on to serve as intermediaries between Native and nonNative worlds and expected to provide counselling to that end while carrying on their regular duties. Some Aboriginal teachers find the challenge unduly harsh and suffer premature burnout. In the final analysis, it is those individuals, Native or nonNative, who can help Aboriginal students to bridge the gap between the traditional Indigenous world and that of contemporary society who are most successful as teachers.

The fundamental question is, "Who is a successful teacher in an Aboriginal community? "The answer is quite complex, because cultural factors that are at play pose a unique challenge. It is perhaps safe to say that effective teachers of children, Aboriginal or nonAboriginal, are characterized by their ability to create a climate of warmth and to demand a high quality of academic work. They often take the role of facilitator or encourager, rather than that of impersonal professional. They use a variety of methods and approaches in teaching such as providing positive nonverbal messages, being pleasant, and frequently maintaining close body distance to communicate engagement and warmth. These teachers are successful, not because of their social status or ethnic background, but because of their instructional style (Barman, Hébert, and McCaskill, 1987: 13).

The mark of a good teacher is the ability to deal effectively one on one with students in a manner that motivates students to think well enough of themselves so they will be able to harness their energies toward self-devised directions. Goulet (2001: 68) calls the end result of such an experience the ability to enact "responsible self-direction." In classrooms presided over by these teachers, students will:

1. See themselves as worthwhile human beings;
2. Recognize their origin and cultural background as assets;
3. Attack meaningful tasks with the expectation of success;
4. Interact positively with other children in the classroom; and,
5. Recognize that the cultural backgrounds of others are valuable aspects of the pluralistic North American society (Tiedt and Tiedt, 1979: 15).

When nineteenth century American President James H. Garfield learned of the success of educator Mark Hopkins (1882-1887), working with students one on one, he coined a much-quoted preference for an ideal educational setting. Garfield asked for "only a simple bench – Mark Hopkins on one end and the student on the other – and you may have all the buildings apparatus and libraries without him" (Mayer, 1963: 32). Hopkins' approach of one on one is best adopted even today in terms of an effective relationship between any teacher and any student.

The Teaching Milieu

One of the key recommendations of the Hawthorn Report (1967) was that teachers should be encouraged to learn as much as possible about the background and culture of First Nations students and take the initiative in getting to know individual students. This recommendation has perpetually been reiterated during the past three decades and is still a necessary emphasis (Wolcott, 1967; Friesen, 1977; Elofson and 1988; Friesen, 1993; Reyhner, 1992; Duquette, 2000). The need to become familiar with Indigenous cultures is important because the majority of teachers in Aboriginal communities are still nonNative, and in many cases their knowledge of Native culture is quite limited. Taylor (1995) estimates that 90 percent of Native children will, at one time or another, be taught by a nonNative teacher.

Although many well-meaning and successful nonAboriginal individuals have been effective teachers in Aboriginal communities, a number of recurring nonproductive practices which some teachers have engaged in must be noted. The primary concern has to do with the fact that some teachers still contract employment in Native communities because they have not been able to find positions elsewhere (Friesen, 1987). As the school year gets underway teachers new to the vicissitudes of the Aboriginal lifestyle sometimes believe that if they can survive this kind of experience, they can survive anything. Unprepared for what they will encounter in a unique cultural milieu, the cultural gap simply overwhelms them and they fall prey to severe culture shock (Kowalsky, Verhoef, Thurston, and Rutherford, 1996: 269). The usual reaction is to shrink into a cocoon, function ineffectively, or simply resign and leave the community. The cocoon phenomenon occurs when nonNative teachers ignore the community and only interact with one another (Friesen and Boberg, 1990: 149). By doing this they effectively form a private subculture in the community and are viewed as such. Some of their members may even entertain the perspective that since they are only temporary dwellers in the community, why bother becoming part of it?

A unique and useful concept emphasized by Taylor (1995) is the notion of low-context and high-context cultures. Taylor points out that Aboriginal cultures are generally high-context cultures in that Aboriginal culture relies less on the spoken word and more on the context of existing, nonverbal information. Much is left unsaid in such cultural contexts because to some extent, "everybody knows what everybody else is thinking." Conversely, EuroCanadian culture is low-context and relies a great deal on verbal interaction, body language, and gestures. NonNative teachers often experience frustration when they find that their students "simply won't open up." Similarly, they discover that their Native colleagues will offer little help by way of explanation for puzzling or enigmatic events, customs, or happenings. The obvious solution to this dilemma is for nonNative teachers to form a working relationship with a community informant and be willing to learn from this liaison. Naturally, the extent to which learning can occur will depend on the sincerity of the nonNative teacher and the degree to which people from the two very different backgrounds can trust one another.

The element of trust will also be significant in terms of teacher-student relationships. Many Aboriginal students are quite used to being taught by a rotating teaching staff, that is, they may have to work with several incoming teachers in the course of a year. Fortunately, this phenomenon is on a decline, partially because jobs are more scarce than they were a few decades ago, and partly because nonNative teachers are entering the arena of First Nations education better prepared. Regardless of the situation, the bottom line is that any student who reaches out to a teacher should never be discouraged.

Today many Indian bands are developing supplemental or substitute curricula for their schools through curriculum committees with the hope that Indigenous students will have greater opportunity to learn about their heritage. This is a positive development, but it poses a special challenge to nonNative teachers who may be unfamiliar with Aboriginal culture. In some respects it may also offer teachers a second opportunity to learn about Indigenous ways. The new curriculum may also supplement what teachers have studied in their teacher training programs. Native-originated curricula may serve to reduce the cultural gap for First Nations students between school and community. It may help them feel more comfortable in school and possibly reduce the tension that may occur when the two cultures of nonNative and Native (teacher and student) meet.

Teacher Training

University Programs

The effectiveness with which teachers function has significant implications for teacher education programs delivered by universities and colleges. Several decades ago, a number of universities experimented with off-campus teacher education programs delivered on Indian reserves. This meant that university instructors and professors travelled to Native communities and taught accredited courses or conducted workshops onsite. Many of these programs were quite successful. The most appealing aspect of these programs was that First Nations postsecondary students no longer had to leave their communities to obtain university education until their last year of study. Before long, many Aboriginal individuals became qualified teachers in their home community schools (Friesen, 1991; Grant, 1996).

Off-campus teacher education programs were not without unique benefits and challenges. One of the most obvious benefits was for university personnel to learn firsthand about Native community life. As regular visitors they soon became aware of aspects of local functioning which they could not learn about through textbook reading. Native students, on the other hand, particularly older students with family responsibilities, enjoyed the opportunity of studying close to home. A unique challenge implicit in the program for teachers was finding out how to make the program relevant to local needs and interests. Initially, most university instructors who participated in the first off-campus teacher education programs were not acquainted with Indigenous ways, and they tended to function much in the way they did on campus. Few attempts were made to relate course content to local history or culture and the first university graduates from these programs usually received a typical nonNative-oriented kind of education. They were essentially being assimilated into a EuroCanadian way of thinking. This changed as university instructors "learned on the job," and attempted to adapt the objectives of the subject matter they were teaching to a more relevant slant. Grant (1996) and Hare and Barman (1998: 351) stress the need for instructors in such situations to become culturally sensitive, nonjudgmental, and open to personal learning and growth (Littlebear, 1992: 109; Sawyer, 1991: 102-103). Hampton is less optimistic and charges that "Most, if not all, university education in Canada today is education for assimilation" (Hampton, 2000: 210).

A number of university off-campus programs are operating in First Nations communities today, although their emphasis has shifted from strictly concentrating on teacher education. Students who enroll in these programs are now able to pursue degrees in a variety of fields. The number of graduates from these programs has steadily risen, providing proof for the efficacy of this approach. Despite this success, the need for additional on campus course offerings in First Nations history, language, and culture, still exists.

It is imperative that Canadian teacher training institutions continue to follow the watershed work of Brandon University, the University of Alberta, the University of British Columbia, the University of Saskatchewan, and Trent University in promoting courses in Aboriginal education. Kirkness (1999: 62) expresses concern about negative attitudes of teachers who may be called on to teach in Native communities without adequate preparation. Knowledge about Canada's wider First Nations community is mandatory as well as specific tribal information about values, spirituality, and learning styles. This knowledge will not require that teachers be any less professional. In fact, the most successful teachers are those who are actively demanding, yet friendly and caring. Being demanding may be defined as having high expectations of students (Littlebear, 1992: 108).

Learning on the Job

Several years ago, Christina Mader (1999) was researching teacher education in a remote northern Alberta Aboriginal community and determined to find an answer to the question, "What is important for people to know around here?" She summarized her twelve week experience in four photographs entitled, "We value our future" (picture of two cousins), "We value our homeland" (marshland scene), "We value our spiritual traditions" (picture of a Roman Catholic Church built in the shape of a teepee), and "We value our old ways" (picture of a Woodland Cree mother and baby daughter)." Mader concluded her study by discovering that reverence for the ordinary and appreciating unhurried time were keys to successful teaching in Woodland (Bush) Cree country.

We reached a similar conclusion to that which Mader expressed, and the following excerpts substantiate this. During the fall term of 2003 we co-taught a course at Old Sun College on the Siksika (Blackfoot) First Nation Reserve entitled, "Canadian Culture and Humor." The course was offered by the Faculty of Communication and Culture through the University of Calgary's Native Outreach Program which was established in 1972. Twenty-six Blackfoot students were enrolled in the course, and during one written assignment we requested that students write a few paragraphs in answer to the question, "What should teachers know before coming to a First Nations community to teach?" Sample student statements follow, and are subdivided into five sections encapsulating the nature of their responses. Every one of the students expressed concern that teachers should first familiarize themselves with local Blackfoot culture.

(i) Culture and History

Teachers should know that Aboriginal cultural values are based on respect for self, others, the Creator, and Mother Earth. This is the basis for the First Nations way of life.

Know a bit about the culture. If you don't know, be open to know about the culture. Try to understand the social behavior and interaction patterns of the people. That way no one will be offended.

Teachers should be familiar with first Nations people; do some research on their lifestyle, cultural ways, and language.

Teachers should learn about the traditions and protocols of First Nations. They may unknowingly insult people, especially elders at an interview or on the job. This is very important since schools involve elders and spiritual leaders on a regular basis.

Teachers should learn about the customs of the people (which behavior may be right or wrong). There are certain protocols to keep in mind.

Respect is a prime factor in our way of life—respect toward people, Mother Nature, the Creator and the ceremonies.

Teachers should understand our culture which is basically our way of life. It is what our elders pass on to us.

Culture is important to reinforce the idea of being proud to know that who we are is great. Today's youth need empowerment and the knowledge of their culture to truly have an identity.

Teachers should have some background knowledge of the First Nations community in Canada as a whole. They should be familiar with regional First Nations groups, and knowing about the First Nations communities that they would be teaching is an absolute must. Not all Natives are the same. We use storytelling and legends, even humor, to educate our youth.

(ii) Community Relations

Teachers should become an extended part of the community, making themselves open to new experiences, not only to teach their ways to First Nations students.

Teachers should realize that First Nations schools are much different from those off-reserve. The social problems on reserve come out in class and affect students.

Teachers should also know our humorous side since as Native people we tend to laugh at things that most would find offensive. They say that laughter is the best medicine.

Be humorous; don't be so serious and hard to get along with. First Nations people are more friendly to people who know how to have a sense of humor. Be courteous and considerate of others. Do not be insulting.

Teachers should know the Native value system because they are quite a few differences between First Nations communities, let alone if a nonNative individual goes into a Native community to teach. Native people have their own forms of art and music that are just as distinct as that of other cultures. For us, family always comes first in an Aboriginal community.

Reserves are sometimes very isolated and nonNative teachers may find that nonNative faces are few and far between.

Teachers need to keep in mind that Native people are different people who think differently than EuroCanadians; be patient.

Be ready to face cultural differences and cultural shock if necessary.

Teachers should become familiar with the socioeconomic conditions of the community they work in. They should be aware that reserve life is not the same as that of Indian life in the city. The norms are quite different.

Teachers should be personable and try to get along with the people. Natives tease you if they like you.

(iii) Teacher-Student Relations

Teachers should understand that although we are Native, it does not mean that we are any different from everybody else. We just have different cultural backgrounds. We can be quite friendly.

Positive encouragement in education is needed. Everyone wants it. Teachers need to learn how to make learning fun; they need to remind students that school is not jail, but a place to develop ideas, learn, and make each individual confident and more knowledgeable.

Be ready to teach and don't make all the class discussions so boring or we lose track of the issue and fall asleep.

(iv) Language

Language such as Blackfoot is a key to First Nations survival. Our youth should be able to speak our language. Reinforcement of such a beautiful thing should be practiced by all if possible.

Teachers should know the basic language skills in the community where they teach. First Nations language is very important to our people.

Teacher need to keep in mind that sometimes English is not our first language, and at times may be different to comprehend; sometimes it takes a few minutes for something to register.

First Nations people believe that language is a big part of their cultural heritage.

(v) Child-rearing

Teachers should educate themselves on First Nations traditional child-rearing. Our children are seen and respected as individuals to be taught and moulded by example. They are not property of parents or school; they are born with natural rights, not legislated ones.

Teaching Mandate

As the literature related to effective teaching in Native settings continues to grow (Wolcott, 1967; Barman, Hébert, and McCaskill, 1986 and 1987; Reyhner, 1990; Sawyer, 1991; Battiste and Barman, 1995; Battiste, 2000; Castellano, Davis, and Lahache, 2000; Binda and Calliou, 2001; Friesen and Friesen, 2002), it becomes possible to identify reliable pedagogical principles that will ensure the creation of a healthy learning atmosphere for Aboriginal children.

First, teachers need to encourage students to accept themselves in terms of their total identity—spiritually, physically, culturally, and emotionally, particularly with regard to what their nonNative peers or superiors might perceive as atypical traits. This perspective can help reduce the emphasis on cultural or individual differences and encourage the development of meaningful community.

Second, teachers should be prepared to present and accept alternative cultural explanations for normative behavior. Most children are curious about different ways to celebrate Christmas, for example, but the lesson will be more appreciated if such variations in practice can be demonstrated. Fear of the unknown may be a very real phenomenon, but an inclusive approach may widen students' perspectives of what are often perceived as common phenomena.

Third, students should be encouraged to learn about and appreciate the unique contributions of their own culture. This is a tall order, especially if one is not familiar with the historical development or cultural theme of a given culture. This may require a little research, but without exception, it will be fruitful. For the better part of this century, Native youngsters have been taught in school curricula that their people accomplished very little by way of technology before the Europeans came. Even a little historical digging quickly shows the fallacy of such a view, for before the European invasion, North American First Nations did very well in such areas as agriculture, architecture, and engineering, and in making other scientific advances. Their mountainside cities, mounds, pueblo remains, and other ruins attest to a significant period of development. As our society gradually absorbs the benefits of varying value systems into its very essence, hopefully, First Nations will feel increasingly at ease in sharing their way of life with mainstream Canadian society.

Fourth, teachers need to assist First Nations students in realizing that they are worthy of making unique contributions to society. At first glance this statement appears to suggest that each individual ought to make a certain kind of contribution to our society, but that is not what is meant. The fact, nature, and extent of that contribution is not important. What is essential, however, is for each student to believe that they can make a contribution if they so desire, along the lines they choose, and that contribution will be appreciated.

Fifth, students need to be made to feel part of a group while at the same time maintaining their own cultural identity. No group identity is so important (not even mainstream culture), that it can demand a complete obliteration of personal uniqueness and a total melding into the body politic.

Sixth, teachers need to be themselves in terms of acting out their own values and cultural identity (Wolcott, 1967: 130; Littlebear, 1992: 107). Those who are insincere about their own identity will easily be detected by even the youngest student. It is one thing to be sensitive and understanding, but an obvious case of oversell can occur when individuals try to appear too enamored of a lifestyle different than their own. Such a position may encourage them either to pretend that their own way of life is somehow inferior, or not worthy of adherence. Neither stance is honest; neither stance is justified.

Seventh, teachers must learn to accept each student as an individual. It is entirely possible to make too much of individual differences, of course, be they culturally derived or in references to a unique physical or personality trait. On the other hand, however, to eliminate references to differences entirely by suggesting that "people are people" is too simplistic. The starting point of good teaching is to determine where each student is at in terms of a particular learning situation. This is done not by cataloguing unique personal qualities but by an overall professional assessment of the student's readiness, and orientation. The ultimate criterion for measuring one's success in attempting to promote self-appreciation on the part of an individual student is to witness their seeing themselves as worthwhile (Littlebear, 1992: 108-109). On that basis their interactions with others can be positive and they will be able to attack meaningful tasks with every expectation of success.

Tips for Teachers

Onsite university education is only one facet of the effort to understand alternate lifestyles. To become effective teachers it will be necessary to go beyond the university campus for supplemental ideas. Reading good books about First Nations' history and culture is a good starting point. There are plenty of reliable sources available, many of them written by Aboriginal people. A visit to a museum to examine a relevant display can also be beneficial. Even more importantly, teachers should arrange to meet informed First Nations individuals. This can be done by visiting a Native friendship centre or attending a powwow or some other event during a local Indian Awareness Week. Many such events are open to nonAboriginals who are interested in learning about Indigenous ways.

"Three Generations," Elder Clara Rollinmud, daughter Amy, and granddaughter

On arriving in a Native school it is essential that local customs be considered. For example, Indigenous students may not be at school every day nor necessarily always be on time. This may be because they have not been taught that time per se is a commodity of top priority, or a more important obligation has arisen. Other things like family events or responsibilities are always much more significant. It is also important that teachers learn something about Indian protocol. They will need to know that Indigenous people respect age; they respect their elders and grandparents because they possess a lot of valuable knowledge and experience. Other practical items to keep in mind include the following.

First, Aboriginal students tend not to want to look teachers directly in the eye. This is because they have been taught to respect those in authority.

Second, Aboriginal students do not usually like to respond to questions if they do not know the answer. They should not be pushed to "guess." Their traditional cultural background never emphasized the virtues of direct confrontation. Direct confrontation was viewed as being disrespectful to others.

Third, Native students like to work cooperatively, so teachers should assign as many group projects as possible. Amerindian children are taught to work together, help one another, and learn from one another. Older children are usually expected to help younger ones especially if they are in the same vicinity.

Fourth, Aboriginal people generally do not trust anything to do with "the system." They have been misled by EuroCanadian institutions (including the school), for so long that school personnel may find that teachers first have to earn the trust of Aboriginal students and their parents.

Fifth, Native students tend not to be fooled by prestige; they are more easily convinced by true performance.

Sixth, it may appear that Native students lack what might be called "middle class rules of etiquette." This is simply because their forms of etiquette are unique to their culture. Indigenous people do not necessarily appreciate the EuroCanadian penchant for etiquette detail.

Seventh, the traditional Indian way of thinking is holistic which means that individuals perceive everything in spiritual terms. Everything is connected to everything else, so it is important to live in the "perennial now," and appreciate the moment. The future will take care of itself. Only the immediate moment is available for thought and action.

Eighth, teachers must be open to attempting different teaching methods such a sharing circles, learning journals, field trips, creative dramatics, and peer tutoring. Student participation should always be voluntary if possible.

Ninth, teachers need to make connections to the local community. This can be done by inviting speakers from the community to the classroom. Alternately, a class field trip to a museum or Indian cultural centre should be planned. If speakers are invited, elders, for example, it will be important to know which ones to contact. This will require familiarity with the respective community. Sometimes "commercial elders" or "circus elders" are available who will gladly participate in speaking engagements for money, but they are not necessarily respected by their constituents.

Tenth, teachers should try to keep their classroom atmosphere informal and allow plenty of freedom of movement. Desks may be arranged in small semicircles, or students may be encouraged to sit on the floor or work in small groups. Many Aboriginal people are still struggling with the formalities foisted on them by the incoming powers of the past.

It is useful to remember that all children are children to some extent, regardless of cultural background. Classrooms should be laboratories where individuals can discover things about each other—students about students, teachers about students, and students about teachers. It is important that teachers share something of themselves because this will give opportunity for students to learn about alternate ways of thinking and behaving. To some extent, for them the classroom should be a miniature universe of ideas and practice.

Future Outlook

The frontier of teacher training cannot be regarded as a separate challenge, but must be viewed within the context of Native self-government. West (1995) warns that the conceptual framework of most Native aspirations, including self-government, economic self-sufficiency, and education has been defined by nonAboriginal sources. Labelled, "epistemological dependency," it means that specific ideas for reform are usually originated by colonizing sources even though they may be promulgated by First Nations leaders who themselves have been educated in colonizing institutions.

The need for additional Aboriginal input into teacher training is mandatory. First Nations views on such important areas as spirituality, child-rearing practices, learning styles, and teaching methodology, differ from those currently being propounded in teacher training institutions and they must be studied (Ralph, 1993). Curriculum content, teacher certification, and educational standards are also viewed differently by Native leaders and educators and their input on those matters should be viewed as a source of enrichment, not as a threat. After all, university education is supposed to be about appropriating knowledge from the "universe of ideas." There is no doubt that Aboriginal input into these important areas comprises a rich source of knowledge.

References

Aikenhead, Glen, and Bente Huntley. (1999). Teachers' Views on Aboriginal Students Learning Western and Aboriginal Science. *Canadian Journal of Native Education*, 23:2, 159-175.

Barman, Jean, Yvonne Hébert, and Don McCaskill, eds. (1986 and 1987). *Native Education in Canada, Volume 1: The Legacy;* and *Volume 2: The Challenge.* Vancouver, BC: University of British Columbia.

Barman, Jean, Yvonne Hébert, and Don McCaskill. (1987). The Challenge of Indian Education: An Overview. *Indian Education in Canada, Volume 2: The Challenge.* Jean Barman, Yvonne Hébert, and Don McCaskill, eds. Vancouver, BC: University of British Columbia, 1-21.

Battiste, Marie. (2000). *Protecting Indigenous Knowledge and Heritage: A Global Challenge.* Saskatoon, SK: Purich.

Battiste, Marie, and Jean Barman, eds. (1995). *First Nations Education in Canada: The Circle Unfolds.* Vancouver, BC: University of British Columbia.

Binda, K. P., and Sharilyn Calliou, eds. (2001). *Aboriginal Education in Canada: A Study in Decolonization.* Mississauga, ON: Canadian Educators' Press.

Castellano, Marlene Brant, Lynne Davis, and Louise Lahache, eds. (2000). *Aboriginal Education: Fulfilling the Promise.* Vancouver, BC: University of British Columbia.

Duquette, Cheryl. (2000). Becoming a Teacher: Experiences of First Nations Student Teachers in Isolated Communities. *Canadian Journal of Native Education*, 24:2, 134-143

Elofson, Warren, and Betty-Lou Elofson. (1988). Improving Native Education in the Province of Alberta. *Canadian Journal of Native Education*, 15:1, 31-38.

Friesen, John W. (1977). *People, Culture and Learning.* Calgary, AB: Detselig Enterprises.

Friesen, John W. (1987). *Rose of the North.* Ottawa, ON: Borealis.

Friesen, John W. 1991). Teaching in a University Native Education Program. *The Cultural Maze: Complex Questions on Native Destiny in Western Canada.* John W. Friesen, ed. Calgary, AB: Detselig Enterprises, 229-242.

Friesen, John W. (1993). *When Cultures Clash: Case Studies in Multiculturalism.* Calgary, AB: Detselig Enterprises.

Friesen, John W., and Alice L. Boberg. (1990). *Introduction to Teaching: A Socio-Cultural Approach.* Dubuque, IA: Kendall/Hunt.

Friesen, John W., and Virginia Lyons Friesen. (2002). *Aboriginal Education in Canada: A Plea for Integration.* Calgary, AB: Detselig Enterprises.

Goulet, Linda. (2001). Two Teachers of Aboriginal students: Effective Practice in Sociohistorial Realities. *Canadian Journal of Native Education,* 25:1, 68-82.

Grant, Agnes. (1996). *No End of Grief: Indian Residential Schools in Canada.* Winnipeg, MB: Pemmican.

Hampton, Eber. (2000). First Nations Controlled University Education in Canada. *Aboriginal Education: Fulfilling the Promise.* Marlene Brant Castellano, Lynne Davis, and Louise Lahache, eds. Vancouver, BC: University of British Columbia, 208-223.

Hare, Jan, and Jean Barman. (1998). Aboriginal Education: Is There a Way Ahead? *Visions of the Heart: Canadian Aboriginal Issues.* David Long and Olive Patricia Dickason, eds. Toronto, ON: Nelson Canada, 331-360.

Hawthorn, Harry B. (1967). *Survey of Contemporary Indians of Canada.* Two volumes. Ottawa, ON: Department of Indian Affairs and Northern Development.

Kirkness, Verna J. (1999). Native Indian Teachers: A Key to Progress. *Canadian Journal of Native Education,* 23:1, 57-63.

Kowalsky, Laura O., Marja J. Verhoef, Wilfreda E. Thurston, and Gayle E. Rutherford. (1996). Guidelines for Entry into an Aboriginal Community. *The Canadian Journal of Native Studies,* XVI:2, 267-282.

Littlebear, Dick. (1992). Getting Teachers and Parents to Work Together. *Teaching American Indian Students.* Jon Reyhner, ed. Norman, OK: University of Oklahoma, 104-114.

Mader, Christina. (1999). Taking it Back, Passing it on: Reverence for the Ordinary in Bush Cree Teacher Education. *Canadian Journal of Native Studies,* XIX:1, 91-118.

Maina, Faith. (1997). Culturally-Relevant Pedagogy: First Nations Education in Canada. *The Canadian Journal of Native Studies,* XVII:2, 293-314.

Mayer, Martin. (1963). *The Schools.* New York, NY: Anchor Books.

McAlpine, Lynn. (2001). Teacher Training for the new Wilderness: Quantum Leaps. *Aboriginal Education in Canada: A Study in Decolonization.* K.P. Binda and Sharilyn Calliou, eds. Mississauga, ON: Canadian Educators, 105-120.

Ralph, Edwin G. (1993). Enhancing Aboriginal Teacher Education: One Promising Approach. *Canadian Journal of Native Education,* 20:1, 44-62.

Reyhner, John, ed. (1992). *Teaching American Indian Students.* Norman, OK: University of Oklahoma.

Sawyer, Don. (1991). Native Learning Styles: Shorthand for Instructional Adaptations. *Canadian Journal of Native Education,* 18:1, 99-105.

Sterling, Shirley. (2002). Yetko and Sophie: Nlakapamux Cultural Professors. *Canadian Journal of Native Education,* 26:1, 4-10

Taylor, John. (1995). Non-Native Teachers Teaching in Native Communities. *First Nations Education in Canada: The Circle Unfolds.* Marie Battiste and Jean Barman, eds. Vancouver, BC: University of British Columbia, 224-242.

Tiedt, Pamela L., and Iris M. Tiedt. (1979). *Multicultural Teaching: A Handbook of Activities, Information, and Resources.* Boston, MA: Allyn and Bacon.

West, Douglas A. (1995). Epistemological Dependency and Native Peoples: An Essay on the Future of Native/NonNative Relations in Canada. The *Canadian Journal of Native Studies,* XV:2, 279-291.

Wolcott, Harry F. (1967). *A Kwakiutl Village and School.* New York, NY: Holt, Rinehart and Winston.

York, Geoffrey. (1989). *The Dispossessed: Life and Death in Native Canada.* Toronto, ON: Lester & Orpen Dennys.

About the Authors

John W. Friesen, Ph.D., D.Min., D.R.S., a native of Duck Lake, Saskatchewan, is a Profesor in the Faculty of Education and the Faculty of Communication and Culture at the University of Calgary where he teaches courses and conducts research in Aboriginal history and education. He is the author or co-author of more than forty books, including:

The Métis of Canada: An Annotated Bibliography (co-editor). OISE, 1980

Rose of the North, Borealis, 1987

You Can't Get There From here: The Mystique of the North American Plains Indians Culture & Philosophy, Kendall/Hunt, 1995

The Real/Riel Story: An Interpretive History of the Métis People of Canada, second edition, Borealis, 1966

The Community Doukhobors: A People in Transition (co-author), Borealis, 1996

Rediscovering the First Nations of Canada, Detselig Enterprises, 1997

Sayings of the Elders: An Anthology of first Nation's Wisdom, Detselig Enterprises, 1998

First Nations of the Plains: Creative, Adaptable and Enduring, Detselig Enterprises, 1999

Aboriginal Spirituality and Biblical Theology: Closer Than You Think, Detselig Enterprises, 2000

Legends of the Elders, Detselig Enterprises, 2000

Do Christians Forgive? Well, Some Do . . ., Borealis, 2000

Aboriginal Education in Canada: A Pleas for Integration, (co-author), Detselig Enterprises, 2002

Canadian Society in the Twenty-First Century: An Historical Sociological Approach, (co-author), Pearson Canada, 2003

The Palgrave Companion to Utopian Communities in North America, Palgrave Macmillan, 2004

We Are Included: The Métis of Canada Realize Riel's Vision, (co-author), Detselig Enterprises, 2004

Virginia Lyons Friesen, Ph.D., is a Sessional Instructor in the Faculty of Communication and Culture at the University of Calgary where she teaches courses in Canadian culture and Aboriginal education. She is a specialist in Early Childhood Education, and holds a

Certificate in Counseling from the Institute of Pastoral Counseling in Akron, Ohio.

She has co-presented a number of papers at academic conferences, and co-authored several books, including:

Grade Expectations: A Multicultural Handbook for Teachers, Alberta Teachers' Association, 1995

In Defense of Public Schools in North America, Detselig Enterprises, 2001

Aboriginal Education in Canada: A Plea for Integration, Detselig Enterprises, 2002

The Palgrave Companion to Utiopian Communities in North America, Palgrave Macmillan, 2004

More Legends of the Elders, Detselig Enterprises, 2004

Even More Legends of the Elders, Detselig Enterprises, 2005

Still More Legends of the Elders, Detselig Enterprises, 2005

Bibliography

Adams, Howard. (1999). *Tortured People: The Politics of Colonization.* Revised edition. Penticton, BC: Theytus.

Aikenhead, Glen, and Bente Huntley. (1999). Teachers' Views on Aboriginal Students Learning Western and Aboriginal Science. *Canadian Journal of Native Education,* 23:2, 159-175.

Antone, Eileen M. (2000). Empowering Aboriginal Views in Aboriginal Education. *Canadian Journal of Native Education,* 24:2, 92-101.

Antone, Eileen. (2003). Culturally Framing Aboriginal Literacy and Learning. *Canadian Journal of Native Education,* 27:1, 7-15.

Archibald, Jo-ann. (1995). Locally Developed Native Studies Curriculum: An Historical and Philosophical Rationale. *First Nations Education in Canada: The Circle Unfolds.* Marie Battiste and Jean Barman, eds. Vancouver, BC: University of British Columbia, 288-312.

Ashworth, Mary. (1979). *The Forces Which Shaped Them: A History of Minority Group Children in British Columbia.* Vancouver, BC: New Star.

Ashworth, Mary. (1988). *Blessed With Bilingual Brains: Education of Immigrant Children With English as a Second Language.* Vancouver, BC: Pacific Educational.

Barman, Jean. (1986). Separate and Unequal: Indian and White Girls at All Hallows School, 1884-1920. *Indian Education in Canada, Volume 1: The Legacy.* Jean Barman, Yvonne Hébert, and Don McCaskill, eds. Vancouver, BC: University of British Columbia, 110-131.

Barman, Jean, Yvonne Hébert, and Don McCaskill, eds. (1986 and 1987). Native Education in Canada, Volume 1: *The Legacy; and Volume 2: The Challenge.* Vancouver, BC: University of British Columbia.

Barman, Jean, Yvonne Hébert, and Don McCaskill, eds. (1987). The Challenge of Indian Education: An Overview. *Indian Education in Canada, Volume 2: The Challenge.* Jean Barman, Yvonne Hébert, and Don McCaskill, eds. Vancouver, BC: University of British Columbia, 1-21.

Barron, F. Laurie and Joseph Garcea. (1999). The Genesis of Urban Reserves and the Role of Governmental Self-Interest. *Urban Indian Reserves: Forging New Relationships in Saskatchewan.* F. Laurie Barron and Joseph Garcea, eds. Saskatoon, SK: Purich Publishing, 22-52.

Bashford, Lucy, and Hands Heinzerling. (1987). Blue Quills Native Education Centre: A Case Study. *Indian Education in Canada:, Volume 2: The Challenge.* Jean Barman, et. al., eds. Vancouver, BC: University of BrItish Columbia, 126-141.

Battiste, Marie. (1986). Mik'maq Literacy and Cognitive Assimilation. *Indian Education in Canada, Volume 1: The Legacy.* Jean Barman, Yvonne Hébert, and Don McCaskill, eds. Vancouver, BC: University of British Columbia, 23-44.

Battiste, Marie. (2000). Maintaining Aboriginal Identity, Language, and Culture. *Reclaiming Indigenous Voice and Vision.* Marie Battiste, ed. Vancouver, BC: University of British Columbia, 192-208.

Battiste, Marie, ed. (2000). *Reclaiming Indigenous Voice and Vision.* Vancouver, BC: University of British Columbia.

Battiste, Marie (2000). *Protecting Indigenous Knowledge and Heritage: A Global Challenge.* Saskatoon, SK: Purich.

Battiste, Marie, and Jean Barman, eds. (1995). *First Nations Education in Canada: The Circle Unfolds.* Vancouver, BC: University of British Columbia.

Battiste, Marie and James (Sa'ke'j) Youngblood Henderson, eds. (2000). *Protecting Indigenous Knowledge and Heritage.* Saskatoon, SK: Purich.

Bazylak, Darryl. (2002). Journeys to Success: Perceptions of Five Female Aboriginal High School Graduates. *Canadian Journal of Native Education,* 26:2, 134-151.

Bear Heart. (1998). *The Wind Is My Mother: The Life and Teachings of a Native American Shaman.* New York, NY: Berkley.

Benedict, Ruth. (1934). *Patterns of Culture.* Boston, MA: Houghton-Mifflin.

Bennett, Christian I. (1995). *Comprehensive Multicultural Education: Theory and Practice.* Third edition. Boston, MA: Allyn and Bacon.

Berry, J.W. (1999). Aboriginal Cultural Identity. *The Canadian Journal of Native Studies,* XIX:1, 1-36.

Berton, Pierre. (1974). *The National Dream: The Last Spike.* Toronto, ON: McClelland and Stewart.

Binda, K.P., and Sharilyn Calliou, eds. (2001). *Aboriginal Education in Canada: A Study in Decolonization.* Mississauga, ON: Canadian Educators.

Boldt, Menno. (1993). *Surviving as Indians: The Challenge of Self-Government.* Toronto, ON: University of Toronto.

Brascoupé, Simon. (2000). Aboriginal Peoples' Vision of the Future: Interweaving Traditional Knowledge and New Technologies. *Visions of the Heart: Canadian Aboriginal Issues.* David Long and Olive Patricia Dickason, eds. Toronto, ON: Harcourt Canada, 411-432.

Breton, M. (1994). On the Meaning of Empowerment and Empowerment-Oriented Social Work Practice. *Social Work With Groups,* 17:3, 23-37.

Brookes, Sonia. (1990). An Analysis of Indian Education Policy, 1960-1989. Unpublished Master's Thesis, Calgary, AB: University of Calgary.

Brookes, Sonia. (1991). The Persistence of Native Educational Policy in Canada. *The Cultural Maze: Complex Questions on Native Destiny in Western Canada.* John W. Friesen, ed. Calgary, AB: Detselig Enterprises, 163-180.

Brookes, Sonia. (1990). An Analysis of Indian Education Policy, 1960-1989. Unpublished M.A. Thesis, Calgary, AB: The University of Calgary.

Brown, Dee. (1981). *Bury My Heart at Wounded Knee.* New York: Pocket Books.

Bruchac, Joseph. (1993). *The Native American Sweat-lodge: History and Legends.* Freedom, CA: The Crossing Press.

Buckley, Helen. (1993). *From Wooden Ploughs to Welfare: Why Indian Policy Failed in the Prairie Provinces.* Montreal, PQ: McGill-Queen's University.

Burns, George E. (1998). Factors and Themes in Native Education and School Boards/First Nations Tuiition Negotiations and Tuition Agreement Schooling. *Canadian Journal of Native Education,* 22:1, 53-66.

Burrell, Gordon, Robert Young, and Richard Price, eds. (1975). *Indian Treaties and the Law: An Interpretation for Laymen.* Edmonton, AB: Indian Association of Alberta, 1-10.

Cajete, Gregory. (1994). *Look to the Mountain: An Ecology of Indigenous Education.* Durango, CO: Kivakí Press.

Callahan, Raymond E. (1964). *Education and the Cult of Efficiency: A Study of the Social Forces that have Shaped the Administration of the Public Schools.* Chicago, IL: University of Chicago.

Campbell, Maria. (1973). *Halfbreed: A Proud and Bitter Canadian Legacy.* Toronto, ON: McClelland and Stewart.

Cardinal, Harold. (1969). *The Unjust Society: The Tragedy of Canada's Indians.* Edmonton, AB: Hurtig.

Cardinal, Harold. (1977). *The Rebirth of Canada's Indians.* Edmonton, AB: Hurtig.

Carlson, Paul H. (1998). *The Plains Indians.* College Station, TX: Texas A & M University.

Castellano, Marlene Brant, Lynne Davis, and Louise Lahache. (2000). Innovations in Education Practice. *Aboriginal Education: Fulfilling the*

Promise. Castellano, Marlene Brant, Lynne Davis, and Louise Lahache, eds. Vancouver, BC: University of British Columbia, 97-100.

Castellano, Marlene Brant, Lynne Davis, and Louise Lahache, eds. (2000). *Aboriginal Education: Fulfilling the Promise.* Vancouver, BC: University of British Columbia.

Chalmers, John W. (1972). *Education Behind the Buckskin Curtain.* Edmonton, AB: University of Alberta.

Chalmers, J. W. (1974). Marguerite Bourgeoys: Preceptress of New France. *Profiles of Canadian Educators.* Robert S. Patterson, John W. Chalmers, and John W. Friesen, eds. Toronto, ON: D.C. Heath, 4-20.

Churchill, Ward. (1998). *A little Matter of Genocide: Holocaust and Denial in the Americas 1492 to the Present.* Winnipeg, MB: Arbeiter Ring.

Citizens Plus, The Indian Chiefs of Alberta. A Presentation by the Indian Chiefs of Alberta to the Right Honourable Pierre Elliott Trudeau, Prime Minister and the Government of Canada, June, 1970; also known as "The Red Paper."

Clarke, Jean Illsley. (1978). *Self-esteem: A Family Affair.* Minneapolis, MN: Winston.

Colorado, Pam. (1988). Bridging Native and Western Science. *Convergence,* 21:2-3, 57.

Communities First: First Nations Governance Under the Indian Act. (2001). Ottawa, ON: Published under the authority of the Minister of Indian Affairs and Northern Development.

Conrad, Margaret, Alvin Finkel, and Cornelius Jaenen. (1993). *History of Canadian Peoples: Beginnings to 1867.* Toronto, ON: Copp Clark Pitman.

Cornish, George H. (1881). *Encyclopedia of Methodism in Canada.* Toronto, ON: Methodist Book.

Couture, Joseph E. (1985). Traditional Thinking, Feeling, and Learning. *Multicultural Education Journal,* 3:2, 4-16.

Couture, Joseph E. (1991). Explorations in Native Knowing. *The Cultural Maze: Complex Questions on Native Destiny in Western Canada.* John W. Friesen, ed. Calgary, AB: Detselig Enterprises, 53-76.

Couture, Joseph E. (1991). The Role of Native Elders: Emergent Issues. *The Cultural Maze: Complex Questions on Native Destiny in Western Canada,* John W. Friesen, ed. Calgary, AB: Detselig Enterprises, 201-218.

Cummins, J. and M. Swain. (1986). *Bilingualism in Education.* London, UK: Longman.

Deloria, Jr., Vine. (1995). *Red Earth, White Lies: Native Americans and the Myth of Scientific Fact.* New York, NY: Scribner.

Dempsey, Hugh A. (1979). *Indian Tribes of Alberta.* Calgary, AB: The Glenbow Museum.

Dempsey, Hugh A. (1976). *Crowfoot: Chief of the Blackfoot.* Edmonton, AB: Hurtig.

Dickason, Olive Patricia. (1984). *The Myth of the Savage and the Beginnings of French Colonialism in the Americas.* Edmonton, AB: University of Alberta.

Dickason, Olive Patricia. (1993). *Canada's First Nations: A History of Founding Peoples From Earliest Times.* Toronto, ON: McClelland and Stewart.

Dion, Joseph F. (1979). *My Tribe: The Crees.* Calgary, AB: Glenbow Museum.

Doige, Lynda A. Curwen. (2003). A Missing link Between Traditional Aboriginal Education and the Western System of Education. *Canadian Journal of Native Education,* 27:2, 144-160.

Dorais, Louis-Jacques. (1995). Language, Culture and Identity: Some Inuit Examples. *The Canadian Journal of Native Studies,* XV:2, 293-308.

Driver, Harold E. (1968). *Indians of North America.* Chicago, IL: University of Chicago.

Duff, Wilson. (1997). *The Indian History of British Columbia: The Impact of the White Man.* Victoria, BC: The Royal British Columbia Museum.

Duquette, Cheryl. (2000). Becoming a Teacher: Experiences of First Nations Student Teachers in Isolated Communities. *Canadian Journal of Native Education,* 24:2, 134-14.

Dyck, Noel. (1997). *Differing Visions: Administering Indian Residential Schooling in Prince Albert, 1867-1995.* Halifax, NS: Fernwood.

Elofson, Warren, and Betty-Lou Elofson. (1988). Improving Native Education in the Province of Alberta. *Canadian Journal of Native Education,* 15:1, 31-38.

Erasmus, George. (1989). The Solution We Favour for Change. *Drumbeat: Anger and Renewal in Indian Country.* Boyce Richardson, ed. Toronto, ON: Summerhill, 295-302.

Erdoes, Richard. (1972). *The Sun Dance People: The Plains Indians, Their Past and Present.* New York, NY: Random House.

Ermine, Willie. (1995). Aboriginal Epistemology. *First Nations Education in Canada: The Circle Unfolds.* Marie Battiste and Jean Barman, eds. Vancouver, BC: University of British Columbia, 101-112.

Evans, Mike, James McDonald, and Deanna Nyce. (1999). Acting Across Boundaries in Aboriginal Curricuum Development: Examples from Northern British Columbia. *Canadian Jorumal of Native Education,* 23:2, 190-205.

Ewers, John C. (1989). *The Blackfeet: Raiders on the Northwestern Plains.* Norman, OK: University of Oklahoma.

Fettes, Mark, and Ruth Norton. (2000). Voices of Winter: Aboriginal Languages and Public Policy in Canada. *Aboriginal Education: Fulfilling the Promise.* Marlene Brant Castellano, Lynne Davis and Louise Lahache, eds. Vancouver, BC: University of British Columbia, 29-54.

Findley, L. M. (2000). Foreword. *Reclaiming Indigenous Voice and Vision.* Marie Battiste, ed. Vancouver, BC: University of British Columbia, ix-xiii.

Fisher, Robin. (1978).*Contact and Conflict: Indian-European Relations in British Columbia, 1774-1890.* Vancouver, BC: University of British Columbia.

Flanagan, Thomas. (2000). *First Nations? Second Thoughts.* Montreal, PQ: McGill-Queen's University.

Fleras, Augie. (2000). The Politics of Jurisdiction: Pathway or Predicament. *Visions of the Heart: Canadian Aboriginal Issues.* Second edition. David Long and Olive Patricia Dickason, eds. Toronto, ON: Harcourt Canada, 107-142.

Fox, Terry, and David Long. (2000). Struggles within the Circle: Violence, Healing and Health on a First Nations Reserve. *Visions of the Heart: Canadian Aboriginal Issues.* Second edition. David Long and Olive Patricia Dickason, eds. Toronto, ON: Harcourt Canada, 271-301.

Francis, R. Douglas, Richard Jones, and Donald B. Smith. (1988). *Origins: Canadian History to Confederation.* Vol. 1, Toronto, ON: Holt, Rinehart and Winston.

Frideres, James. (1983). *Native People in Canada.* Second edition. Scarborough, ON: Prentice-Hall.

Frideres, James S. (1988). *Native Peoples in Canada: Contemporary Conflicts.* Third Edition. Scarborough, ON: Prentice-Hall.

Frideres, James S. (1993). *Native Peoples in Canada: Contemporary Conflicts.* Fourth edition. Scarborough, ON: Prentice-Hall.

Frideres, James S., and René Gadacz. (2001). *Native Peoples in Canada: Contemporary conflicts.* Sixth edition. Scarborough, ON: Prentice-Hall.

Friesen, John W. (Spring, 1974). John McDougall: The Spirit of a Pioneer. *Alberta Historical Review,* 2:2, 9-17.

Friesen, John W. (1974). John McDougall, Educator of Indians. *Profiles of Canadian Educators.* Robert S. Patterson, John W. Chalmers and John W. Friesen, eds. Toronto: D. C. Heath, 57-76.

Friesen, John W. (1977). *People, Culture and Learning.* Calgary, AB: Detselig Enterprises.

Friesen, John W. (1983). *Schools With A Purpose.* Calgary, AB: Detselig Enterprises.

Friesen, John W. (1985). *When Cultures Clash: Case Studies in Multiculturalism.* Calgary, AB: Detselig Enterprises.

Friesen, John W. (1987). *Rose of the North.* Ottawa, ON: Borealis.

Friesen, John W. (November, 1989). The Human Side of Prairie Settlement. *Multicultural Education Journal,* 7:2, 28-36.

Friesen, John W. (1991). Highlights of Western Canadian Indian History. *The Cultural Maze: Complex Questions on Native Destiny in Western Canada.* John W. Friesen, ed. Calgary, AB: Detselig Enterprises, 1-22.

Friesen, John W. (1991). Teaching in a University Native Education Program. *The Cultural Maze: Complex Questions on Native Destiny in Western Canada.* John W. Friesen, ed. Calgary, AB: Detselig Enterprises, 229-242.

Friesen, John W. (1993). Formal Schooling Among the Ancient Ones: The Mystique of the Kiva. *American Indian Culture and Research Journal,* 17:4, 55-68.

Friesen, John W. (1993). *When Cultures Clash: Case Studies in Multiculturalism.* Second edition. Calgary, AB: Detselig Enterprises.

Friesen, John W. (1994). *The Riel (Real) Story: An Interpretive History of the Métis People of Canada.* Ottawa, ON: Borealis.

Friesen, John W. (1995). *You Can't Get There From Here: The Mystique of North American Plains Indians' Culture & Philosophy.* Dubuque, IA: Kendall/Hunt.

Friesen, John W. (1995). *Pick One: A User-Friendly Guide to Religion.* Calgary, AB: Detselig Enterprises.

Friesen, John W. (1998). *Sayings of the Elders: An Anthology of First Nations' Wisdom.* Calgary, AB: Detselig Enterprises.

Friesen, John W., and Alice L. Boberg. (1990). *Introduction to Teaching: A Socio-cultural Approach.* Dubuque, IA: Kendall-Hunt.

Friesen, John W., and Virginia Lyons Friesen. (2002). *Aboriginal Education in Canada: A Plea for Integration.* Calgary, AB: Detselig Enterprises.

Friesen, John W., and Virginia Lyons Friesen. (2004). *We Are Included: The Métis People of Canada Realize Riel's Vision.* Calgary, AB: Detselig Enterprises.

Friesen, John W., and Terry Lusty. (1980). *The Métis of Canada: An Annotated Bibliography.* Toronto, ON: Ontario Institute for Studies in Education.

Furniss, Elizabeth. (1995). *Victims of Benevolence: The Dark Legacy of the Williams Lake Residential School.* Vancouver, BC: Arsenal Pulp.

Gamlin, Peter. (2003). Transformation and Aboriginal Literacy. *Canadian Journal of Native Education,* 27:1, 16-22.

Glazer, Nathan. (1980). Toward a Sociology of Small Ethnic Groups, a Discourse and Discussion. *Canadian Ethnic Studies,* XII:2, 1-16.

Goddard, John. (1992). *Last Stand of the Lubicon Cree.* Vancouver, BC: Douglas and McIntyre.

Goddard, J. Tim. (2002). Ethnoculturally Relevant Programming in Northern Schools. *Canadian Journal of Native Education,* 26:32, 124-133.

Goulet, Linda. (2001). Two Teachers of Aboriginal students: Effective Practice in Sociohistorial Realities. *Canadian Journal of Native Education,* 25:1, 68-82.

Goulet, Linda, Marjorie Dressyman-Lavalee, and Yvonne McLeod. (2001).*Aboriginal Education in Canada: A Study in Decolonization.* K. P. Binda and Sharilyn Calliou, eds. Mississauga, ON: Canadian Educators, 137-153.

Grant, Agnes. (1995). The Challenge for Universities. *First Nations Education in Canada: The Circle Unfolds.* Marie Battiste and Jean Barman, eds. Vancouver, BC: University of British Columbia, 208-223.

Grant, Agnes. (1996). *No End of Grief: Indian Residential Schools in Canada.* Winnipeg, MB: Pemmican.

Gresko, Jacqueline. (1986). Creating Little Dominions Within the Dominion: Early Catholic Indian Schools in Saskatchewan and British Columbia. *Indian Education in Canada, Volume 1: The Legacy.* Jean Barman, Yvonne Hébert, and Don McCaskill, eds. Vancouver, BC: University of British Columbia, 88-109.

Grinnell, George Bird. (1900). *The North American Indians of To-day.* London, UK: C. Arthur Pearson, Ltd.

Haig-Brown, Celia. (1993). *Resistance and Renewal: Surviving the Indian Residential School.* Vancouver, BC: Tillacum Library.

Hampton, Eber. (1995). Towards a Redefinition of Indian Education. *First Nations Education in Canada: The Circle Unfolds.* Marie Battiste and Jean Barman, eds. Vancouver, BC: University of British Columbia, 5-46.

Hampton, Eber. (2000). First Nations Controlled University Education in Canada. *Aboriginal Education: Fulfilling the Promise.* Marlene Brant Castellano, Lynne Davis, and Louise Lahache, eds. Vancouver, BC: University of British Columbia, 208-223.

Hanks, Lucien M. Jr., and Jane Richardson Hanks. (1950). *Tribe Under Trust: A Study of the Blackfoot Reserve of Alberta.* Toronto, ON: University of Toronto.

Hanohano, Peter. (1999). The Spiritual Imperative of Native Epistemology: Restoring Harmony and Balance to Education. *Canadian Journal of Native Education*, 23:2, 206-219.

Hare, Jan, and Jean Barman. (1998). Aboriginal Education: Is There a Way Ahead? *Visions of the Heart: Canadian Aboriginal Issues*. David Long and Olive Patricia Dickason, eds. Toronto, ON: Nelson Canada, 331-360.

Harrod, Howard L. (1992). *Renewing the World: Plains Indians Religion and Morality*. Tucson, AZ: University of Arizona.

Hart, E. J. (1983). *The Selling of Canada: The CPR and the Beginning of Canadian Tourism*. Banff, AB: Altitude.

Hawthorn, Harry B. (1967). *Survey of Contemporary Indians of Canada*. Two volumes. Ottawa, ON: Department of Indian Affairs and Northern Development.

Henderson, James (Sa'ke'j) Youngblood. (2000). Postcolonial Ledger Drawing: Legal Reform. *Protecting Indigenous Knowledge and Heritage*. Marie Battiste and James (Sa'ke'j) Youngblood, eds. Saskatoon, SK: Purich, 172-178.

Higham, C. L. (2000). *Noble, Wretched & Redeemable: Protestant Missionaries to the Indians in Canada and the United States, 1820-1900*. Albuquerque, NM: University of New Mexico.

Hoebel, E. Adamson. (1965). *The Cheyennes: Indians of the Great Plains*. New York: Holt, Rinehart and Winston.

Horse Capture, George P. (1989). *Pow wow*. Cody, WY: Buffalo Bill Historical Center.

Hylton, John H. (1999). Future Prospects for Aboriginal Self-Government in Canada.*Aboriginal Self-Government in Canada*. John H. Hylton, ed. Saskatoon, SK: Purich. 432-455.

Illich, Ivan. (1971). The DeSchooling of Society. *Alternatives in Education*. Bruce Rusk, ed. Toronto, oN: General, 105-106.

Indian Affairs Branch. (1952). *Annual Report*. Ottawa, ON: Department of Citizenship and Development.

Jaenen, Cornelius. (1986). Education for Francization: The Case of New France in the Seventeenth Century. *Indian Education in Canada*, Vol. I: *The Legacy*. Jean Barman, Don McCaskill, and Yvonne Hébert, eds. Vancouver, BC: University of British Columbia, 45-63.

Jenness, Diamond. (1986). *The Indians of Canada*. Toronto, ON: University of Toronto.

Jennings, Jesse D. (1978). *Ancient Native Americans*. Sanfrancisco, CA: Freeman.

Johnson, F. Henry. (1968). *A Brief History of Canadian Education*. Toronto, ON: McGraw-Hill.

Johnston, Basil. *(1988). Ojibway Heritage: The Ceremonies, Rituals, Songs, Dances, Prayers, and Legends of the Ojibway*. Toronto, ON: McClelland and Stewart.

Johnston, Basil. (1995). *The Manitous: The Spiritual World of the Ojibway*. Vancouver, BC: Key Porter.

Jones, Christianna. (2003). Self-Management and Self-Direction in the Success of Native Literacy Learners. *Canadian Journal of Native Education*, 27:1, 45-54.

Josephy, Alvin M. Jr. (1968). *The Indian Heritage of America*. New York: Alfred A. Knopf.

Kimura, Takashi. (1998). The Cayuga Chief Jacob E. Thomas: Walking a Narrow Path Between Two Worlds. *The Canadian Journal of Native Studies*, XVII:2, 313-333.

King, A. Richard. (1967). *The School At Mopass: A Problem of Identity*. New York, NY: Holt, Rinehart & Winston.

Kirkness, Verna J. (July/August, 1981). *The Education of Canadian Indian* Children. Child Welfare, LX:7, 446-455.-

Kirkness, Verna J. (1998). The Critical State of Aboriginal Languages in Canada. *Canadian Journal of Native Education*, 22:1, 93-107.

Kirkness, Verna J. (1998). Our Peoples' Education: Cut the Shackles, Cut the Crap; Cut the Mustard. *Canadian Journal of Native Education*, 22:1, 10-15.

Kirkness, Verna J. (1999). Native Indian Teachers: A Key to Progress. *Canadian Journal of Native Education*, 23:1, 57-63.

Knudtson, Peter and David Suzuki. (1992). *Wisdom of the Elders*. Toronto, ON: Stoddart.

Kowalsky, Laura O., Marja J. Verhoef, Wilfreda E. Thurston, and Gayle E. Rutherford. (1996). Guidelines for Entry into an Aboriginal Community. *The Canadian Journal of Native Studies*, XVI:2, 267-282.

Krotz, Larry. (1990). *Indian Country: Inside Another Canada*. Toronto,ON: McClelland and Stewart.

Laenui, Poka. (2000). Processes of Decolonization. *Reclaiming Indigenous Voice and Vision*. Marie Battiste, ed. Vancouver, BC: University of British Columbia, 150-160.

Lambert, W.E. (1983). Deciding on Languages of Instruction: Psychological and Social Considerations. *Multicultural and Multilingual Education in Immigrant Countries*. by Torsten Husen and Susan Oppe, eds. Oxford, UK: Pergamon Press, 93-104.

Lambert, W. E., and G. R. Tucker. (1972). *Bilingual Education of Children: The St. Lambert Experiment*. Rowley, MA: Newbury House.

LaRoque, Emma. (1975). *Defeathering the Indian*. Agincourt, ON: The Book Society of Canada.

Leavitt, Robert. (1995). Language and Cultural Content in Native Education. *First Nations in Canada: The Circle Unfolds*. Marie Battiste and Jean Barman, eds. Vancouver, BC: University of British Columbia, 124-138.

Lincoln, Kenneth. (1985). *Native American Renaissance*. Berkeley, CA: University of California.

Little Bear, Leroy. (2000). Jagged Worldviews Colliding. *Reclaiming Indigenous Voice and Vision*. Marie Battiste, ed. Vancouver, BC: University of British Columbia, 77-85.

Littlebear, Dick. (1992). Getting Teachers and Parents to Work Together. *Teaching American Indian Students*. Jon Reyhner, ed. Norman, OK: University of Oklahoma, 104-114.

Littlejohn, Catharine, and Shirley Fredeen. (1993). Indian Language Programs in Saskatchewan: A Survey. *Aboriginal Languages and Education: The Canadian Experience*. Sonia Morris, Keith McLeod, and Marcel Danesi, eds. Oakville, ON: Mosaic, 57-84.

Long, David and Patricia Dickason, eds. (2000). *Visions of the Heart: Canadian Aboriginal Issues*. Second edition. Toronto, ON: Harcourt Canada.

Lowie, Robert. (1924). *Primitive Religion*. New York: Grosset and Dunlop.

Lowie, Robert M. (1963). *Indians of the Plains*. New York, NY: The Natural History Press.

Lucas, Christopher. (1984). *Foundations of Education: Schooling and the Social Order*. Englewood Cliffs, NJ: Prentice-Hall.

Lupul, Manoly, R. (1970). Education in Western Canada Before 1873. *Canadian Education: A History*. J. Donald Wilson, Robert M. Stamp. and Louis Philippe Audet, eds. Scarborough, ON: Prentice-Hall, 241-264.

Lyons, Oren. (1984). Spirituality, Equality, and Natural Law. *Pathways to Self-Determination: Canadian Indians and the Canadian State*. Leroy LittleBear, Menno Boldt, and J. Anthony Long, eds Toronto, ON: University of Toronto, 5-13.

MacLean, John. (1896). *Canada's Savage Folk*. London: William Briggs.

Mader, Christina. (1999). Taking it Back, Passing it on: Reverence for the Ordinary in Bush Cree Teacher Education. *Canadian Journal of Native Studies*, XIX:1, 91-118.

Maina, Faith. (1997). Culturally-Relevant Pedagogy: First Nations Education in Canada. *The Canadian Journal of Native Studies*, XVII:2, 293-314.

Manitoba Association for Native Languages. (1986). *Report of the Native Education Concerns Group on the Native Language Enrichment Project.* Winnipeg, MB: MANL Annual Report, April 1985 to March 1986.

Manuel, George, and Michael Posluns. (1974). *The Fourth World: An Indian Reality.* Don Mills, ON: Collier Macmillan Canada.

Marker, Michael. (2000). Economics and Local Self-Determination: Describing the Clash Zone in First Nations Education. *Canadian Journal of Native Education*, 24:1, 30-44.

Matthews, Maureen, and Roger Roulette. (1998). Fair Wind's Dream: *Naamiwan Obawaajigewin. Reading Beyond Words: Contexts for Native History.* Jennifer S. H. Brown and Elizabeth Vibert, eds. Peterborough, ON: Broadview, 330-363.

Mayer, Martin. (1963). *The Schools.* New York, NY: Anchor Books.

McAlpine, Lynn. (2001). Teacher Training for the new Wilderness: Quantum Leaps. *Aboriginal Education in Canada: A Study in Decolonization.* K. P. Binda and Sharilyn Calliou, eds. Mississauga, ON: Canadian Educators, 105-120.

McClintock, Walter. (1992). *The Old North Trail.* Lincoln, NB: University of Nebraska.

McDonald, N.G. (1974). David J. Goggin: Promoter of National Schools. *Profiles of Canadian Educators.* Robert S. Patterson, John W. Chalmers and John W. Friesen, eds. Toronto, ON: D C. Heath, 167-191.

McDonald, N.G. (1974). Alexandre Tache: Defender of the Old Regime. *Profiles of Canadian Educators.* Robert S. Patterson, John W. Chalmers, and John W. Friesen, eds. Toronto, ON: D.C. Heath, 141-166.

McDonnell, R.F., and R.C. Depew. (1999). Self-Government and Self-Determination in Canada: A Critical Commentary. *Aboriginal Self-Government in Canada.* John H. Hylton, ed. Saskatoon, SK: Purich Publishing, 352-376.

McDougall, John. (1903). *In the Days of the Red River Rebellion.* Toronto, ON: William Briggs.

McFarlane, Peter. (1998). Aboriginal Leadership. *Visions of the Heart: Canadian Aboriginal Issues.* David Long and Olive Patricia Dickason, eds. Second edition. Scarborough, ON: Nelson Canada, 49-80.

McGaa, Ed Eagle Man. (1995). *Native Wisdom: Perceptions of the Natural Way.* Minneapolis, MN: Four Directions.

McMillan, Alan D (1988). *Native Peoples and Cultures of Canada.* Vancouver, BC: Douglas & McIntyre.

McMillan, Alan D. (1995). *Native Peoples and Cultures in Canada: An Anthropological Overview.* Revised edition. Vancouver, BC: Douglas & McIntyre.

Medicine, Beatrice. (1987). My Elders Tell Me. *Indian Education inCanada, The Challenge, Volume One: The Legacy.* Jean Barman, Yvonne Hébert, and Don McCaskill, eds. Vancouver, BC: University of British Columbia, 142-152.

Meili, Diane. (1991). *Those Who Know: Profiles of Alberta Elders.* Edmonton, AB: NeWest.

Melling, John. (1967). *Right to a Future: the Native Peoples of Canada.* Toronto, ON: T.H. Best.

Miller, Alan D. (1995). *Native Peoples and Cultures of Canada.* Revised edition. Vancouver, BC: Douglas and McIntyre.

Miller, J. R. (1987). The Irony of Residential Schooling. *Canadian Journal of Native Education.* 14:2, 3-14.

Miller, J. R. (2000). *Skyscrapers Hide the Heavens: A History of Indian-White Relations in Canada.* Third edition. Toronto, ON: University of Toronto.

Mollica, Anthony. (1989). Language Learning: the Key to Understanding and Harmony. *Language and Society.* 26: 40-41.

Moore, Patrick J. (2003). Lessons on the Land: The Role of Kaska Elders in a University Course. *Canadian Journal of Native Education,* 27:1, 127-139.

Morris, Joann Sebastien and Richard T. Price. (1991). Community Control Issues and the Experience of Alexander's Kipohtakaw Education Centre. *The Cultural Maze: Complex Questions on Native Destiny in Western Canada.* John W. Friesen, ed. Calgary, AB: Detselig Enterprises, 181-198.

Morrison, R. Bruce, and C. Roderick Wilson. (1986). *Native Peoples: The Canadian Experience.* Toronto, ON: McClelland and Stewart.

Morrison, R. Bruce, and C. Roderick Wilson. (1995). *Native Peoples: The Canadian Experience.* Revised edition. Toronto, ON: McClelland and Stewart.

Nicholas, Andrea Bear (2001). Canada's Colonial Mission: The Great White Bird. *Aboriginal Education in Canada: A Study in Decolonization.* K. P. Binda, and Sharilyn Calliou, eds. Mississauga, ON: Canadian Educators, 9-34.

Norris, Mary Jane. (1998). Aboriginal Peoples in Canada: Demographic and Linguistic Perspectives. *Visions of the Heart: Canadian Aboriginal Issues.*

Second edition. David Long and Olive Patricia Dickason, eds. Toronto, ON: Nelson Canada, 167-236.

Norton, Ruth W. (1989). Analysis of Policy on Native Languages: A Comparison of Government Policy and Native Preferences of Native Language Policy. Unpublished paper. Calgary, AB: University of Calgary, 35 pp.

O'Keefe, Michael. (1990). *An Analysis of Attitudes Towards Official Languages Policy Among Anglophones.* Ottawa, ON: Office of the Commissioner of Official Languages.

Okadale, Suzanne. (May/June, 2002). Creating Continuity Between Self and the Other: First Person Narration in an Amazonian Ritual Context. *Ethos,* 30:1-2, 158-175.

Oskaboose, Gilbert. (1980). To be Indian. *Indian News.* 21:8, (November), 3.

Owen, Roger C., James Deetz, and Anthony D. Fisher, eds. (1968). *The North American Indians: A Sourcebook.* New York: Macmillan.

Palmer, Howard. (1982). *Patterns of Prejudice: A History of Nativism in Alberta.* Toronto, ON: McClelland and Stewart.

Pattanayak, D. P. (1987). *Multilingualism and Multiculturalism: Britain and India.* Occasional Paper No. 1, London, UK: International Association for Intercultural Education.

Paulsen, Rhonda. (2003). Native Literacy: A Living Language. *Canadian Journal of Native Education,* 27:1, 23-28.

Paupanekis, Kenneth, and David Westfall. (2001). Teaching Native language Programs: Survival Strategies. *Aboriginal Education in Canada: A Study in Decolonization.* K. P. Binda and Sharilyn Calliou, eds. Mississauga, ON: Canadian Educators, 89-104.

Patterson, E. Palmer. (1972). *The Canadian Indian.* Toronto, ON: Macmillan.

Pelletier, Wilfred. (n.d.) Two articles. Toronto, ON: Neewin Publishing Co., quoted in J. S. Frideres. (1974). *Canada's Indians: Contemporary conflicts.* Scarborough, ON: Prentice-Hall, 105-106.

Pelletier, Wilfred, and Ted Poole. (1973). *No Foreign Land: The Biography of a North American Indian.* Torotono, ON: McClelland and Stewart.

Persson, Diane. (1986). The Changing Experience of Indian Residential Schooling: Blue Quills, 1931-1970. *Indian Education in Canada, Vol. I, The Legacy.* Jean Barman, et. al., eds. Vancouver, BC: University of British Columbia, 150-168.

Ponting, J. Rick, ed). (1986). *Arduous Journey: Canadian Indians and Decolonization.* Toronto, ON: McClelland and Stewart.

Ponting, J. Rick. (1997). Getting a Handle on Recommendations of the Royal Commission on Aboriginal Peoples. *First Nations in Canada:*

Perspectives on Opportunity, Empowerment, and Self-Determination J. Rick Ponting, ed. Toronto, ON: McGraw-Hill Ryerson, 445-472.

Poonwassie. Anne, and Ann Charter. (2001). Counselling Aboriginal Students: Bridging of Conflicting Worldviews. *Aboriginal Education in Canada.* K. P. Binda and Sharilyn Callious, eds. Mississauga, ON: Canadian Educators, 121-136.

Porterfield, Amanda. (1990). American Indian Spirituality as a Countercultural Movement. *Religion in North America.* Christopher Vecsey, ed. Moscow, ID: University of Idaho, 136-151.

Purich, Donald. (1986). *Our Land: Native Rights in Canada.* Toronto, ON: James Lorimer.

Purich, Donald. (1988). *The Métis.* Toronto: ON: James Lorimer.

Radin, Paul. (1937). *Primitive Religion: Its Nature and Origin.* New York: Viking.

Ralph, Edwin G. (1993). Enhancing Aboriginal Teacher Education: One Promising Approach. *Canadian Journal of Native Education,* 20:1, 44-62.

Ray, Arthur J. (1974). *Indians in the Fur Trade: Their Role as Trappers, Hunters and Middlemen in the Lands Southwest of Hudson Bay, 1660-1870.* Toronto, ON: University of Toronto.

Red Fox, Cief William. (1971). *The Memoirs of Chief Red Fox.* New York, NY: McGraw-Hill.

Regnier, Robert. (1995). The Sacred Circle: An Aboriginal Approach to Healing Education at an Urban High School. *First Nations in Canada: The Circle Unfolds.* Marie Battiste and Jean Barman, eds. Vancouver, BC: University of British Columbia, 313-329.

Restoule, Jean-Paul. (2000). Aboriginal Identity: the Need for Historical and Contextual Perspectives. *Canadian Journal of Native Education,* 24:2, 102-112.

Reyhner, John, ed. (1992). *Teaching American Indian* Students. Norman, OK: University of Oklahoma.

Reyhner, John, ed. (1992). *Adapting Curriculumn to Culture. Teaching American Indian Students.* Norman, OK: University of Oklahoma, 96-103.

Rich, E. E. (1976). *The Fur Trade and the Northwest to 1857.* Toronto, ON: McClelland and Stewart.

Richardson, Boyce, ed. (1989). *Drumbeat: Anger and Renewal in Indian Country.* Toronto, ON: Summerhill.

Riley, Del. (1984). What Canada's Indians Want and the Difficulties of Getting It. *Pathways to Self-Determinaiton: Canadian Indians and the*

Canadian State. Leroy Littlebear, Menno Boldt, and Anthony Long, eds. Toronto, ON: University of Toronto, 159-163.

Roberts=Faiti, Gloria. (1997). Encouraging Self-Esteem in Early Childhood. *Include Me Too! Human Diversity in Early Childhood.* Kenise Murphy Kilbride, ed. Toronto, ON: Harcourt Brace, Canada, 83-105.

Ross, Rupert. (1992). *Dancing With a Ghost: Exploring Indian Reality.* Markham, ON: Reed Books.

Sawyer, Don. (1991). Native Learning Styles: Shorthand for Instructional Adaptations.*Canadian Journal of Native Education,* 18:1, 99-105.

Schmidt, Wilhelm. (1965). The Nature, Attributes, and Worship of the Primitive High God. *Reader in Comparative Religion: An Anthropological Approach.* William A. Lessa and Evon Z. Vogt, eds. New York, NY: Harper and Row, 21-33.

Schukltz, Marylou, and Miriam Kroeger, eds. (June, 1996). *Teaching and Learning with Native Americans: A Hndbook for Non-Native American Adult Educators.* Phoenix, AZ: Arizona Adult Literacy and Technology Resource Center.

Sciara, Frank J., and Richard K. Jantz. (1972). *Accountibility in American Education.* Boston, MA: Allyn and Bacon.

Scott, Andrew. (1997). *The Promise of Paradise: Utopian Communities in B.C.* Vancouver, BC: Whitecap.

Sealey, D. Bruce, and Verna J. Kirkness. (1973). *Indians Without Tipis: A Resource Book by Indians and Métis.* Vancouver, BC: William Clare.

Sealey, D. Bruce, and Antoine S. Lussier. (1975). *The Métis: Canada's Forgotten People.* Winnipeg, MB: Manitoba Métis Federation.

Seton, Ernest Thompson, and Julia M. Seton. (1966). *The Gospel of the Redman: A Way of Life.* Santa Fe, NM: Seton Village.

Siccone, Frank. (1995). *Celebrating Diversity: Building Self-Esteem in Today's Multicultural Classrooms.* Boston, MA: Allyn and Bacon.

Slobodin, Richard. (1966). *Métis of the MacKenzie District.* Ottawa, ON: Centre Canadien de Recherches en Anthropologie, Universite Saint-Paul.

Smith, W. Alan. (Spring, 1995). A Cherokee Way of Knowing: Can Native American Spirituality Impact Religious Education? *Religious Education,* 90:2, 241-253.

Smith, Murray. (2001). Relevant Curricula and School Knowledge: New Horizons. *Aboriginal Education in Canada.* K. P. Binda and Sharilyn Callious, eds. Mississauga, ON: Canadian Educators, 77-88.

Snow, Chief John. (1977). *These Mountains Are Our Sacred Places: The Story of the Stoney Indians.* Toronto, ON: Samuel Stevens.

Spence, Lewis. (1994). *North American Indians: Myths and Legends*. London, UK: Senate.

Stamp, Robert M. (1974). John Seath, Advocate of Vocational Preparation. *Profiles of Canadian Educators*. Robert S. Patterson, John W. Chalmers, and John W. Friesen, eds. Toronto, ON: D. C. Heath, 233-252.

Steckley, John L., and Bryan D. Cummins. (2001). *Full Circle: Canada's First Nations*. Toronto, ON: Prentice-Hall.

Steigelbauer, S. M. (1996). What is an Elder? What Do Elders Do? First Nation Elders as Teachers in Culture-based Urban Organizations. *The Canadian Journal of Native Studies*, XVI:1, 37-66.

Sterling, Shirley. (2002). Yetko and Sophie: Nlakapamux Cultural Professors. *Canadian Journal of Native Education*, 26:1, 4-10

Surtees, R. J. (1969). *The Development of an Indian Reserve Policy in Canada*. Ontario Historical Society, LXI, 87-99.

Suzuki, David. (1992). A Personal Foreword: The Value of Native Ecologies. *Wisdom of the Elders*. Peter Knudtson and David Suzuki. Toronto, ON: Stoddart, xxi-xvi.

Swanson, Sharon. (2003). Motivating Learners in Northern Communities. *Canadian Journal of Native Education*, 27:1, 61-73.

Symington, F. (1969). *The Canadian Indian*. Toronto, ON: McClelland and Stewart.

Taylor, Fraser. (1989). *Standing Alone: A Contemporary Blackfoot Indian*. Halfmoon Bay, BC: Arbutus Bay.

Taylor, J. Garth. (1994). North Algonquians on the Frontiers of "New Ontario, 1890-1945." *Aboriginal Ontario: Historical Perspectives on the First Nations*. Edward S. Rogers and Donald B. Smith, eds. Toronto, ON: Dundurn, 307-343.

Taylor, John. (1995). Non-Native Teachers Teaching in Native Communities. First *Nations Education in Canada: The Circle Unfolds*. Marie Battiste and Jean Barman, eds. Vancouver, BC: University of British Columbia, 224-242.

Thomas, Rodney. (August, 2004). Quoted in TeknoWave Prepares Aboriginal Workers for the Twenty-first Century by H. C. Miller. *Alberta Native News*, 21:8, 13.

Tiedt, Pamela L., and Iris M. Tiedt. (1979). *Multicultural Teaching: A Handbook of Activities, Information, and Resources*. Boston, MA: Allyn and Bacon.

Tiedt, Pamela L., and Iris M. Tiedt. (1995). *Multicultural Teaching: A Handbook of Activities, Information, and Resources*. Fourth edition. Boston, MA: Allyn and Bacon.

Titley, E. Brian. (1992). Red Deer Indian Industrial School: A Case Study in the History of Native Education. *Exploring Our Educational Past.* Nick Kach and Kas Mazurek, eds. Calgary, AB: Detselig Enterprises, 55-72.

Tremblay, Paulette C. (2001). First Nations Educational Jurisdiction: National Background Paper. Ottawa, ON: Educational Sector,

Tsuji, Leonard J. S. (2000). Modified School Years: An Important Issue of Local Control. *Canadian Journal of Native Education,* 24:2, 158-168.

Underhill, Ruth. (1953). *Red Man's Religion.* Chicago., IL: University of Chicago.

Underhill, Ruth. (1965). *Red Man's America.* Chicago, IL: University of Chicago.

Wall, Denis. (2000). Aboriginal Self-Government in Canada: The Cases of Nunavut and the Alberta Métis Settlements. *Visions of the Heart: Canadian Aboriginal Issues.* Second edition. David Long and Olive Patricia Dickason, eds. Toronto, ON: Harcourt Canada, 143-166.

Weaver, Jace, ed. (1998). *Native American Religious Identity: Unforgotten Gods.* Maryknoll, NY: Orbis Books.

Webb, Walter Prescott. (1931). *The Great Plains.* New York: Gosset and Dunlop.

Wedel, Waldo R. (1978). *The Prehistoric Plains: Ancient Native Americans.* Jesse D. Jennings, ed. San Francisco, CA: Freeman, 183-220.

West, Douglas A. (1995). Epistemological Dependency and Native Peoples: An Essay on the Future of Native/NonNative Relations in Canada. *The Canadian Journal of Native Studies,* XV:2, 279-291.

Wiggin, Gladys A. (1962). *Education and Nationalism: An Historical Interpretation of American Education.* New York: McGraw-Hill.

Wissler, Clark. (1966). *Indians of the United Sates.* Revised edition. New York: Doubleday and Winston.

Witt, Norbert. (1998). Promoting Self-Esteem, Defining Culture. *Canadian Journal of Native Education,* 22:2, 260-273.

Wolcott, Harry F. (1967). *A Kwakiutl Village and School.* New York: Holt, Rinehart and Winston.

Wuttunee, William I. C. (1971). *Ruffled Feathers.* Calgary, AB: Bell Books.

Yazzie, Robert. (2000). Indigenous Peoples and Postcolonial Colonialism. *Reclaiming Indigenous Knowledge Voice and Vision.* Marie Battiste, ed. Vancouver, BC: University of British Columbia, 39-49.

York, Geoffrey. (1989). *The Dispossessed: Life and Death in Native Canada.* Toronto, ON: Lester & Orpen Dennys.

Index